HUMOR AND NONVIOLENT STRUGGLE IN SERBIA

Syracuse Studies on Peace and Conflict Resolution
Robert A. Rubinstein, *Series Editor*

Humor & Nonviolent Struggle in SERBIA

Janjira Sombatpoonsiri

Syracuse University Press

For a listing of books published and distributed by Syracuse University Press,
visit www.SyracuseUniversityPress.syr.edu.

ISBN: 978-0-8156-3407-2 (cloth)   978-0-8156-5340-0 (e-book)

Library of Congress Cataloging-in-Publication Data
Chanchira Sombatphunsiri.
    Humor and nonviolent struggle in Serbia / Janjira Sombatpoonsiri. — First edition.
      pages cm — (Syracuse studies on peace and conflict resolution)
      Summary: "'If I had no sense of humor, I should long ago have committed suicide,' wrote the late Mahatma Gandhi, expressing the potent power of humor to sustain and uplift. Less obvious is humor's ability to operate as a cunning weapon in nonviolent protest movements. Over the last few decades, activists are increasingly incorporating subversive laughter in their protest repertoires, realizing the ways in which it challenges the ruling elite's propaganda, defuses antagonism, and inspires both participants and the greater population. In this highly original and engaging work, Sombatpoonsiri explores the nexus between humor and nonviolent protest, aiming to enhance our understanding of the growing popularity of humor in protest movements around the world. Drawing on insights from the pioneering Otpor activists in Serbia, she provides a detailed account of the protesters' systematic use of humor to topple Slobadan Milošević in 2000. Interviews with activists, protest newsletters, and documentaries of the movement combine to illustrate how humor played a pivotal role by reflecting the absurdity of the regime's propaganda and, in turn, by delegitimizing its authority. Sombatpoonsiri highlights the Otpor activists' ability to internationalize their nonviolent crusade, influencing youth movements in the Ukraine, Georgia, Iran, and Egypt. Globally, Otpor's successful use of humor became an inspiration for a later generation of protest movements"—From publisher's website.
    Includes bibliographical references and index.
    ISBN 978-0-8156-3407-2 (cloth : alkaline paper) — ISBN 978-0-8156-5340-0 (e-book)
 1. Otpor (Organization : Serbia)—History.   2. Milošević, Slobodan, 1941-2006.   3. Protest movements—Serbia—History.   4. Student movements—Serbia—History.   5. Wit and humor—Political aspects—Serbia—History.   6. Nonviolence—Political aspects—Serbia—History.   7. Political activists—Serbia—History.   8. Government, Resistance to—Serbia—History.   9. Serbia—Politics and government—1992-2006.   I. Title.
    DR2051.C52 2015
      949.7103—dc23   2015024120

Manufactured in the United States of America

For my parents and Marko Simić.

Contents

Illustrations

Figures

Table

Prologue

ime creeps in Kanjiža, a small town bordering northern Serbia and southern Hungary. During my five months of field research in Serbia, I took several trips to virtually all regions in the country—from Belgrade to Leskovac, from Kragujevac to Sombor, from Novi Sad to Čačak, from Smederevo to Niš, and many more—in an attempt to interview as many activists as I could. But Kanjiža was the fondest memory, perhaps because of my encounter with the mystique of the frontier that refined my understanding of humor. As a life-long resident of big cities (Bangkok and Melbourne), I have always been anxious about time, particularly when there are meetings to attend. In the city, time is limited and highly valuable, while transportation and traffic can work against this imperative. Many urbanites like me are convinced that temporal uncertainty must be managed—if not controlled. Hence, spending almost three hours on a local bus to cover only thirty-nine kilometers (from the northern city of Subotica to Kanjiža) was anathema to me. I was very nervous because I was running late for the interview with an ex-Otpor activist, being afraid that he would feel insulted and cancel the interview. Upon my arrival at Kanjiža's town hall, Roberto Knjur stood there and smiled at me gently. He had been waiting for nearly two hours. I apologized for wasting his time, asking whether he had other affairs scheduled for the day. He replied, "I only go fishing afterwards. There are always fish in the river, so I have plenty of time to waste." The frontier showed me the uncontrollable—in this case, it was time—and more importantly, how to embrace or even celebrate it. Beyond jokes and laughter, a sense of humor is basically an outlook enabling one to enjoy uncertainty. It was a Serbian lesson I learned.

Why consider humor in Serbia? This is the most common question posed to me when anyone learns that my PhD dissertation examines the use of humor in nonviolent protests. My typically academic (and boring) answer would discuss literature review, research methodology, and other serious stuff. But in fact, the initial impetus for this study was simply my love of adventure, to test my epistemological limits and cultural boundaries. I encountered concerns, warnings, and skepticism time and again as to whether a young "Asian female" could undertake a study about and in such a faraway land as Serbia. In Serbia, I often struggled to explain my identity to people—an Australian student, but a Thai citizen of Chinese heritage—unless they had at least five minutes. At times, I was known as "the Thai girl," and later my Indonesian diplomat friend told me that there were only two Thais living in Serbia. One was a maid, and the other a PhD student. Back in Thailand, I was the lone researcher and lecturer on Yugoslav/Serbian politics. When discussing Serbia with my students and colleagues, most of the time I have to provide them with a map of southeastern Europe. Or else, I simply tell them that Serbia is next to Vietnam!

Amidst some oddities, Serbia is a fantastic place for nonviolence research. In the West, Serbs gained the reputation of being wild and atrocious. Seen through the eyes of a "Western" European, Serbia is Europe's Africa. The Yugoslav wars in the 1990s contributed substantially to constructing these images. Marshal Tito's death in 1980, followed by the economic recession and ethno-nationalist mobilization, led to the violent breakup of a seventy-year-old "United States" of "South Slavs" (dubbed the "Kingdom of Yugoslavia" in 1929, and the "Socialist Federal Republic of Yugoslavia" from 1963 to 1991). Vivid in the global public mind was the brutality Serbs inflicted upon millions of Bosnian Muslims. Little noticed were the endless attempts by those in Serbian civil society to raise their pro-peace voices and resist the regime's war-mongering propaganda. Of course, these voices were the minority in Serbia, but they gradually created an alternative platform for imagining a democratic and nonviolent Serbia. The Otpor movement was one such unsung, yet heroic voice. Its struggle was not only at the level of domestic political change, but also of global perception about Serbs and Serbia. Otpor's creative nonviolent resistance has thus far inspired activists across the globe. This legacy serves to remind

Serbians that they, too, took part in a long history of nonviolent action, while also challenging the global image of the "violent Serbs."

Why nonviolence in Serbia? My reasons are personal. Thai society needs Serbian experiences. For almost a decade, the Thai polity has faced increasingly acute conflicts over governance, which has already claimed hundreds of lives. Nonviolent protests have been the instrument of choice of power struggle between two political camps divided along diverging fault lines. Activists and politicians of both camps have, at times, felt that nonviolent methods have been exhausted, and that violent tactics therefore should be introduced to exert pressure. In fact this assumption results from an inability to see beyond paradigms of violence which views nonviolence as weakness and as having limited application. The problem with nonviolent action, however, does not derive from a dearth of options or opportunities so much as a lack of creativity in searching ongoingly for nonviolent alternatives. Serbians' civil resistance astonishes me with the abundance of their creativity and wit, and I wish to humbly demonstrate to Thai society and others the great breadth of possibility within nonviolent activism. If Serbians were able to enlist humor in their resistance campaigns, there must also be other unexplored terrains of nonviolent action appropriate and perhaps effective for many different conflicts. Finding those possibilities requires courage to explore unfamiliar frontiers—to confront the unknown—in order to discover novel realms of nonviolent action.

Many important figures made this book possible. At Melbourne's La Trobe University, Dr. Thomas Weber and Dr. Robert Horvath's excellent support and caring attitude have carried me along a rough road in undertaking my doctoral degree. In Serbia, my first debt is to my devoted research assistant and dear friend, Jelena Vukičević. My heartfelt thanks go to former Otpor activists whose kindness and wonderful hospitality tremendously facilitated my research in Serbia: Aleksandar Pavlović, Dalibor Glišović, Dušan Koćić, Goran Dašković, Ivan Marović, Petar Lacmanović, Roberto Knjur, Siniša Šikman, Srđa Popović, Stanko Lazendić, Vladimir Marović, Vladimir Stojković, Zoran Matović, and Žejlko Trifunović. I would like to dedicate this book to Marko Simić from Otpor Užice, who passed away in a car accident a few days after his final interview with me.

I would like to extend my sincere gratitude to veterans of the 1996–97 protests (especially Vladimir Đumić, Saša Mladenović, Čedomir Antić, and Milan Stefanović), Serbian NGO members, scholars, and journalists who helped me expand networks of interviewees and eagerly offered me their personal collections of protest material. My special thanks go to Staša Zajović from Belgrade's "Women in Black," who allowed me to observe the group's protest actions. This experience provided me with some insights into the nature of protest campaigns in Serbia.

In Thailand, Professor Chaiwat Satha-Anand, director of the Peace Information Center and lecturer in violence and nonviolence in politics at the Political Science Faculty, Thammasat University, inspired my scholarly and activist passion in nonviolence. Without his profound pedagogy and extensive support since my undergraduate studies, I would not have come this far. Nor would I have learned the power of humor without the delightful work experience I had at his center.

My greatest gratitude is for my family and friends in Bangkok. There are several decisions I have made that have not been easy for my parents to understand. Nevertheless, they have always been proud of me, their eldest daughter. I owe them the unconstrained love that has shaped the person I am. Finally, I would like to thank Marc Saxer for being there for me throughout the process of making the book manuscript. His love, wisdom, and sense of adventure have enriched my life.

Note

An early version of chapter 6, entitled "Nonviolent Action as the Interplay between Political Context and 'Insider's Knowledge': Exploring Otpor's Preference for Humorous Protest across Serbian Towns," was published in Kurt Schock, ed., *Comparative Perspectives on Civil Resistance* (Minneapolis: University of Minnesota Press, 2015).

Abbreviations

ACT UP   AID's Coalition to Unleash Power
ANEM   Association of Independent Electronic Media (Asocijacija nezavisnih elektronskih medija)
CANVAS   Center for Applied Non-Violent Actions and Strategies
CeSID   Center for Free Elections and Democracy (Centar za slobodne izbore i demokratiju)
CNR   Center for Nonviolent Resistance
DOS   Democratic Opposition of Serbia (Demokratska opozicija Srbije)
DS   Democratic Party (Demokratska stranka)
DSP   Democratic Party of Socialists of Montenegro (Demokratska partija socijalista crne Gore)
DSS   Democratic Party of Serbia (Demokratska stranka Srbije)
FRY   Federal Republic of Yugoslavia
GSS   Civic Alliance of Serbia (Građanski savez Srbije)
IRI   International Republican Institute
JUL   Yugoslav United Left (Jugoslovenska udružena levica)
KV   Vojvodina Coalition (Koalicija Vojvodina)
LDP   Liberal Democratic Party (Liberalno demokratska partija)
LSV   League of Social Democrats of Vojvodina (Liga socijaldemokrata Vojvodina)
NATO   North Atlantic Treaty Organization
ND   New Democracy (Nova demonkratija)
NGO   nongovernmental organization
NS   New Serbia (Nova Srbija)

NSK	New Slovenian Art (Neue Slowenische kunst)
SNS	Serbian Progressive Party (Srpska napredna stranka)
SPO	Serbian Renewal Movement (Srpski pokret obnove)
SPS	Socialist Party of Serbia (Socialistička partija Srbije)
SRS	Serbian Radical Party (Srpska radikalna stranka)
RTS	Radio Television of Serbia (Radio-televizija Srbije)
VMSZ	Alliance of Vojvodina Hungarians (Vajdasági Magyar Szövetség)

Humor and Nonviolent Struggle in Serbia

Introduction

f I had no sense of humor, I should long ago have committed suicide," wrote the late Mahatma Gandhi. But there is one thing he forgot to mention. While humor lifts up a desperate soul, it can also sabotage a dictator's authority. Humor is potentially an effective nonviolent "weapon."

Over the past few decades, nonviolent social movements have incorporated "subversive laughter" in their protest repertoires. In Western democracies, tactical carnivals and avant-garde street theater have become increasingly prominent, especially among anti-globalization and anti-militarism campaigners. The "Absurd Response" activists, for instance, opposed the United States-led war in Iraq by dressing in "fluorescent colored gowns, opera-length gloves, and two-foot high Marge Simpson-type wigs." They carried a banner that read "An Absurd Answer to an Absurd War." Rather than chanting "give peace a chance," they were sarcastic: "We Need Oil! We Need Gas! . . . Watch Out, World, We'll Kick Your Ass!" and "We Love BUSH! We Love DICK! All You Peaceniks Make Us SICK!"[1]

In central Europe, humorous protest actions played a conspicuous role in the struggle against Soviet communism. The Polish Orange Alternative's absurd street performances provide an inspiring example in this context. On the Soviet-nominated "Children's Day," for instance, activists dressed in elf outfits (red shoes, red caps, and, if possible, red nails) took to the street. They handed out candy, sang children's songs and danced in a circle. As the police moved to detain "the elves," they willingly surrendered, loading themselves into the police cars where they merrily waved to the onlookers. Then they kissed the police.[2]

In Thailand, waves of protests staged between 2005 and 2010 were characterized by activities and theater performances that ridiculed the

1

ruling elites. For example, after the protest crackdown in 2010, demonstrators opted for cheeky street actions to circumvent the consequences of the emergency decree imposed to prohibit public gatherings. On every Sunday, they carried out non-political activities such as aerobic dancing or bicycle riding and proclaimed that these actions were lawful because they were only a form of group physical exercise.[3]

This book examines the nexus between humor and nonviolent protest, aiming to enhance our understanding of the growing popularity of humor in the protest repertoires of activists around the world. Drawing on the insights of the 1996–97 protesters and Otpor activists in Serbia, it theorizes how humor operates in nonviolent conflicts in three ways. First, forms of humor such as satire and parody challenge the ruling elites' propaganda by annexing its form in order to adapt and reconstruct it in an absurd version that undermines its original purpose. Second, carnivalesque activities can transform the protest atmosphere from one of antagonism to cheerfulness. This emotive shift can influence protesters to refrain from provoking security forces, and thus pre-empt the government's justification for a crackdown. Third, carnivalesque protests contain the metaphor of participants' emancipation from an oppressive situation. This metaphor can generate popular awareness of the possibilities of changing the status quo, and inspire activists to turn these possibilities into reality.

Achieving the aforementioned conceptual task may be trailblazing due to the near pedagogical silence regarding humor's potential in non-violent resistance campaigns. On the one hand, nonviolence studies have largely neglected this subject because of assumptions about the possible ethical and tactical drawbacks of humor. For instance, proponents of principled nonviolence—those regarding nonviolence as an ethical imperative[4]—may not consider humor nonviolent, given its association with ridicule and humiliation. In a conflict situation, humiliating an opposing party can damage relationships, hindering long-term conflict resolution.[5]

The proponents of pragmatic nonviolence—those viewing nonviolence as a set of unarmed techniques used in a struggle—have generally acknowledged forms of humorous nonviolent actions such as street skits, pranks, and satirical songs.[6] However, one possibility for the dismissal of humor in pragmatic nonviolence lies in its theoretical foundation, which largely derives from Etienne de La Boétie's book *The Politics of Obedience: The Discourse of Voluntary Servitude*. La Boétie's central argument is that a tyrant can maintain his power because people willingly and habitually render him obedience or "voluntary servitude." Rituals and entertainment manifested in the form of comic theater, farce, feasts, and plays are powerful tools for the manipulation of subjects. By maneuvering entertainment to strengthen his popularity, and hence his legitimacy, a tyrant does not need to rely on terror or violence to achieve remain in power.[7]

In humor studies, safety-valve theory became a conceptual barrier, blocking scholars from acknowledging the subversive potential of humor.[8] The theory regards anti-elite jokes as merely a psychological release of popular resentment, which serves to prevent the eruption of a mass uprising. This is the reason elites allow the circulation of jokes against themselves.[9] From this perspective, political jokes are not a form of resistance. They reflect "no political programme and . . . will mobilise no one."[10]

Despite this dismissal of humor's potential, recent works of social movement scholarship have drawn increasing attention to the use of humor in protest activism. This focus shifts from assessment of the jokes' subversive contents to the tactical use of humor by organized movements pursuing social change. It is the political purpose behind the use of humor to resist domination that shapes its subversive character.[11]

In a similar vein, the use of humorous protest to impugn a movement's opponent has become a topic of interest for a new breed of nonviolent action scholars.[12] An underlying concept in existing studies relates to the function of nonviolence as a tool to subvert an oppressive ruler as a person, rather than confronting a broader process of domination. Humor serves this function by unmasking a ruler's hypocrisy and by making repression appear ridiculous and excessive in the eyes of the public. By undermining the figurehead oppressor, the oppressive mechanism is hindered.

While sharing certain positions with these earlier works, the present volume applies a different analytical framework. It analyzes the impact of humorous protest actions on changes at the level of popular discourse and perception. It adopts the understanding that domination is a process larger than any one individual actor, involving an array of influences on a community's ways of thinking. Accordingly, nonviolent resistance to domination is here defined as an action plan that can deal with the manipulation of public opinion by means other than merely overthrowing individual ruling elites. Arriving at this understanding will require a refinement of existing theories explaining the power of nonviolent action.

Humor, Excorporation, and Political Imagination in Nonviolent Contexts

Power theory underpinning nonviolent activism is rooted in the maxim that power is dichotomized and flows between the ruler and the ruled. This dichotomy is virtually irrelevant when power exercises itself at the level of perception. Domination is associated with the ability to monopolize the construction of truths. Accordingly, resistance may imply a challenge to this monopoly.

Nonviolent action theory generally regards obedience as voluntary, and the ruled are equipped with the ability to entirely withdraw consent from the ruler so as to resist a ruler's domination. Gene Sharp—a "founding father" of pragmatic nonviolence theory—postulates that power is spread throughout society. A tyrant's power comes from authority, human resources, material resources, punishment, and other "intangible" factors such as ideology and popular faith in the ruler. Underlying all of these sources are obedience and consent rendered by the ruled. Logically, when the ruled cease to obey and withdraw their consent, the power of the ruler can be weakened.[13] This understanding is underpinned with the trust in agency. The ruling person monopolizes domination. Despite that, the people or the ruled is equipped with free will to totally uproot the ruler's domination.

Based on the association of domination with the ruling person, nonviolent resistance is understood as the search for unarmed "techniques" that work to foster the withdrawal of mass support from the ruler.[14] Techniques such as mass demonstrations, economic sanction, and establishment of parallel state institutions are applied to inflict a political, economic, and social damage on the opposing party. The pressure may reach a point where the antagonist chooses to grant activists some of their demands rather than continue the conflict.[15] If compromise is not reached, nonviolent activists are suggested to carry on with applying nonviolent methods until the damage spreads to a large enough scale. This may cause groups upon which the ruler depends (e.g. bureaucrats, the police force, the army, business sectors, and foreign governments) to withdraw their support. At some point, the ruler is forced to grant activists all of their demands.[16] This theorizing of nonviolent methods' functions is, again, based on the conception that domination stems from a ruler. Therefore, those resisting it should rely on offensive tactics undercutting material bases from which the ruler derives his or her power.

In a nutshell, existing explanations of how nonviolent struggle works are influenced by the "contractarian" notion of power. That is, power is clearly dichotomized between the ruler and the ruled. "Change" of power relations has the undercurrent of ceasing the social contract allowing a person to rule. Presumably, if the ruler is removed from power, it follows that his or her influence dissipates, thereby cracking the entire system of domination. In addition, this logic associating an overthrow of the ruling person with annulling domination assumes that nonviolent activists are free from webs of influence that once strengthened the ruler's power. Put differently, a nonviolent social change, according to the existing theorem, is oriented towards a change at the actor level, rather than the level of perceiving political truths.

In this sense, the contractarian conception of power overlooks the discursive terrain of domination.[17] The power of discourse lies in ways in which our thoughts and practices are influenced by certain sets of belief, value, and knowledge. Unquestioned knowledge and norms become the truth which arranges and normalizes how things and persons are related in society. For example, psychopathology as knowledge and practice shapes our perception about mentally healthy persons and those with a mental disability. This perception leads us to believe in the actual scientific differences between the "normal" and the "abnormal," thereby treating the two groups differently. Such categorization of social groups sustains the system that provides economic benefits or political rights for one group over another. But this is just the surface of a discursive form of domination. For a discourse to operate, it must convince the populace to equate social inequality with "order." Therefore, changing this order implies the emergence of chaos. And when our worldview is shaped to regard chaos as life-threatening, we tend to prefer the status quo and disregard social inequality as not being a problem.[18]

The discursive analysis of domination dismisses a possibility that individuals have complete access to free will enabling them to give or withdraw their consent from a rule. Networks of discursive domination are entrenched at the level of popular consciousness. Rather than the blatant use of force being the means of maneuvering collective obedience, the powerful rely on existing sets of "truth" to achieve "governmentality." This implies that the "people" are led to believe that they can fully exercise autonomy to decide upon issues in the private and public spheres of their lives, and that they possess the total freedom to grant or take back consent from a ruling person. In contrast to this belief, the ostensible availability of free will is constructed to camouflage discursive domination.

Nonetheless, the pervasiveness of discursive domination does not imply complete subordination. Influence is dynamic. There are "no relations of power without resistance . . . [and it] exists all the more by being in the same place as the power."[19] While reality can be manipulated so popular consent is constructed to sustain domination, there remains space within the system of domination whereby people always do things they want to regardless of the system's expectation.

Daily activities such as reading, cooking, and walking are prime examples. These activities contain some rules of operation: linguistic codes of reading, recipes for cooking, and maps for walking. The rules are conceived by faceless systems, be they certain sets of knowledge, consumerism, or the state. However, there can never be a guarantee that the rules will be followed precisely. While reading, readers interpret meanings from the text according to what they have in mind; while cooking, recipes are adjusted to one's preference; while walking, one may get lost and discover sites unidentified on the map.[20] As an act, deviating from established rules connotes the stubbornness of "doing things as I like," making it hard for a dominant system to keep its logic coherent and influence consistent entirely.

Rule distortion constitutes a part of the consumption process, reflecting the "parasite-like" nature of subversive power. Production is the realm wherein domination operates: the production of propaganda, ideology, and knowledge. The process of this production is completed by the process of consumption which covers a wide range of activities that are "using things."[21] This process carves out a space for resistance. Put differently, consumption indicates a location of resistance within the system of domination. Because of this location, the act of resistance connotes ways in which subordinates can embrace what has initially strengthened the dominant in order to use it against them. Those that are subordinate are consumers of the vast system of production. And in the process of consuming, the original production modes, dictated by the dominant system, can subtly be altered to the subordinates' ends. The resistant power of the consumption process lies in the producer being disabled from totalizing his or her influence over the consumer.[22]

The process of consumption offers an analogy of resistance from within the space of domination, as an alternative to the all-out withdrawal of cooperation from the opponent that underpins nonviolent action theory. The concept of "excorporation" can illuminate this analogy. It denotes ways in which subordinates can subvert the dominant by relying on resources initially strengthening domination. They incorporate into their tactics of resistance the political ideology and popular culture which was originally manipulated by the ruling elites to foster collective acceptance of their rule. In this process, the subordinates also distort the core meaning of the elites' culture, replacing it with their own political message. As a result, the elite discourse loses its convincing tone.[23] In effectively diminishing the power of the dominant discourse, it allows further acts of subversion by subordinates.[24] Although many art forms have the potential to excorporate dominant sources of power, those with humorous elements tend to be largely effective.[25] Humor can amplify this effect of excorporation.

Satire, parody, and carnivals are forms of humor selected for the exploration of humor's subversive role. On the one hand, components of these forms featured in humorous protest actions staged in Serbia's

1996–97 protests and Otpor's campaigns, on which this study bases its analysis. On the other, satire, parody, and carnivals are acknowledged in the humor studies literature as being subversive and empowering the less powerful party in a conflict situation.[26]

Satire and parody contain subversive potential. Out of these types of humor, satire is arguably the most ferocious when deliberately used to attack the adversary. The political statement underlying satire is more explicit than for the other genres of humor that will be discussed subsequently.[27] In modern time, satire is most well known in forms of literature with the aim of criticizing particular groups of elites and popular belief. Its method of criticism is usually positioned as an attack from a higher ethical viewpoint. The context from which satire is derived is always that of political conflict.[28]

Mimesis and distortion denote ways in which satire works to subvert domination.[29] Satirical joke is usually based on the rhetoric of a joke's target, but ends with the gist of the claim being twisted. The absurdity arises when the twisted claim is juxtaposed with ideological claims from a rival ideology. The end product is the emphasis on hypocrisy of the ideological rhetoric attacked by the joke. In a nutshell, satire works to "defeat the opponent on his own ground by pretending to accept his premises, his values, his methods of reasoning, in order to expose their implicit absurdity."[30]

In a similar vein, parody operates on the basis of taking advantage of the adversary's resources to emasculate the adversary. While satire is explicit in its ethical claim and attacking message, parody subtly weakens its target of attack through mimicry.[31] The "object" of parody is usually a piece of artwork, or a specific rhetoric, which claims its position of authenticity in asserting to reflect nature and reality. By imitating the original artwork, a parody may seek to make disjoint the originally intended fusion between its form and content. This process can result in the original content being removed and replaced with an absurd image or version which inverts its original meaning.[32] The subversive characteristic of parody lies in the subtle act of deforming to absurdity the essence which renders the artwork's apparent authenticity to be genuine. The subtlety of parody is due to the fact that its identity fully depends on imitation of the already legitimized target. But parody is subversive because while mimicking the original object, it twists characteristics of the object which have hitherto enabled claims that it is a "genuine" reflection of reality. Fundamentally, parody suspends the truth claim of its imitated object. It does so by distorting elements that consolidate the truth claim in the first place.

The concept of "excorporation," which suggests mounting resistance from within a space of domination, can be applied to comprehend subversive characteristics of satire and parody. These genres of humor reflect ways in which the less powerful employ the resources of their mightier opponents to strike back at them. The subordinates co-opt the opponent's rhetoric and symbolism while distorting them to the absurd. Often, the distortion works to suspend the truth claim underpinning the rhetoric, and at times the claim is replaced with the subordinates' message of subversion.

In contrast to satire and parody, carnivals generally contain the transformative capacity of humor. They counter domination by providing a metaphor of alternative realities. In ancient and medieval carnivals, role inversion and temporary transgression of established norms are common. Men dress as women and vice versa. The young can scold the old. People of low caste are permitted to beat up those from the ruling class. Masters serve slaves while slaves are invited to join the banquet of elites.[33] Jesters were proclaimed bishops while clerics were allowed to be follies, dancing, and hopping through the church.[34]

Typical for these role inversions is the wearing of clothes and masks that exaggerates a social image of particular elite groups. For instance, in some carnivals during Europe's Middle Ages, the pseudo kings and queens were elected from the peasantry. They deliberately donned clothes turned inside out and hats inscribed with mocking parodies.[35] At times, the mimesis of the powerful personalities took the form of effigies made in a ridiculous fashion.[36]

Carnivals provide a space for both an open conflict and a dialogue between the antagonists. The free speech in medieval carnivals enabled the subordinates to insult the elites who were immune from criticisms at other times. Numerous accounts note the events in which unpopular rulers, abusive soldiers, corrupt local officials, and priests were cursed by peasants during carnivals. Abusive terms and satirical chants, common in carnivals, were used to maximize the insult of these elites. The scale of verbal abuse could be so extensive that some of the nobles refused to participate in carnivals, fearing that the verbal threats would erupt into physical assaults.[37]

The subversive space offered in carnivals is facilitated by processes that encourage the subordinate to imagine their triumph over an oppressive situation. Carnivals provide a metaphor of power-relations inversion (e.g. subjects became rulers). When this metaphor seems to achieve nothing visible, it can nevertheless fulfill the imaginative aspirations of the subordinate: "[Carnivals] do, at least at the level of thought, create an imaginative breathing space in which the normal categories of order and hierarchy are less than completely inevitable."[38] In the carnivalesque space, hierarchy is dismissed, gender roles are reversed, and taboo violation is allowed. Hence, carnivals at least serve to remind us of the possibility of a change of status quo when the reality of oppression seems to occupy our perceptions. The opportunity for "carnivalesque humor" generates a scenario wherein a change of power relations can be contemplated, however fleetingly, but perhaps realized in time to come.

Resisting power-holders aside, the opportunity for free speech inherent in the nature of carnivals can facilitate a dialogue between carnival participants and their antagonists. Medieval carnivals did not only postulate the destruction of officialdom, but they also generated new perspectives. This is why the image of the lower parts of the human body, such as the belly and buttocks, are central to the carnivalesque image. They connote the continuum between releasing wastes and producing energy, between death and birth, and between ending and renewal.[39] The regenerative image of carnivals provides the metaphor of constant change. The end of something always marks the beginning of something else. From this viewpoint, multiple possibilities can always emerge. The carnivalesque world offers a scenario where alternative realities to the seemingly fixed present one may just be possible.[40]

Ways in which carnivals foster dialogue between protagonists and antagonists is through the creation of opportunities for exchanging conversations and interacting, despite existing prejudices. Through interactive activities, carnivals create a dialogical space among the participants and between the participants and their antagonists. The medieval feasts exemplified how a frank conversation with the enemies was carried out over the dining table. However, acute antagonism was abated by the act of eating and drinking together. The feasts could unite people, encouraging them to overcome past hostilities. These feasts carried with them the prospect of reconstructing relationships, suggesting "looking into better days to come."[41] Carnivals transform our imagination of the "Other."

The excorporation process and transformative power of humor are put at work when an organized movement strategically plans their use of humor, incorporating it in their overarching strategy. The Serbian Otpor Movement serves as the case in point in this book. It showed ways in which humor could subvert discursive domination under the Milošević regime, and at the same time opened up an imaginative space for Serbians. This process of changing power relations inherently denotes the core meaning of nonviolent struggle.

Otpor: A Brief History

Otpor is characteristically an avant-garde mass movement driven by political and life style-based goals. It is a by-product of a decade long civil resistance in Serbia which started in 1991 in response to vote rigging by the ruling Socialist Party. When Slobodan Milošević moved to re-consolidate his power in the 1996 municipal election, students in Belgrade and other regions organized nationwide demonstrations for four months, dubbed "The Winter of Discontent." Despite the euphoria of possible change, student activists found themselves trapped in the usual cycle of political stalemate marked by Milošević's resilient regime and opposition parties' infighting. These incidents shaped the emergence of the popular movement Otpor (the Serbian term for resistance). Founding activists were determined to remove Milošević from the Serbian political landscape by utilizing a wide range of nonviolent actions in their anti-regime campaigns.

Unique was Otpor's strategic use of satire, parody and festivals to subvert the regime's authority, and promulgate its democratic messages to the Serbian populace. Humor became the signature of Otpor boosting activists' popularity, especially among Serbian youngsters. At its peak, the movement attracted between thirty thousand and sixty thousand activists and supporters, with approximately 130 branches in twenty-four cities and 150 municipalities in Serbia.

In 2000, Otpor collaborated with the opposition coalition in several election campaigns which were conducive to victory over Milošević's Socialist Party. Predictably, votes were manipulated to reverse this outcome which in turn triggered the popular uprising. Between October 2 and 5, Otpor activists together with opposition politicians in different towns mobilized their supporters in nationwide strikes and eventually the nonviolent blockade of Belgrade. The epic event ended with Milošević's capitulation and subsequently his trials for crimes against humanity by the International Criminal Tribunal for the former Yugoslavia.

Chapters Outline

This book assesses the power of humor used as a vehicle of nonviolent struggle by focusing on humorous protests in Serbia's 1990s which reached the peak in Otpor campaigns between 1998 and 2000. Chapters 1 to 3 trace the history of Serbian humor in the 1990s that influenced humorous protest actions in Otpor's campaigns. It shows that using humor as a protest method was an emerging trend in Serbia from the time of the antiwar demonstrations in 1991, and later the student protest in 1992. This trend was influenced by the genre of absurd theater popular among critical art movements in the former Yugoslavia, the satirical lyrics of rock 'n' roll music, tragicomic films, and most importantly the popularity of black humor in everyday life. The 1996–97 demonstrations saw this development of subversive humor reached its zenith. Numerous actions were organized by student protesters who contemplated in advance what effect the humor could have on the regime. This knowledge was used to develop Otpor's core political strategy.

Chapters 4 to 5 examine the development, characteristics and local dynamics of Otpor's humorous nonviolent actions. The outcome of the 1996–97 protests which failed to topple the Milošević regime propelled a group of student activists to found the Otpor (Resistance) movement. They put forward the goal of regime change, shifted the protest methodology from taking to the street to staging media campaigns, and reached out to the young in the regime's stronghold towns. These changes enhanced the effects of humorous protest actions. The actions were schematically designed and executed, and encapsulated coherent messages that aimed to convince the Serbian public to vote against Milošević. In addition, the widespread nature of Otpor branches across Serbia enabled the proliferation of these actions. Activists from hundreds of Otpor branches were encouraged to create innovative satirical street performances to mock the regime's propaganda and organized a host of concerts and parties to promote the resistance campaigns. Parody became an emerging form of humor utilized by activists to co-opt national symbols and historical narratives, which were once maneuvered to consolidate the regime's power.

Despite effective coordination, chapter 6 demonstrates that humor was not the preferred choice of tactics in every town. The extent to which independent media, NGO members, and opposition politicians were active in different areas shaped activists' tactical decisions. Situations that are favorable and not favorable for employing humorous tactics are assessed by these local observations.

Theoretical implications of humor used as a vehicle for nonviolent struggle are discussed in chapters 3 and 5 detailing humorous protests. I point out that in the conduct of nonviolent resistance campaigns, humor is effective for mobilizing a campaign's supporters, while also constituting a useful media toolkit to promote the campaign's messages. In response to regime repression, using humor can bring to the fore the absurdity of this repression, thereby furthering a movement's claim of a regime's illegitimacy. The theoretical analysis sheds light on the operation of humor as a form of power in nonviolent conflicts. Satirical street theater and parodic protest actions worked to desecrate the regime's truth claims. Carnivalesque protest activities produced a different effect from these two genres, generating the joyful atmosphere conducive to preventing clashes between protesters and security forces. Moreover, carnivalesque protests offered a metaphor of reality inversion which potentially encouraged protesters to realize the possibilities of emancipation from the oppressive regime. This process of seeing multiple possibilities can be regarded as a primary step toward a nonviolent "revolution."

PART ONE

A History of the Serbian Sense of Humor

1

Laughing at the Misery
Serbian Comedic Culture

This chapter demonstrates the cultural construction of intuitive humor, which provides fertile ground for humorous protest actions in Serbia's 1990s. Various forms of comedic culture have been popular in this region from the time of the former Socialist Yugoslavia. These forms included absurd theater genre, rock 'n' roll music, and television comedy shows. But it was the widespread nature of established anti-authoritarian and self-deprecating jokes in everyday Serbian life that set the stage for comedic pop art to flourish. These jokes familiarized people with the subversive potential of humor, and enabled them to maximize this potential. As we shall see in subsequent chapters, Serbian protesters in the early 1990s initiated humorous actions out of spontaneity rather than meticulous planning. They "felt" that humor could be used to defy the authorities, and this heartfelt knowledge was largely shaped by everyday jokes and comedic pop art.

Absurd Theater in the Former Yugoslavia

Art groups in the former Yugoslavia contributed to the development of humorous protest methods by amplifying the potential of absurd theater in criticizing authorities. Since the 1930s, Yugoslav artists—particularly from "avant-garde" circles—have played a major role in expressing disagreement with the authorities, despite the control exerted by the communist regime of the time.[1] For them, art and political life were not two separate entities. Artists were responsible for reflecting on and criticizing what has gone wrong in society. To do so, satire and absurd expression was integrated into their artworks. Renowned for playing this role was "Dada," the avant-garde art movement that came into being in Western Europe as early as 1916.[2] In February 1921, Dada was introduced into the former Yugoslavia by the poet Ljubomir Micić, who also founded the magazine *Zenit* in the Croatian capital of Zagreb. The magazine soon became a mouthpiece for painters, designers, theatrical artists, filmmakers, and musicians in criticizing the militarization of Yugoslavia and Europe as a whole during and after the First World War.[3] Puns, humorous verses, and the combination of incongruent words with absurd meanings were typical of the writing style in the magazine. The end product was aimed at countering state propaganda.[4]

In the late 1970s, avant-garde art reemerged in Yugoslavia, paving the way for artists' involvement in protest campaigns. Prominent avant-garde artists in this period included the Slovenian art group OHO, Croatian filmmaker Tom Gotovac, the student satirical theater group Kugla glumište, Novi Sad-based artist and political scientist Branko Andrić Andrla, and playwright Zorica Jevremović. All these artists actively engaged in civic protests.[5] Another influential avant-garde collective that formed in this period was "New Slovenian Art" (Neue Slowenische Kunst or "NSK"). The group housed artists from various fields such as punk band Laibach, visual art group IRWIN, theater group Scipion Nasice Sisters Theater (later known as Noordung), and the graphic artists group New Collective Studio.[6]

Through making parody of what it opposed, NSK art challenged oppressive ideologies through its early focus on fascism and communism in the former Yugoslavia. It operated within the system of institutionalized ideology, which enabled its subtle distortion of ideological symbols and rhetoric to absurdity.[7] Typically, NSK artists juxtaposed symbols from the different and often incompatible political ideologies, and would at times deliberately exaggerate the ideological undertone of the totalitarian regime it opposed. In the NSK's constitution, membership rules epitomized the latter approach: "Once a member is inducted, the association denies each member his own freedom of choice regarding his religious persuasion, and political and aesthetic affiliation."[8] Another example from within the NSK collective was IRWIN's poster designed for the Socialist

Youth Relay in 1987. The poster design contained the image of a strapping youth bounding forward with a huge Yugoslav flag in hand, surrounded by a dove and six torches symbolizing the Yugoslav republics. These images were borrowed from a famous Nazi poster of 1936, but with some twists. The Nazi flag was replaced by a Yugoslav flag and the title—"The Third Reich"—was replaced with "Youth Day." Despite the outright parody that equated the Yugoslav regime with its historical Nazi antagonist, the NSK won the poster competition.[9]

The influence of Yugoslav avant-garde artists persists in contemporary art groups in Serbia such as Dah Teatar, Škart, and Magnet. Similar to *Zenit*, which was founded in the aftermath of the First World War, Dah Teatar came into existence in the context of the 1990s Yugoslav wars. Dijana Milošević—a founder of Dah Teatar—believed that theater could constitute a powerful way to communicate to the Serbian republic about the destructiveness of war and nationalist propaganda.[10] During the Bosnian war in 1992, the group staged its first performance, "This Babylonian Confusion," in Belgrade's pedestrian square. The performance served as an antiwar manifesto despite the then "hyper-patriotic context" in which any challenge to the Serbian state's justification of the wars was perceived as an act of treason.[11] Dah Teatar often traveled across Serbia to promote a pacifist, cosmopolitan spirit against the backdrop of the "barbarian, war-prone, blood thirsty" stereotype of Serbs.[12] The street performances choreographed by Dah Teatar were aimed at provoking questioning thought by onlookers about the nationalist rhetoric that justified the wars.[13]

This nascent artistic project to raise awareness within the Serbian populace was soon joined by the design group Škart (the Serbian term for "trash"). In December 1992, the group began its "sadness" (*tuga*) project, in an attempt to bring home the disastrous reality of the wars. Škart printed weekly hand-made "sadness" cardboard booklets, which emphasized the impact of the wars on the private sphere of life of Serbians. The booklets were given away to passersby at different locations in Belgrade. This later became Škart's key methodology for engaging ordinary citizens in politics. Artists designed paraphernalia (e.g., matchboxes, badges, and stamps) on which a short satirical or absurd message were printed, which were then distributed to pedestrians, shoppers, and passengers on trams and buses.[14]

Avant-garde theater shaped the "style" of street protest in the 1990s. Despite its artistic origin, this genre of theater was arguably the most popular among rank-and-file protesters in the 1990s. In many ways its popularity was a consequence of continuous engagement by the "alternative" stream of artists, especially from avant-garde art movements.[15] The convergence of dramaturgy and protest campaigns would reach its apogee in the 1996–97 protests and in Otpor's campaigns.

Pop Culture: Satirical Rock 'n' Roll, Tragicomic Films, and Comedy Television Shows

The realm of popular culture had been a battleground between urban dissidents and the Milošević regime. To a great extent the regime was able to maintain its power, not only by using force, but by maneuvering nationalist rhetoric through different forms of pop culture, such as folk epics, poems, novels, songs, and theater. In the regime's domain of popular culture, tragedy and hatred constituted the main language.[16] This language was particularly devised to fabricate the image of Milošević as a legitimate leader capable of defending Serbs from their enemies.[17]

To undermine the regime's propaganda, as it was promulgated through forms of pop culture, dissidents opted for the language that made light of tragedy. This was the kind of language that dismissed the tragic undertone of national narratives that were used to justify the wars and gain the regime its desired legitimacy. In the Serbian struggles of the 1990s, the comedic language vocally expressed in rock 'n' roll music, tragicomic films, and comedy television shows served this purpose.

Rock 'n' Roll

Rock was generally despised by the regime because of its association with "multi-ethnic" and westernized Yugoslavia. In the quest for a "true and greater Serbia," novelist Dobrica Ćosić and other conservative artists publicly condemned rock as an unpatriotic cultural expression: "Yugoslavism in its 'evil incarnation' is an expression of a political parvenu mentality; of the snobbery of the rock-and-roll generation; of the cosmopolitanism of liberal intellectuals; of a legitimate and 'progressivist' and 'democratic' mask for anationality and anti-Serbianism."[18] In countering the rise of rock culture among Yugoslav youth, the Milošević regime promoted an emerging form of folk music dubbed "turbo folk." The regime embraced this genre's juxtaposition of traditional Serbian arabesque motifs alongside contemporary "techno beat" sounds as an expression of true Serb identity in opposition to the "fake" cosmopolitan persona of rock music.[19]

The history of Yugoslav rock music coincided with the emergence of dissidents in Serbia. Rock came into being in the former Yugoslavia toward the mid-1960s, and reached the peak of its popularity in the 1980s. In 1981, for instance, the British magazine *New Musical Express* listed the Belgrade art student's club, Academia (Akademija), as one of the finest music clubs in Europe. With the dominance of nationalist rhetoric in the context of the Yugoslav break-up, rock bands became identified with dissidents, and also acted as their mouthpiece. In the late 1990s, rock bands remained influential among dissidents, despite the continuous censorship and lack of financial resources. Emerging bands that often performed for opposition demonstrations included Darkwood Dub, Deca Loših Muzičara, Eyesburn, Love Hunters, Atheist Rap and Kanda, and Kodža i Nebojša. Their musical productions had been bolstered by Rex, the music production company behind the rebellious radio station B92.[20]

Prominent rockers and persistent dissidents who perfectly combined rock music and satire included Antonije Pušić, commonly known as "Rambo Amadeus," and Đorđe Balašević. A graduate from the Tourism Faculty of Belgrade University, Pušić admitted that he was involved in the music industry because of his interest in caricaturing political figures. His inspiration derived from his disdain for turbo folk, which could be heard on every radio station when he first moved to Belgrade: "In the late 1980s, somehow the media was open to peasants' music, some kind of primitive bullshit. And it really got to my nerves. So, I produced a song to mock this kind of music. The song was pretty much like turbo folk, but it tried to say that turbo folk was a crappy music. . . . I didn't care about rock music. I only cared about caricature!"[21]

Pušić's songs were unique in that their lyrics ferociously satirized the regime's propaganda. His musical style was eclectic, ranging from rock, rap, jazz, funk, reggae, and folk to techno, but it was his satirical lyrics that made him particularly popular among Serbian dissidents. They highlighted "the madness, paranoia, kitsch, and inauthenticity of the neofolk" being fanned by the regime. Typically, the songs revealed the absurdity underlying Milošević's propaganda.[22] For instance, the lyrics of the track "My Friend, My Friend" (*Prijatelju, prijatelju*) were based on excerpts from speeches delivered by Milošević and Franjo Tuđman, the Serbian and Croatian leaders that led their nations into destructive wars.[23] Pušić mockingly drew on these speeches, which sounded very much alike in their nationalist and war rhetoric despite the Serbian and Croatian leaders' hostility toward each other. "My Friend, My Friend" ironically demonstrated that a kind of "friendship" between two enemies could be constructed from the nationalist rhetoric that separated them in the first place.

The song that possibly best represents Pušić's mockery of the regime is "Goodness Gracious" (*Karamba, karambita*). Repeatedly performed in his concerts during the protests of the 1990s, the song narrates the "polluted" environment of that decade—be it the media propaganda, the wars, the submissiveness of the Serbian populace, or the endemic nature of "kitsch" culture. Beyond the cynical criticisms, the song motivated people to change these destructive circumstances: "Turn off the TV—don't you see it's poisoning you."[24]

The ridicule and cursing which often featured prominently in Pušić's music were also common practice in his concert performances. One example comes from the "Belgrade Rock Winner" concert, organized by a state-run TV program in 1992. While the singer Bebi Dol was performing, Pušić jumped onto the stage, snatching the mike from her. Then he aimed a tirade of abuse at the TV audience: "While we are here playing music, bombs are falling on Dubrovnik, and Sarajevo! I don't want to entertain the electorate! Fuck you all!"[25] In another event, he declared on stage that "rock and roll in Serbia died the moment Slobodan Milošević appeared."[26] Following those events, Pušić was excluded from appearing on any state-run media, but according to the music guru, Petar Janjatović, the ban only increased his popularity.[27]

Pušić had been actively involved in the 1992 and 1996–97 student demonstrations as a performer for the protest concerts, and as a protest participant. His first concert was organized as part of the antiwar demonstrations in 1992. In the 1996–97 protests, he not only performed for the students, but also participated in the street actions. Pero Jelić, then a student protester charged with organizing cultural events and concerts for the 1996–97 protests, recalls: "I met Rambo Amadeus for the first time during the protest. He supported the protest and was at the Faculty of Philosophy [building] every day. He had some ideas [for street actions]. One of them was that students were here not to destroy, but to construct. Then he re-painted the toilet wall of the Faculty of Philosophy."[28]

Đorđe Balašević became an emblem for cultural resistance in the 1990s due to his satirical songs and persistent engagement in student protests. As early as 1988, Balašević composed songs that manifested the absurdity of the wars, the regime's hypocrisy, and life under dictatorship. Throughout the 1990s, Balašević released tracks that either explicitly criticized social problems precipitated by the regime, or exposed "the regime's rhetoric regarding war, nationalism, oppression, and destruction of the country in ways that ranged from nostalgic and reflective to piercingly ironic."[29] The song "Freedom—No" (*Sloboda-ne*), released in 1992, was repeatedly performed at Belgrade's Terazije Square in the course of the 1992 demonstrations. The title of the song is based on a wordplay with *Slobodan* (Slobodan Milošević and the Serbian word for "freedom").[30] The background music to the song is typical of the Serbian folk genre found in the regime's officially sanctioned music, but by incorporating folk music with anti-regime lyrics, "Freedom—No" tacitly attacks the cultural manipulation by the regime. The song's "hook" phrase explicitly unveils Milošević's rhetoric that there is no war, and that he is only protecting the Serbs in Croatia and Bosnia.[31]

The album simply titled *1990s* (*Devedesete*) became an all-time hit, inspiring many protesters in the late 1990s. In the song "Legend of Geda the Stupid" (*Legenda o Gedi gluperdi*), Balašević impersonates Milošević (as "Geda") and exaggerates his ignorant attitude to the absurd. Moreover, he successfully utilizes allegory and humor to speak of an unspeakable subject at the time—the possible downfall of the Milošević regime. From January 1998 to the regime's fall on October 5, 2000, the song was performed at numerous anti-regime demonstrations across Serbia.[32] Brana

Mijatović notes that "Legend of Geda the Stupid" became an anthem of people's power. It changed "the people's attitude towards the regime from fear to courage, and it reached its peak of popularity in the months and weeks before the September 2000 elections which toppled the Milošević regime." The key phrase in the song reads as follows: "Gedo, you idiot. You gambled away the whole land. . . . But who is crazy here—is it Geda, or us?"[33]

During Otpor's campaigns in 2000, Balašević's song "To live Freely" (Živeti slobodno) was composed exclusively to boost the morale of young activists. The lyrics are powerful in motivating youth to fight for the liberation of life, and to resist the despair of the regime. They depict exactly what tens of thousands of Otpor activists endeavored to achieve through their street actions, staged in Milošević's stronghold towns: "This heart beats an endless rhythm of 'Resistance'. . . . Your banner is on every town where somebody feels delighted for you."[34]

Balašević performed annually in the concert at Belgrade's Sava Center, which eventually became the public site "where the 'normal' people congregated amid the madhouse of surreal everyday life."[35] On the eve of 2000, which became the historic year of regime change, he dedicated his concert particularly to Otpor, praising "those kids of the 'Resistance' who were beaten and arrested by the ruthless regime."[36] After Balašević had performed "To Live Freely," all the concert attendees stood up and raised their clenched fists to salute him.[37]

The Slovene punk band, Laibach, and its ferocious parodic subversion of the Yugoslav regime, inspired Otpor's leading activists—particularly when combining parody with street protest action. The band was formed as a part of the New Slovenian Art collective in the 1980s, as discussed earlier. Unlike Rambo Amadeus or Đorđe Balašević, Laibach did not explicitly attack the regime or its ideology. Instead, the band embraced the ideologies it opposed, completely endorsing their symbolisms in order to distort the original meanings. Laibach's method can be detected in the song "The State" (Država), which praises the state and forces people to fully lay their trust in it: "The state is taking care of the physical education of the nation, . . . It is behaving ever more indulgently, all freedom is allowed."[38]

The lyrics are accompanied with militaristic drum beats, rendering the song similar to the anthem of a totalitarian state, be it Nazi or communist. The band made sure that its incorporation of totalitarian emblems was total by printing the lyrics beside a large swastika made from four axes taken from a World War II poster designed by an anti-Nazi artist. In so doing, the swastika lost its meaning and context: the Nazi ideology and its symbol (swastika) that appear to permeate the song are dismantled by the anti-Nazi imagery (axes) that accompanies it.[39]

At the onset of the Bosnian war, Laibach was outspoken, but in its own way. In 1994 the band released its *NATO* album, on which they remade songs originally from the West, but with an ironic twist. For instance, the song "War," originally a pacifist song performed by Edwin Starr, contains the line: "War . . . , what is it good for? Absolutely nothing."[40] The Laibach version changes the pacifist answers to a list of concepts that provide the grounds for wars (science, religion, domination), including a list of companies reaping profits from wars. Implicitly, Laibach condemns Western powers under NATO for insufficiently implementing measures to mitigate the Bosnian war's atrocities, suggesting that sustaining the war provided increased strategic and economic benefits for them.

Laibach's strategy for subversion relies on symbolically incorporating its ideological opponent. The band essentially opposes totalitarianism not only in its governmental form, but also in its political and economic "cult" forms. By appearing to embrace the "cult" they despise, Laibach changes the meanings of the symbols that have initially supported authority. The change itself, however, is not essentially the act of subversion. Rather, the subversion lies in the "occurrence" of symbolic incorporation, often through satire and irony, which demonstrates the "incompletion" of ideological domination. Through this simple maneuver, Laibach denies "the existence of true totalitarianism."[41]

Yugoslav and Serbian rock 'n' roll music contributed to shaping the forms of humor integrated into the protest repertoires of the late 1990s. Rock artists, especially Antonije Pušić, Đorđe Balašević, and Laibach, demonstrated to protesters in 1996–97 and Otpor activists the power of satire and parody in criticizing the regime's propaganda.[42] Moreover, the approaches adopted by these artists provided young dissidents with a subversive methodology with which to mimic and mock the regime's rhetoric. "Parodied obedience" would become a popular element of humorous protest action carried out in the late 1990s.

Tragicomic Films (1970s to 1990s)

Yugoslav and Serbian tragicomic films produced in the 1970s through the 1990s contributed to cultivating popular awareness of humor's two subversive functions: criticizing the prevailing regime and challenging self-perception among Serbians. Generally, the films revolved around tragic life events under the socialist regime. These events ranged from violent death—common in the Balkans as a result of war atrocities and regime oppression—to the social discrimination of marginalized groups.[43] But tragicomic films typically made light of these tragedies by, for example, portraying highly respected public figures exhibiting absurd behavior, describing ridiculous causes for fatal accidents, or providing optimistic insights into what were otherwise sad film endings. These characteristics of tragicomic films might not have influenced humorous protest methods directly, but they shaped a collective understanding in which humor, particularly satire, constituted the foremost option for undermining the regime's authority or suspending—at least temporarily—widespread depression in times of political instability.[44]

Earlier in this period, between the 1970s and 1980s, Yugoslav tragicomic films typically conveyed criticism of social life under the communist regime. Under the "Black Wave" genre, 1970s film productions were influenced significantly by the Belgrade students rebellion of 1968, and other left-wing student movements in Europe.[45] Popular films produced in this period include *When I Am Dead and Pale* (*Kad budem mrtav i beo*, 1967), *I Even Met Happy Gypsies* (*Skupljači perja*, 1967), and *Doomsday Is Near* (*Biće skoro propast sveta*, 1969). Crucially, these films share similar endings: they either question popular beliefs generated under communism or they symbolically attack the ideology.[46]

"Doomsday is Near" incorporates the latter feature through its ending, with the protagonist's "ethical" death. A kind-hearted swine herder saves a mentally challenged girl from sexual harassment by his fellow villagers. However, under the influence of these villagers, he is involved in further incidents against his will, including murdering the girl he earlier saved. The same group of townspeople later stage a kangaroo court, persecuting him for his crime. The swine herder is battered to death, but his death also symbolizes a kind of "ethical" death, represented by his preparedness to submit his own will to that of popular prejudice. Alongside the death scene of the protagonist is the film's finale depicting the town dwellers mobilizing to vote for the Communist Party in a manipulated election. By juxtaposing these two scenes, the director critiques the mindless, subservient obedience cultivated under communism.[47]

Yugoslav tragicomic films reached the apogee of their international recognition in the 1980s.[48] Award-winning films in this period include: *Who's Singin' over There?* (*Ko to tamo peva*, 1980); *The Balkan Spy* (*Balkanski špijun*, 1981); *The Marathon Family* (*Maratonci trče počasni krug*, 1982); *Strangler vs. Strangler* (*Davitelj protiv davitelja*, 1984); and *The Meeting Point* (*Sabirni centar*, 1989). *Who's Singin' over There?* represents an all-time classic of Yugoslav tragicomic film. The movie revolves around a bus trip to Belgrade and the absurd behavior of the passengers, representing stereotypes across different social groups (e.g., two Gypsy musicians, a World War I veteran, a Germanophile, a budding singer, and a hunter with a rifle). Along the way, they encounter various difficulties that slow the bus down (e.g., a flat tire, a shaky bridge, a farmer who ploughs over the road, a funeral, and two feuding families). The ludicrous traits of each passenger cause further trouble. The movie, however, ends with the deaths of the protagonists (except for the two Gypsies) when, upon arrival in Belgrade, World War II begins. The bus is bombed by the first airstrike that hit the capital city.[49]

But it is the *Balkan Spy* that successfully satirizes the paranoid temperament of the communist regime. The leading character, Ilija Čvorović, is accused of being a Soviet spy and is jailed for many years. When he is released and returns home, he suspects the tenant of his rented house of being a French spy. Despite the unfounded suspicion, Čvorović makes up evidence based on his illusion. Čvorović goes so far as to detain his tenant and tortures him to extract a confession. When the tenant plans to flee the country, Čvorović orders his wife to call the airport seeking the cancellation of "all flights." The film bases its absurd comic edge on mimicry of the Yugoslav regime's obsession with witch-hunts for Soviet communists.[50]

In the context of the Yugoslav wars and the rise of nationalism, the tragicomic films of the 1990s generally questioned the values that established grounds for waging war. The films typically based their comedy on nostalgia, military mobilization, war profiteering, and inhumane conduct by militia. Films such as *Underground* (*Podzemlje*, 1995), *Pretty Village, Pretty Flame* (*Lepo sela, lepo gore*, 1996), *Black Cat, White Cat* (*Crna mačka, beli mačor*, 1998), and *War Live* (*Rat uživo*, 2000) are prime examples. They are all "war" movies, per se, with the exception of *Black Cat, White Cat*, which centers on the romantic relationship of a war profiteering Gypsy couple in the 1990s. However, their comic lines can usually be found amidst the scenes of war and destruction. For instance, *Pretty Village, Pretty Flame* depicts the Bosnian war. Despite melodramatic events, especially when two friends—a Bosnian Serb and a Muslim Bosnian—turn against each other, the character "Viljuška" lights up the generally depressive mood of the film. Viljuška's nickname is "Fork" because he carries a fork around his neck to symbolize the claim that Serbs had invented the fork—implying achievement of civilization before other European nations emerged from the Middle Ages. This claim was fanned to mobilize nationalist sentiments in support of wars for a "greater Serbia."[51] *Pretty Village, Pretty Flame* successfully mocks the claim through the character of Viljuška, while highlighting the association of national myths with war mobilization.[52]

Comedy Television Shows

The popularity of British television comedy shows, particularly *Monty Python's Flying Circus*, evidently offered the 1990s protesters ammunition in terms of ideas for humorous street actions.[53] *Monty Python* was initially broadcast in the former Yugoslavia in the 1970s. Famously acknowledged for being the most "surreal, nonsensical, and carnivalesque" of TV comedies, *Monty Python* sketches cast state ideologies, their authorities, and Catholicism in Western Europe in an absurd light.[54] For instance, in the skit "The Communist Quiz," Karl Marx, Lenin, Che Guevara, and Mao Zedong are reduced to jesters competing to answer a senseless quiz in a pseudo TV game show. The skit "Hitler in England" exposes moral errors within the Nazi ideology by exaggerating it to the absurd. Other skits, such as "Ministry of Silly Walks" and "Court Sketch," unveil the universally absurd characteristics of bureaucracy. Numerous sketches—such as "I Wish to Report the Burglary," "Probe around on Crime," "Crunch Frog," "Police Raid," and "Fairy Story about the Police"—contemptuously juxtapose the seriousness of the police with the silliness of police tasks. The comic and exaggerated performance of the *Python* members expresses the unspeakable, that is, the nonsensical nature of police duties, such as the excessive use of force in the "Police Raid" skit, despite unfounded allegations.[55]

The "Pythonesque" style of dark humor, upending the seriousness of established norms, fits well with the tradition of Yugoslav avant-garde theater and the tragicomic film genre.[56] While other British comedy shows, such as *Allo Allo* and *Doctor Who*, managed to become popular in the former Yugoslavia, the odd combination of rebelliousness and silliness central to *Monty Python*, remained an inspiration for young protesters in the 1990s.[57] Time and again *Monty Python's Flying Circus* is referenced as a crucial source of inspiration for Otpor's street skits.[58] As we shall see in later chapters, the disclosure of the nonsensical nature of the state's apparatus in serving the regime was the approach Otpor adopted from *Monty Python*.

The Serbian Sense of (Black) Humor

"Life has never been easy here, but we manage to laugh" is a common expression in Serbia. Black humor flourishes in places where life is hard. The historical episodes of war, mass exodus, dictatorship, poverty, media censorship—and the list goes on—provide rich material for black humor. Consequently, humor that teases with matters of life and death has here become the force that "invalidates power of all existential obstacles and of death itself."[59] In the Balkan region, where six wars have raged within the past century—in the Second World War alone, eleven percent of the total population of Yugoslavia was lost[60]—a black sense of humor has become a mechanism for survival.[61] Serb protesters learned to harness the power of black humor in assuaging their fear of death, a fate threatened regularly by the authorities.

While the consequences of war in Croatia and Bosnia were disastrous,[62] Serbians also bore the impact of war to a great degree. By mid-1993 there were approximately 540,000 refugees, most of them Croatian and Bosnian Serbs who had migrated into Serbia. And international sanctions from 1992 through the Dayton Peace Agreement in 1995 pushed domestic industry to the edge of bankruptcy. Only ten percent of factories were able to work normally, while the unemployment rate rose to 44 percent in 1998.[63] During the period of sanctions, inappropriate financial policy led to hyper-inflation, reaching its peak in 1992 through to late 1993. At one point, fifty million Serbian dinars were worth only a few loaves of bread.[64] In January 1994, inflation rose by 313,563,558 percent per month. Electricity was subsequently restricted during the winter of 1994.[65] The widespread shortage of food in shops also forced many to rely on food distributed by charities.[66] Serbian society had turned into a mafia fiefdom. Warlords and black market profiteers became respected figures, while the rule of law was replaced with gang assassination.[67] This period also saw a significant "brain-drain" from Serbia, with an estimated 150,000 to 300,000 émigrés who were highly educated young professionals.[68]

Under these circumstances of war and destruction, black humor flourished in Serbia, as well as other Yugoslav states. Black humor has the reputation of being perverse in the sense that it often involves saying the opposite of what one actually means, and making fun of deadly situations. An example of this black humor is discernible in the jokes poking fun at the stereotypes of rural population and ethnic groups in Yugoslavia (e.g., southern Serbians as misers, central Serbians as capricious and malicious, Montenegrins as lazy and pushy, Bosniaks as crude and stupid, and Macedonians as jolly).[69] As much as ethnic jokes can demonstrate the prejudice of one ethnic group toward another, they are considered prototypical of Yugoslav black humor because the jokes contain "self-racism," where an ethnic group mocks its own stereotype.[70] Jokes circulated among Bosnians during the Serbian siege in the early 1990s epitomized this interplay between ethnic stereotype and self-deprecating black humor. The following Bosnian joke pokes fun at war atrocities and at the same time highlights Bosniaks' mockery of themselves as being "dull":

> Cigarettes are in very short supply and Mujo had put his last one behind his ear. . . . Mujo and Suljo are running over the Drvenija Bridge when a [Serb] sniper opens up on them. Mujo takes a hit, which shears off his ear. He stops frantically in the middle of the bridge looking at the ground.
>
> Suljo yells, "Get under cover, idiot! You've got two ears!"
>
> Mujo responds, "Fuck the ear, I am looking for the cigarette!"[71]

In Serbia, during the 1990s, the anti-authoritarian and self-disparaging elements of black humor have been popular, evidence of which can be found in many funny aphorisms. Found springing from a society going through upheaval, these aphorisms are satirical, short, and sharp sayings. Their contents contain ironic statements that praise the existing socially distressing conditions. In Serbian society, aphorisms could be found anonymously written on the walls in many different places, or circulating amongst friends. If witty enough, they would be picked up by newspapers, radio shows, and notably by street protesters.[72]

The popular themes of aphorisms in the 1990s revolved around wars and the Serbian share of the guilt for generating the wars, the sanctions, shortages of basic goods, and the hypocritical and repressive nature of the Milošević regime. The theme of war primarily dealt with the absurd causes of the Yugoslav wars. Examples of these are as follows: "Fake patriotism is bothering me. I love my country exactly because I don't know why;" "The conflict could not have been avoided. You were fighting for peace, we were fighting against war;" "We wanted the war to finish as soon as possible. That's why we started it first;" "We didn't have any reason to slaughter each other. That motivated us even further;" "Is a new war possible? I don't know. All the previous ones were impossible;" and "The longer the war, the closer we are to peace."

Other aphorisms deal with Serbian responsibility for instigating the wars. Examples include the following: "We never take responsibility for our acts—we are not a terrorist organization;" "It is ridiculous to accuse us of having planned a genocide. We never plan anything in advance;"

and "The war criminal has double-parked. Such a thing cannot go unpunished in this country."[73]

The international sanctions that induced economic recession enriched the creation of humorous aphorisms. During the hyperinflation of 1994, the government cut off the entire country's electricity supply. The following phrases were found in response: "The only good thing about not having electricity is that there is no television to tell us that we *have* electricity," [which was common government propaganda at the time, despite the obvious falsehood]; "Serbia is at this moment the most romantic country in the world—we all live by candlelight;"[74] and "Without regular power cuts, there won't be enough electricity."[75] The high rate of unemployment due to the economic crisis gave rise to aphorisms such as: "I realized that time was money. I never have time to eat;" "Workers are paid miserably. Luckily, this doesn't happen very often."

Numerous satirical sayings reflected popular resentment toward repression by the regime. Examples are: "Stop! We will shoot!—the policemen warned the demonstrators. The demonstrators stopped. The police fired warning shots in the air. It's not their fault that some demonstrators inhaled them;" "When a policeman can't remember something, he hits the first passer-by in the head;" "You will have full freedom of speech. That will somewhat restrict your freedom of movement;" "Do you have freedom of speech?—Yes, but I'd rather not talk about it over the phone;" and "The opposition had good results at the elections. No one got killed."[76]

Finally, the Serb's traumatic history—which in many ways provided the ground for the rise of Serb nationalism—was at the top of the satirists' target-list: "Our past is awful, our present terrible: it's lucky that we don't have a future;"[77] "I am afraid that we will have a stormy past even in the future;" and "Once I went so far into the future that I arrived at the beginning of the past."[78]

The proliferation of everyday satirical jokes underpinned the development of humorous street actions in the 1996–97 protests and Otpor's campaigns. Veteran protesters and activists alike congruently stated that the dark period in the 1990s sharpened a popular sense of humor as a strategy for survival: "[you] either sit down, cry and kill yourself or start to make jokes out of it."[79] But beyond being merely a survival strategy, as the following chapters will demonstrate, protesters and activists in the 1990s were aware of the power of humor to subvert Milošević's dictatorial rule.

Cultural Construction of Intuitive Humor

The popularity of defiant and black humor in the former Yugoslavia and Serbia—manifested in theater, music, movies and comedy TV shows—generally helped construct a popular mindset conducive to the development of humorous protest tactics in Serbia in the 1990s. This development of tactical humor exhibits the crucial nexus between intuition and culture that constitutes an entry point to understand the terrain of humor's operation in a nonviolent struggle. Intuition is where the skill of joke creation develops. It is the ability to carry out an activity and make a judgment by drawing on one's experience bodily, emotionally, and intellectually. Rather than being based in rationality, intuition flows from an "inner" knowledge—a heartfelt awareness of what to do in a certain situation. Creative activities such as playing musical instruments and making handcrafted art are arguably intuitive; analytical skills are largely unrelated to these activities. This inner knowledge requires the reference to past experiences, the knowledge stored in parts of the brain and mind usually not reached by conscious thought processes.[80] The ability to create a humorous moment through jokes or comedic performance arises from this intuitive terrain.[81]

Despite the intuitive basis, culture influences the collective understanding of what is regarded as humorous. On the one hand, this understanding determines the content of popular jokes in one society in contrast to others. On the other hand, a collective understanding also delineates how some jokes are regarded as culturally appropriate, while others are seen to be "crossing the line."[82] Take, for example, the subjects permitted for mockery. In a culture with an egalitarian tendency, mocking political and religious figures may be acceptable. However, in a culture with a strong hierarchy, doing so may be considered a serious insult, causing public outrage.[83] Due to the influence of this collective cultural understanding, joke creators draw on their cultural background in order to provoke laughter in the audience from their particular society. In other words, the intuition, discussed above, that aids in creating humor must be understood as an intuition that operates relative to a given culture.[84] The skill of creating jokes depends on an awareness of what triggers laughter in a specific cultural setting.

Culture draws a boundary for one's creation of jokes at the same time that it provides material for jokes to proliferate. In terms of "getting" a joke, culture may pose limits to an outsider. For a cross-cultural understanding of a joke to be possible, there must be extended insight into the symbolism, language, and historical context of the society wherein the joke has developed. Nevertheless, jokes have traveled among and between civilizations, indicating that comic culture may be transferred, despite the cultural particularity of a given joke's origins.[85] The relation between culture and jokes may be considered from a productive viewpoint. Symbolism, language, and historical knowledge are resources for joke contents. They provide tools for making fun of somebody or something by relating to symbolic or linguistic systems commonly understood by one's cultural fellows. In this sense, cultural settings are the market of ideas for joke creators.[86]

The cultural construction of intuitive humor provides an explanation about the relationship between proliferation of comedic culture in the former Yugoslavia, and the invention of tactical humor by Serbian protesters in the 1990s. For them, infusing political protests with a touch of humor was intuitive, spontaneous (at least in the early 1990s), and yet collective. It was something they felt was ingrained in their "Serb nature" or even their "genes."[87] Hence their use of humor was "natural."[88] Nevertheless, this "natural" sense of humor was to a large extent shaped by social and political experiences that many Serbians shared.[89]

Black humor, characterized by poking fun at otherwise depressing moments, has long been a mechanism of coping with everyday difficulties in Serbia such as poverty, war atrocities, and limited civil freedom. The prevalence of black humor helps explain the popularity of comedy films, satirical rock songs, and absurd theatre in the former Yugoslavia and present Serbia. These different forms of comedic pop culture constituted a vehicle for artists to express their discontent toward the regime. This artistic resistance provided diverse sources of inspiration and an arsenal of ideas upon which 1990s' protesters and activists would draw. As I will elaborate, some humorous actions mimicked Yugoslav artists' productions, while other methods of speaking mirth to power resonated with Laibach and *Monty Python*.

Conclusion

The proliferation of humor in everyday Serbian life provided the key underpinning factor for the development of humorous protest actions in the 1996–97 protests and Otpor's campaigns. The subversive content contained in satirical jokes and forms of pop culture (e.g., absurdist theater, satirical rock lyrics, tragicomic films, and comedy television shows) helped to cultivate anti-regime sentiment among the general public. These forms of everyday humor would expose dissidents and seasoned activists to the possibilities of incorporating humor into their protest repertoires. Expressed differently, everyday experiences of humor created the vast pool of ideational resources for activists. Despite the general perception that their use of defiant humor was intuitive, this chapter has shed light on the important role culture has in shaping intuitive humor. When combined in protest repertoires, culturally influenced humor could offer an effective tool to challenge discursive domination.

2

Coming to the Fore

Humorous Protest Actions in Serbia in the Early 1990s

The sites of struggle in Serbia in the 1990s were not only formal institutions of politics, but also political culture. Whereas Slobodan Milošević could consolidate his power through manipulation of popular perception, especially regarding the survival of Serbia, dissidents attempted to undermine his rhetoric by tactically instrumentalizing cultural resources at their disposal. This chapter shows the initial incorporation of everyday life humor into protest repertoires in 1991 and 1992. Although various humorous actions were created spontaneously—as a reaction to vote manipulation and simmering Yugoslav wars—they reflected collective awareness of humor's subversive potential. The cultural realm of humor that had developed in the former Yugoslavia was coming to the fore, offering dissidents a tool to wrestle with the regime's promulgation of nationalist culture.

Serbia under Milošević

In the media prank entitled "Tito among the Serbs for the Second Time," one Serbian passerby complained to (pseudo) Marshall Tito roaming in Belgrade's center that his life was so much in misery after Tito's death because there were too many "Titos." He would prefer to have only one Tito. "The one was good," he affirms.[1] This view could represent an aspect of Serbian authoritarian personality: the popular trust in strong leadership and a commitment to obedience.[2] Slobodan Milošević came to power in the late 1980s through several political maneuverings so as to centralize his authority. More importantly, he managed to capture the Serbian public

36

mind searching for the psychological assurance of certainty in the wake of Yugoslav decline. This assurance, however, came at a cost. Throughout the 1990s, Milošević launched wars with neighboring countries that, among other things, led to international sanctions, manipulation of the Serbian currency rate followed by hyperinflation, and a strengthening of the security forces coupled with the militarization of civilians. In dissipating growing dissatisfaction among the populace, Milošević promulgated a series of propaganda based on distorted history that consequently reinforced ethnic fault lines, Serb victimization, and fear of "enemies" both inside and outside Serbian borders. The propaganda influenced a popular perception of Milošević as the defender of the Serbs, providing him with a great deal of legitimacy and justification to suppress challengers. Serbians' desire for conformity combined with Milošević's schematic manipulation of public opinion posed challenges to Serbian opposition fronts. Despite this backdrop, ideas to strike the regime at its own discursive ground emerged in the 1991 and 1992 demonstrations. Satire and parody were forms of resistance that came in handy.[3]

Street Actions in the Early 1990s

The nascent incorporation of humor in street protests was witnessed in two periods: during opposition-led demonstrations in 1991 and student demonstrations in 1992. The latter was characterized by satirical performances, parody in slogans, and street parties that would be replicated and multiplied in the 1996–97 anti-vote-rigging protests. Apart from student and opposition demonstrations, antiwar activists and journalists were inspired to develop their own style of defiant humor. Some of their actions could be labeled as sardonic, while others were rather thought provoking.

The 1991 demonstrations were triggered by the growing anti-regime sentiment following the Milošević-led Socialist Party of Serbia's (Socijalistička partija Srbije or "SPS") dubious victory in parliamentary and presidential elections.[4] Vuk Drašković, leader of the Serbian Renewal Movement (Srpski pokret obnove or "SPO"), realized that the SPS's control over the media contributed to his defeat. On March 9, 1991, he led a mass demonstration, which the regime crushed harshly. From March 10 to 14, students occupied Terazije Square, demanding the release of those arrested during the crackdown. Aiming to differentiate themselves from the opposition parties, students to some degree invented comic symbols, which were then used in place of national banners. For instance, the "velvet panda bears" banner was commonly seen at the protest site, which conferred on the 1991 protest the title, "the Velvet (R)evolution" (*Plišana (r)evolucija*).[5]

When the Bosnian war broke out in May 1992, satirical street performance became a vital method for many civil society groups to criticize the Milošević regime's gross involvement in the Yugoslav wars. The independent radio station B92 was one of these groups. At the onset of the Bosnian war, a founder and then chairperson of the board of directors of B92, Veran Matić, set up a parallel war scene in Belgrade in order to expose people to the frontline reality. Barricades were erected in the city center. Matić, in a mocking manner, donned a military uniform—topped with a beret and sun glasses—and patrolled around the fake barricades.

In another incident, a disk jockey at B92 used black humor to show Serbs that the wars caused neighboring countries to feel distrustful and fearful toward them. He called random telephone numbers in the Slovenian capital of Ljubljana, introducing himself as an old Serb friend from the army. To proceed with the prank, the DJ asked whether he and twelve other Serb friends could come and stay overnight at houses of those he called. The recipients of the call were horrified "at the prospect of a dozen 'redneck' nationalists descending upon them[.]"[6]

To bring home the impact of the wars even further, the B92 station crew staged another street skit, which they called "All the President's Babies." The action was an attempt to make public the economic recession that affected household concerns, such as the rise in price of children's products. Parents were invited to bring their babies to Milošević's house in the affluent suburb of Dedinje and offer them to the President, so he could take care of them. A few days after the action, the government reduced the tax on children's products.[7]

In a similar vein, antiwar street actions by various peace movements in Serbia provided a theatrical basis for satirical protests in the late 1990s. The activist group "Women in Black" (Žene u crnom) has been persistently combining nonviolent demonstrations with theatrical performance.

During the Bosnian war, the group's activists gathered in the pedestrian square of Belgrade's center, dressed in black, and carried black banners, candles and flowers. They stood in silence every Wednesday afternoon to show their grief and disagreement with the war precipitated by the Milošević regime.[8] The group's most recognized street action was arguably the "Black Mourning Band" in which a thousand participants held a 1,300 metre-long black ribbon. It was a procession to pay tribute to all victims of war and to mark the first anniversary of the Bosnian war.[9] In another street action held on July 15, 1992, peace activists from Women in Black and other groups collectively held a yellow ribbon and a banner, which read "I am an Orthodox, Catholic, Muslim, Jew, Buddhist, and Atheist," in front of the Federal Assembly building. This performance sought to foster cosmopolitan values against regime-fanned xenophobia and nationalism.[10]

Other peace groups approaching protest actions with theatrical performance included the Center against War and the Civil League. In the street action performance, "The Last Bell," these groups encouraged Serbians to demand a change of regime as the solution to limited civil rights and the ongoing armed conflicts with neighboring countries. The action's inspiration was derived from a common saying that the ringing of the "last bell" signifies the country's leader's resignation. To express their popular desire for regime change, participants in the action were asked to bring along anything that could make a clinking sound. They stood for an hour in front of the Serbian Assembly building, "concertizing with their chimes, carillons, sheep and cow's bells, cymbals, sets of keys, and noisy mechanical alarm clocks."[11]

It was the mass demonstration in 1992 that saw students' leading role in inventing numerous humorous protest actions. Between June and July, around 20,000 students occupied faculty buildings of Belgrade University, demanding immediate elections and the removal of the Milošević regime. Their slogan was "Enough!" (*Dosta!*): enough of the wars, international sanctions, and the regime's restrictions on university freedoms. Throughout the twenty-six days of the protest, continuous music playing and parties generated a festive euphoria, despite the imminent possibility of a regime crackdown, in addition to the existing backdrop of wars and sanctions. Innovative satirical theater and witty slogans invented by the students also gave a festive edge to the protest.[12]

The state control of media, destructive policies, and corrupt regime cronies were the main themes of students' satirical protests. For instance, in the street action performance "The Strolling of the Blind," students walked past the state TV headquarters with their eyes closed, symbolizing the manipulation of the state-run media.[13] They also deliberately dressed in prison uniforms and walked past police headquarters, so people could see that they were "imprisoned" in the "police" state.[14] In the same action, students responded to the regime's accusation that they were being manipulated by pinning prisoners' numbers onto their shirts and walking with one hand holding their student identification cards high in the air.[15] To denounce figures within the corrupt regime, students staged the action, "Washing Up." Each of them left domestic hygiene supplies (such as soap, detergent, and a half-used tube of toothpaste) in front of the Assembly building, for politicians to sanitize their "dirty tongues and gross past deeds." During the action, Vojislav Šešelj, the leader of the Serbian Radical Party (Srpska radikalna stranka or "SRS") and of a paramilitary group, came out of the building, swearing at and threatening the protesters with his revolver. The students responded by pelting him with a barrage of soap bars.[16]

Students walked to Milošević's neighborhood and mockingly invited him and his family to join the protest. On July 7, the anniversary of the Partisan Rebellion Day (which had been symbolically associated with the Yugoslav United Left (Jugoslovenska udružena levica or "JUL"), led by Milošević's wife, Mirjana Marković), students organized a "Peace March." The title indicated the antiwar theme of the 1992 protest at the same time that it parodied the name "Mirjana," which derives from *mir*, the Serbian word for "peace." Students walked for twelve kilometers from the Student Square in Belgrade's center to the Milošević home, claiming that they wanted to "go for a cup of coffee" with Marković. Inhabitants of the area the students strolled through came out to greet them, and some even joined the walk. The students, however, were prevented by cordons of police from reaching Milošević's house.[17] Tired of wrestling with the police, students opted for a different option the following day:

they created a parallel theatrical scene—entitled "Five O'Clock Coffee"—which mockingly depicted reaching the Milošević home. Puppets were made to represent Milošević and his wife and were placed on the stage, which was decorated to resemble the Milošević's residential area. Students then replicated the whole walk they had undertaken on the previous day, presenting the president with flowers and their list of demands.[18]

During the 1992 protest, sculptures and effigies were created and placed around the university campus and in some city locations as an expression of student rebellion. Apart from mocking regime figures, the effigies served as a reflection on the authoritarian mentality of Serbian society. For instance, a sculpture of a TV spectator—whose eyes were blindfolded—was erected in front of the office building of the state-run media. Protesters wanted to show that official media was deliberately ignoring the realities of the war and oppression by blindfolding itself. The sculpture of a soldier—positioned as if to be in the throes of committing suicide—was erected in front of the Defense Ministry building to protest the regime's war-mongering policies. The sculpture of a weary citizen was exhibited in front of the assembly building to reflect the endemic political apathy of broader society. An installation of a male figure was found on the roof of the Faculty of Philosophy building, with his footsteps painted on a long sheet of paper all the way to the ground. It indicated he had climbed up the building toward heaven, but that path led him nowhere except to the ledge. The artwork was named, "A Path to Heavenly Serbia." It was both a parody and a criticism of the way in which the most well-known Serbian epic, depicting Serbia as "the Empire of Heaven," was notoriously appropriated as a rhetorical device for inciting war to expand Serbian territory.[19]

The 1992 protest saw a multitude of witty slogans created to mock government figures, as well as to lighten the protest atmosphere. One of the first satirical creations came in the form of a protest slogan hung on a faculty building: "SPS = Guns n' Roses." Playing on the name of an American rock band, the slogan allegorically associated the regime with violence (guns) and the Socialist Party's monopoly of the country (the rose was the symbol of the SPS). In the following days, creative slogans emerged. Examples include: "Enough with Thanatos, we vote for Eros!"

(associating the regime with Thanatos, the Greek god of hatred and death, and associating democratic change with *eros*, the power of love); "Wanted! Exchange of a student booklet for an agricultural cooperative membership card" (mocking the provincial support of the regime); and "Offer: house with a single story for a house with a basement" (suggesting the possible bombing of Serbia by the international community). Other slogans were based on popular sayings or commercial phrases, such as: "Sloba or wealth? We have decided, have you?" (referring to the original slogan for the health campaign, "Smoking or health?");[20] "One small step for you, one giant leap for Serbia" (a parody of Neil Armstrong's moon-landing proclamation); and "I think, therefore I strike!" (echoing René Descartes's famous phrase). There were also slogans playing with the meaning of the president's name, "Slobodan," which means 'liberal' in Serbian: "If you are 'SLOBODAN,' I don't feel that you really are."[21] This kind of humorous subversion has a long history within Serbian culture, and thereby not entirely innovative. However, its collective use as a constitutive part of an organized protest was unprecedented.

Psychological Safety Valve

The 1991 and 1992 protests demonstrated how humor could move from the private realm of everyday personal interactions to the public arena of street demonstration. As discussed in the previous chapter, anti-regime jokes circulating among friends and family members indicate the operational location of humor in the private sphere. Despite an understanding that these private jokes potentially set the stage for organized resistance movements,[22] there remains a tendency to belittle humor's potential by dismissing it as merely a psychological safety valve. From that perspective, anti-authoritarian humor only serves the oppressed's need for a psychological escape from harsh reality, effectively enabling oppression to be endured and sustained. The emerging tactical use of humor in the 1991 and 1992 protests potentially challenges this argument in two ways.

First, the tactical humor manifested in these protests did not arise in a vacuum, but was instead an outcome of the cumulative experiences of Serbians poking fun at authorities in their everyday lives. While I do not suggest a purely linear relationship between everyday humor and organized protest humor, I have demonstrated that everyday experiences of Serbian humor predated the 1991 and 1992 protests, which were clearly characterized by subversive humor. It is possible that activists and protest participants were inspired by their everyday encounters with defiant humor. In this sense, jokes circulating in the private sphere provided a reservoir of ideas for demonstrators in the 1990s.[23]

Second, the connection between everyday comedic experiences and humorous protests—as discerned in the 1991 and 1992 demonstrations—problematizes the assessment of humor's subversive potential underpinning the safety valve theory. The assumption that anti-regime humor does not actually undermine the regime's legitimacy is generally based on an examination of joke contents. The political motivation underlying jokes is ambiguous, depending on the interpretation of contexts surrounding jokes.[24] In contrast, when humor is used as a tactic in planned resistance campaigns, the degree of its contribution can be better assessed. This is because the unit of analysis is shifted from joke contents to a protest movement utilizing humor instrumentally together with other repertoires so as to achieve stated goals. Whether or not humorous tactics are effective may depend on the movement's conceptualization of humor's function in its overarching strategies. For our purpose, the 1991 and 1992 protesters combined humor into their street actions. However, these demonstrations generally lacked effective organization and achievable goals, which consequently hindered the maximization of humor's subversive potential.

Nonetheless, the infusion of humor into protest repertoires by protesters may be considered an attempt to appropriate the cultural site primarily dominated by the Milošević regime. The 1991 and 1992 protests shed light on how the invention of protest actions was shaped and enriched by the politico-cultural settings within which the activists exist. Ideas for humorous actions are influenced by the intangible asset their knowledge provides that humor can be a powerful method for resisting the dominating power they face. As much as cultural experiences shape ways of thinking, they also provide ideational resources for strategic planning in a political struggle. That is to say, if Milošević could maintain his power by relying on cultural resources to mobilize popular support, the same resources were available to those who sought to resist him.

Street actions such as "All the President's Babies," "Strolling of the Blind," "Washing Up," and "A Path to Heavenly Serbia" were created based on the regime's existing rhetoric, corrupt policies, and the national myth. These domains of influence helped consolidate the regime's legitimacy for years. In completing these actions, protesters however twisted the core meanings of the propaganda to the point of absurdity, potentially contributing to the rhetoric's loss of convincing tone. The regime was fought in its own domains of discursive power.

Other actions, such as "Five O'Clock Coffee" and "Peace March," deliberately mocked a specific regime figure, Mirjana Marković. The ridicule desecrated her persona as a fierce politician, and above all, paved the way for a later generation of protesters to poke fun at her fashion sense and personality in their street performances.

Student protesters' slogans juxtaposed domestic political incidents with unrelated pop culture. This not only resulted in a public manifestation of political absurdity, but also carved out an imaginative space amidst the paramount reality of nationalist mobilization and imminent wars. The two key elements—unsatisfactory Serbian politics and Western achievements—contained in students' slogans reflected Serbian urban youths' aspiration to join the international community, to be "normal" like young people in other societies.

Theoretically, such an imaginative expression provides a vehicle for transporting a familiar reality into an unfamiliar world. The imaginative creation of the humorous moment is intrinsically intertwined with the construction of sub-universes. Paramount reality reminds us day in and day out that it is the only world we are living in. However, imagination expressed in dreams, aesthetic experience, in child's play, and humorous moments enables the existence of other worlds within this reality.[25] Imaginative humor renews the meanings of things that are taken for granted in mundane life.[26] This construction of imaginative space would subsequently be integrated in the 1996–97 protesters' and Otpor's carnivalesque activities, leading to the collective effort to translate young Serbians' wish for a better life into a reality of democratic change.

3

Coming of Age

Carnivalesque Protests

I n 1996 and 1997, Serbia witnessed the nascent carnivalesque revolution. Led by opposition politicians and Belgrade students, the anti-vote-rigging demonstrations featured a variety of creative and cheerful non-violent actions. In one manifestation, ordinary citizens launched several spontaneous "happenings" in response to the regime's refusal to accept its defeat in municipal elections in November 1996. Other actions were organized and staged by students and, unlike the spontaneous "happenings," these actions were informed by a degree of reflection about the possible impact of humor upon the Milošević regime. The most important aspect of these events was the belief among some of the student leaders that humorous actions could dissipate protesters' anger, helping them hold back from provocative behavior. Students anticipated that this effect could discourage the security forces from violent crackdown. Moreover, parallel realities constructed in carnivalesque activities allowed protesters to project their vision of Serbia as democratic and nonviolent society. Both the disarming and imaginative functions of humor would be amplified in Otpor's campaigns.

Chronological Overview of the 1996–1997 Protests

The trigger for protests at this time was the evident rigging of municipal elections in 1996. On November 3, both federal and municipal elections were held.[1] At the federal level, the Left Coalition, comprising Slobodan Milošević's Socialist Party of Serbia (SPS), Mirjana Marković's Yugoslav United Left (JUL), and the New Democracy (Nova demokratija or "ND") beat the opposition coalition (Zajedno or "Together"). This coalition consisted of Zoran Đinđić's Democratic Party (Demokratska stranka or "DS"), Vuk Drašković's Serbian Renewal Movement (SPO), and Vesna Pešić's Civic Alliance of Serbia (Građanski savez Srbije or "GSS").[2] However, at the municipal level, no party received a decisive majority of the vote. The second round of the election was held on November 17, when the Left Coalition gained victories in over 100 municipalities, but lost to the opposition parties in forty-one major cities and municipalities, including Belgrade. These cities formed the backbone of Serbia's economy, were key strongholds for Milošević's popularity, and were the locations where the regime exerted its control over the media.[3] Because of these significant factors, the Electoral Commission—controlled by the ruling parties—moved to annul the electoral victories of the opposition coalition.[4]

The "stolen election" gave legitimate ground for the opposition coalition to call for nationwide demonstrations. On November 19, the first protests erupted in the southern city of Niš, and attracted some 50,000 participants at its peak.[5] On the following days, other protests followed in Užice, Kragujevac, Novi Sad, Čačak, Pirot, and Jagodina. On November 21, the opposition coalition began its first march in Belgrade when it became clear that the authorities were attempting to obstruct the election of Đinđić, who had won the Belgrade mayoral poll.[6]

The eighth day of protest saw Serbians taking to the streets across the country. In Belgrade the number of protesters reached 200,000, while 15,000 people gathered in Kragujevac, and 5,000 in Kraljevo. In SPS-controlled towns such as Valjevo and Leskovac, people also took to the streets.[7] By January 1997, in Belgrade alone, approximately 700,000 persons had taken part in the demonstrations.[8] And by mid-February, close to the end of the opposition protests, around six million people across Serbia had reportedly taken part in "The Winter of Discontent."[9]

Overall the protests were nonviolent, but there was a major clash between SPS supporters and Belgrade protesters on December 24, 1996. Observers noted that around 40,000 to 60,000 SPS supporters were transported from southern and eastern Serbia, including Kosovo.[10] These supporters claimed that they came to Belgrade to defend Serbia from "a handful of hooligans and provocateurs," a line that echoed the propaganda of the state-controlled media.[11] As soon as the SPS protesters got off the buses however, they found themselves surrounded by hundreds of thousands of angry Belgraders who booed at them and made it clear "they were ready to fight."[12] The clash culminated in the shooting of an SPO supporter, Ivica Lazović, the beating to death of Predrag Starčević, and another fifty-eight injuries.[13]

The protests gained increasing political momentum, and by early January received both domestic and international endorsements. In late November 1996, the Organization for Security and Cooperation in Europe (OSCE) and the US government sent letters to Milošević, demanding the recognition of the local election results. On January 2, 1997, the Serbian Orthodox Church released a letter that endorsed the student protests, while condemning the Milošević regime as a "[communist], godless, and satanic regime."[14] A few days later, the Yugoslav Army's chief-of-staff agreed to meet with a student leader, Čedomir Jovanović. Later, he confirmed that the Army would not carry out any action that was against the constitution or the will of citizens.[15]

The second week of January 1997 saw the regime's acknowledgement of the opposition coalition's victories. The election results were first recognized in Niš and Vršac, followed by fourteen other municipalities.[16] On February 11, the Serbian Assembly adopted a special law (*lex specialis*), introduced by the government, as a way out of the growing mass dissatisfaction that might have led to its downfall had it let the protests continue. The law recognized the original election outcomes, but did not hold the Electoral Commission accountable for its unlawful falsification of the opposition coalition's victories.[17] The opposition's protests were concluded on February 23, 1997, and Đinđić was inaugurated as the mayor of Belgrade.[18]

Despite the regime's acceptance of electoral defeat, there remained several thousand students in Belgrade persistently carrying on the "student protests" (*studentski protesti*). The students were known for their political nonpartisanship and commitment to nonviolence. The student networks that emerged during the protests paved the way for the formation of the Otpor ("resistance") movement and its innovative humorous protest tactics.

Organizing the Student Protests

In the 1996–97 protests, the independent students' ad hoc committee, which had been formed in late November, became the catalyst for
establishing student networks across Serbia's major cities.[19] The Belgrade
student organization was the most structured. After the annulment of
election results, students from Belgrade University and the School of Arts
began to boycott classes. This initial act of defiance led to the formation
of the student initiatives boards in faculties such as philology, philosophy,
mathematics, mechanical engineering, and biology. Membership of each
faculty-level board ranged from five to fifteen persons. These boards, now
collectively known as the University Students' Main Board, were tasked
with attending meetings of the university-level board.[20]

Consisting of between seventy and eighty representatives from the
faculty boards, the Students' Main Board oversaw the coordination and
logistics of staging the protests. It held daily meetings to discuss matters such as decisions on walking routes, the nature of street activities
and cultural events, and coordinating their activities with the opposition coalition as well as the police.[21] In terms of logistical management,
the Faculty of Philosophy spearheaded the division of tasks by setting
up teams such as the security team, propaganda and press team, the
program unit and electronic media team, and finance team.[22] According
to Čedomir Antić, then the vice-chairman of the Students' Main Board,
there were around 300 people working on administration in the different
teams. During the peak of the demonstrations, such as the stand-off with
the police on the eve of 1996, the number of student volunteers reached
between 3,000 and 4,000.[23]

The program unit took the lead in organizing humor-based events to
generate a festive atmosphere. The main responsibility of this program
unit was to organize cultural events and concerts after the end of the
daily protest program. Typically, the protest activity began with a gathering and speeches at 12:00 p.m., followed by the student walk and the citizen walk (led by the opposition coalition) from 4:00 to 6:00 p.m. Cultural
events and theater plays or concerts were usually organized at night to
maintain a critical number of participants.[24] The program unit was later

involved in engineering some of the collective street actions by students, and worked collaboratively to help the propaganda and press team, which was charged with contacting the independent media to cover the protest events and student actions.[25] According to Pero Jelić, a member of the program unit's staff, the majority of student street action was humorous, specifically created to generate a festive euphoria. However, Jelić indicated they needed to be careful about the type of humor they used for their protest actions, preferring satire because it could provide an entertaining "edge" to the protests without losing the image of their seriousness.[26]

In the southern city of Niš, student protests were carried out on a smaller scale than in Belgrade, but were similarly well-organized. A few days after the alleged electoral fraud, students from different faculties at University of Niš took to the street. They demanded the acceptance of the opposition's electoral victory and the accountability of authorities who were allegedly involved in vote rigging.[27] According to student leaders Milan Stefanović, Mile Ilić, and Boban Arsenijević, students began setting up the core committee after a few days of separate protests.[28] Due to the smaller number of students compared with those from University of Belgrade, tasks within the Niš Student Committee were not clearly divided or assigned to different teams. Only the security team was properly formed to take care of traffic security during the daily walks, and a group of thirty to forty students led the organization of cultural events, committee meetings, and press conferences. This "action team" put together and implemented a strategy that was media friendly, theatrical, and convenient for ordinary people to participate in.[29] Most importantly, their actions were organized and staged on a basis of nonviolence.[30]

In Novi Sad, the gateway to the Vojvodina region in northern Serbia, student organization was almost without any structure or clear division of tasks. The opposition coalition managed to secure its electoral victory in this northern city. Consequently, students took to the street for reasons other than the fraudulent election. For instance, Stanko Lazendić and Miloš Gagić, who were among the leading student protesters, hoped that the nationwide uprisings could galvanize the potential overthrow of Milošević.[31] But Aleksandar Savanović points out that he took part in the protest because he wanted the abolition of the draconian University Law.[32]

The Novi Sad protest began with around fifty students gathering and spontaneously delivering speeches that condemned the regime for stealing votes in other cities. Later, they were in charge of organizing daily walks and other protest activities, one of which was the march to Belgrade.[33]

Nonviolence and Humorous Street Actions

Serbia's 1996–97 protests are remembered as nonviolent, joyful, and carnivalesque. And, the employment of nonviolence was planned as much as it was intuitive. For the opposition coalition, the use of nonviolence and humor in their actions was generally deliberate. There was agreement among opposition politicians to maintain the nonviolent nature of the protests. Dušan Juvanin, a long-standing member of the DS and a politician in the Northern town of Zrenjanin, points out that *Zajedno*'s reliance on nonviolent action resulted from the lessons they learned from the regime's crackdown against the 1991 protests. The opposition party realized that riots and sabotage could not defeat Milošević, because he controlled the police force, paramilitaries, and the army. More importantly, Milošević's power had been unchallenged because of his maneuvering and use of fear-based rhetoric.[34] Accordingly, there was discussion at the time within the circle of opposition politicians regarding what kind of nonviolent action could effectively deal with the fear generated, with the view taken that protests should be cheerful and positive. A sarcastic and humorous style of protest was chosen to respond to Milošević's politics of fear.[35]

For students, reliance on nonviolent action was both intuitive and deliberate. For many students, nonviolent struggle was an intuitive response to the wars and street crimes that had plagued Serbia during the 1990s. This hostility toward the regime became strong, particularly among male students who were being mobilized to serve as troops on the frontline. During the wars of the 1990s, the Serbian military had to rely on irregular soldiers as only 13 percent of draftees actually served in the military in the period of the wars.[36] In Belgrade alone, 90 percent of young men went into hiding during the military draft.[37] The strong sentiment in opposition to the regime's wars was reflected in one student's testimony in response to the regime's belittling of students by calling them "children": "Students are no children; they are citizens with full rights in this country, who have risen against the abolishment of their rights. You did not worry about our age when you sent us to Vukovar [in Croatia] and other places where the war was on."[38]

Intuition aside, the organizers of student protests were aware of the political necessity of maintaining nonviolent discipline. As did opposition politicians, students understood that provocative behavior or sabotage could play into the hands of the regime, which held complete control of the security forces. Students could have lost their popular support and could have been defeated in the struggle.[39] For Čedomir Antić, the problem of using violence in the fight for democracy runs deeper. He explained that if students had resorted to arms and they had happened to win the struggle, the students' goal of democratic change would not have been achieved.[40]

Students understood that humor could be used as a form of nonviolent action because it could attack the regime symbolically without provoking police repression. For instance, Pero Jelić explains that students became committed to nonviolence because of their general awareness that they could not match the regime's security forces, and that rank-and-file authorities only followed their commander's orders. Nevertheless, students wanted to express their rebellion against the regime. Humor provided students with an effective combination: "We didn't like the police, so what we did was to outwit them, to show them that we were smarter."[41]

This view reflects the way in which humor and nonviolent action were intertwined in the 1996–97 protests. Humorous street actions were staged together with different methods of nonviolent action, such as the use of blinking lights, jamming the phone lines, creating traffic jams, and sit-ins. They were either initiated by ordinary citizens and students, or nationally coordinated by the opposition coalition. Individually initiated actions were spontaneous, while those created by students and encouraged by the opposition coalition were planned. Humorous protest actions carried out in the 1996–97 protests can be categorized as carnivalesque rallies, witty slogans on placards, and satirical street theater.

Carnivalesque Rallies

Food throwing, noise making, parades, fancy costumes, plays, and parties defined the carnivalesque features of the 1996–97 protests.[42] The opposition coalition primarily conceived of egg throwing at buildings as a "symbolic" attack on the regime. This initiative later evolved into an entertaining and yet subversive protest activity. In the protest's early days, during the daily walks, some protesters allegedly threw stones and abused staff of Radio Television of Serbia (Radio-televizija Srbije or "RTS") and the regime-controlled newspaper, *Politika*. To prevent this vandalism, which could provoke a repressive response by the police, and yet maintain ways for protesters to express their anger, the opposition party leaders introduced the activity of throwing eggs at state buildings.[43] The prime targets were the offices of state media, City Hall, the court house, and the assembly buildings.[44] At the peak of the campaign, around 200,000 demonstrators launched eggs at state buildings, which consequently turned yellow and created a disgusting stench.[45] To visually emphasize this, the opposition leaders blocked their noses with their hands, showing a disgusted face every time they strolled past the stinking state buildings.[46]

Another carnivalesque characteristic of the 1996–97 protests was the cacophony of noise made to drown out the regime's propaganda. At the end of November, students launched the campaign "noise is in fashion" (*buka u modi*). They invited citizens in Belgrade and other cities to create noise from any equipment they could find. Because of their portability, whistles became the preferred "weapon" of individuals. They provided a carnivalesque edge to the protests. More importantly, the act of blowing whistles in itself conveyed a political message: whistling gave voice back to protesters whose votes—and therefore voices—were stolen (the noun *glas* in Serbian means both voice and vote). And the protesters managed to bring back their voices by whistling for ninety days.[47] At the same time, they demonstrated that the regime could not successfully silence the citizenry through media manipulation and the threat of a police crackdown. Whistling, in this sense, empowered people symbolically.[48]

Apart from using whistles, people showed their creativity by using a variety of instruments to generate noise. When marchers passed through neighborhoods, residents grabbed anything in their households to then join the caravan of noise. Bells, firecrackers, pots, kettles, pans, rubbish bins, vacuum cleaners, bullhorns, and radios are just a few examples. Of course, bare hands could be the first and last resource for making noise.[49] During the daily protest walks, drummers played Latin and African rhythms that converged with trumpets and even sports fans' rattles. More often than not, rock 'n' roll bands accompanied marchers, playing a kind of punk rock juxtaposed with traditional folk to mock the state-promoted "turbo-folk" of the time.[50]

It was the collective banging of pots and pans during the state news program that marked the apogee of the acoustic rebellion. The basic idea behind this action was that only the noise of a civic multitude could drown out the "noise" of news propaganda broadcast daily by RTS at 7.30 p.m. Pots and pans were popular devices because they were easy to find and use, and could produce the loudest noise.[51] During the news broadcast every day, "walkers"—both students and opposition supporters—would start to beat pots and pans. Then the whole city would follow suit. The elderly, children, housewives, and others who did not take to the street, came out onto their balconies and beat their pots of pans together with the "walkers."[52]

This scene and its sound became a metaphor for "people's power," as it broke the darkness and silence that had been consuming the lives of so many in Serbia. Through this collective action, solidarity was fostered that undermined the widespread sense of isolation.[53]

Flag waving and costume parades characterized the cosmopolitan spirit of carnival in the 1996–97 protests. On January 1, 1997, "Belgrade Is the World" (*Beograd je svet*) became the protest's slogan and served to display the cosmopolitan identity of Belgrade, in contrast with the nationalist image of Serbia generally perceived by the international community.[54] This approach was instigated by people waving international flags, which ranged from those of Yugoslavia and Serbia, France, Japan, Germany, and the United States.[55] These flags were accompanied by "apolitical" flags, such as those of miners, car racing, and commercial logos, the gay pride rainbow flag, American Civil War flag, and the skull and crossbones flag. There were even "improvised" flags made from scarves tied to sticks. It was as if people brought "whatever they had hanging on their walls" to the protest site.[56]

Parade marchers wore ridiculously fancy costumes in an attempt to mock anyone they wished. There was a man wearing a tin helmet with red tulips popping up from this "crown," while some were dressed as Roman gladiators. Others put on comic sunglasses, face masks, and nurse's, military and police uniforms.[57] At one point in January, four sheep were brought in from Mount Zlatibor in western Serbia to a demonstration site, and taken for a "walk" to the Australian embassy.[58] In poking fun at socialist voters, sheep owners hung placards on the sheep's necks, bearing such slogans as "we support the Socialist Party of Serbia" and "the whole world is against us."[59] The parade would have lacked a real spirit of anti-regime demonstration without mocking Milošević. Dejan Bulatović, a student and an SPO supporter, managed to create a life-size sponge effigy of Milošević, dressed in a stripped prison uniform; his small head being rendered in modeling clay and stuck on an umbrella, and his Pinocchio-like nose made from an inflated condom.[60]

The carnivalization of these protests manifested its tactical connection to nonviolence particularly in the "Cordon against Cordon" action held between January 19 and 27, 1997. Theater performance, plays, games, and concerts were staged to ameliorate the nerve-racking stand-off with police that intervened into the street party. A week before the Orthodox New Year celebration, police cordons had blocked Kolarčeva Street in Belgrade's center, a usual walking route of the student protests. Instead of backing down or breaking the cordon with force, students decided to throw a party in front of the police. Confronting sober police officers armed with batons, tear gas launchers, and guns were lines of playful citizens armed with flowers and mirrors. Flowers were handed to the police by flirting female protesters. The mirrors were held up to the police by a group of artists and scholars, so they could see their own "human" faces.[61]

On the following day, students organized a "mini Olympics" in which they played all kinds of sports in front of the police line. There was also the "Cordon of Uniforms" where members of a diverse range of professions put on their outfits to show their positions as scientists, architects, lecturers, or judges, contrasting with the homogenous uniforms of the police. In addition, protesters brought along their dogs and cats, lining them up as the "Cordon of Pets." They proposed that perhaps Milošević,

1. "Cordon against Cordon" action, 1997. (Photographer unknown. Courtesy of *Vreme* magazine, Belgrade.)

who did not like the people's protest walks, might allow these pets to walk through because they were easily manipulated.[62]

To provide entertainment for themselves and the grim security forces, protesters improvised all kinds of games, such as water polo in the heavy rain, "photographing [citizens with the police] and drawing their portraits, playing chess . . . , and fishing fish tins from the surrounding garbage cans."[63] Even cheekier, a group of demonstrators equipped themselves with bicycle wheels and a colorful umbrella, whirling them in front of the police cordon, so the police were hypnotized.[64] At some point, students decided to put up tents, start a bonfire, put out cooking equipment and camp next to the police cordon.[65]

2. "Cordon of Pets" action, 1997. (Photographer unknown. Courtesy of *Vreme* magazine, Belgrade.)

The "Cordon against Cordon" action was most remembered for its party atmosphere. At night when the number of participants tended to decline, students organized the "Discotheque Blue Cordon" (Diskoteka plavi kordon). A sound system was brought in to get the festivity started. For 178 hours, police were witness to the largest ever live Belgrade party, with approximately 30,000 partygoers who ceaselessly danced along to British punk music mixed with traditional Balkan songs. The sound of the music was so loud that "all nightclubs in town that normally catered to a student audience suspended their activities . . . because . . . they could not compete with Diskoteka plavi kordon."[66] The highlight of the discotheque was the "Miss University Contest," which was organized by students in collaboration with a pro-opposition newspaper, *Demokratija*, to elect the best female protester.[67] The event was followed by the "Mister Police Contest," in which the most popular policeman in the view of protesters was selected.[68] The stand-off lasted for eight days. Eventually, the police withdrew from Kolarčeva Street on St. Sava Day,

3. Games and plays enacted before the police cordon, 1997. (Photographer un-known. Courtesy of *Vreme* magazine, Belgrade.)

shortly before the Patriarch of the Serbian Orthodox Church—together with some 30,000 students and protesters—carried out a procession on the street.[69]

Witty Slogans on Placards

The least coordinated and yet most creative and wittiest protest actions were slogans on placards. These slogans were original works created by individuals, or were sometimes adapted from popular commercial advertising slogans, quotations from literature, and lyrics. These placards became a channel to not only express resentment toward the regime, but to exchange "dialogue with other participants."[70] According to Milena Dragičević-Šešić from the University of Arts, these slogans reflected an evolving discourse in Serbia at the time. The early 1990s was filled with socialist slogans focusing on *četnik* iconography, the return to traditional Serbia and its "traumatic" history.[71] The 1996–97 slogans were created to counter this symbolism. They were ideologically eclectic (if not ambiguous), which reflected the emergence of individualism against authoritarianism and collectivism.[72]

The predominant messages were related to the electoral fraud. One example comes from a demonstrator whose banner satirized the court decision relating to the elections. Based on the defeat of the Yugoslav soccer team to the Spanish team in an international match, the banner read: "Yugoslavia beats Spain 2–0. Signed. The Supreme Court of Serbia."[73] In a similar fashion, a student satirically commented on the legal conditions in Serbia: "Who says that Serbia is an undemocratic country? In Serbia, everybody has the equal right to lack access to all information." And with a placard made into the shape of toilet seat cover, a student showed the message: "There is much shit about the election and RTS."[74]

Others mocked the endless repetition of election rounds through messages such as, "Voting from IV to MCMXXX rounds;" "Today the 764th round of elections in Serbia is held—vote with the SPS membership card!;"[75] "On Monday, 6 December, 1999: the 763th round of elections is held;" "Belgrade in the year of 2010: the 857th round of elections is held—however we hold the election in advance."[76]

Students also competed with one another to create the catchiest phrase deriding the vote-stealing. Examples include: "I think; therefore, I am. I can vote; therefore, I know how to count!;" and "Somebody give the Electoral Commission a calculator!" Another student re-conceptualized the mathematical system in Serbia, bearing the placard message: "There are five ways of calculation in Serbia—addition, subtraction, multiplication, division, and stealing."[77]

Slogans with insulting humor often contained messages directly attacking regime figures. The most popular butt of many jokes was unsurprisingly Mirjana Marković and her allegedly bizarre fashion sense. When she was preparing to visit India, students advised her via their placards: "You'll be safe in India; they don't kill cows there." Other suggestions included: "Mira, your flower is wilting" (with reference to the flower often placed in her hair); "Children, beware of the witch with a red flower in her hair!"; or a culturally insulting comment for a woman— "Down with the hens from Dedinje!"[78]

The protesters' other major target was Milošević. A slogan, launched by B92 during the Bosnian war equated him with Saddam Hussein. It read, "Sloba Saddam," to which a protester responded four years later: "Don't insult Saddam!" Similar biting humor could be seen on a placard that read, "Sloba, go home to Loch Ness" [the large lake best known for its "Loch Ness Monster"]. This was hilariously responded to by the slogan: "Don't set me up. Signed, Loch Ness."[79] A student also compared President Bill Clinton with Milošević, whom the US government considered the guarantor of peace in the Balkans. It bore the message: "American people have: Bill Clinton, Stevie WONDER, Johnny CASH, and Bob HOPE. Serbian people have: Slobodan Milošević, no WONDER, no CASH, and no HOPE."[80] A student protester praised the ingenuity of Milošević as a renowned "scientist" for bringing Serbians an international reputation, just as Nikola Tesla did with his extraordinary inventions in the field of electricity: "Our two biggest scientists: (1) Nikola Tesla. He invented [alternating current] electricity. (2) Slobo. He discovered isolation for us."[81] In order to stress the nonpartisanship of protesters, a protester wrote on his placard; "We are not here for Vuk, or Zoran [the opposition leaders], but for Sloba!"[82] When supporters of Milošević chanted, "Sloba, we love you," Milošević bluntly replied, "I love you, too." On the following day, students carried shields with lettering, "I love you, too." They also greeted each other by saying, "I love you" and replying "I love you, too."[83]

Many satirical slogans were derived from the meaning of the names of Slobodan ("freedom") Milošević and Mirjana ("peace") Marković. Placards held during the demonstrations read: "Milošević is free! But what about Serbia?;"[84] "We want *peace* and *freedom*, not *Mira* and *Slobodan;*" "Those who don't have "Peace" [*Mira*] have hope." For Milošević, a student protester reminded him: "Not every man is *free*, and vice and versa" [meaning that not every "Slobodan" is a man].[85] Soon after, stickers were produced and widely circulated with the names of Slobodan and Mira. Perforations were made between the letter "a" and "n" for Slobodan, and between the letter "r" and "a" for Mira. When tearing the "n" from Slobodan and the "a" from Mira, people would achieve real "freedom" and "peace." Needless to say, this word game was intended to motivate

Serbians to "tear down" these two figures if they wanted their own free-dom and peace to come.[86]

The despised regime-run media could not avoid being the target of mockery, either. Being the propaganda machine of the regime, Radio Tele-vision of Serbia (RTS) belittled the demonstrations by broadcasting news of Milošević being a peace advocate who not only signed the Dayton Peace Agreement to end the Bosnian war, but also led Serbians to prosperity and everlasting happiness. To many, this portrait was an imaginative fairy tale, some sort of hallucination. The report was in striking contrast to the harsh everyday reality faced by the populace. These contrasting realities gave rise to banner messages, such as "I want to live in the land of RTS;" "I think; therefore, I don't watch RTS;" "TV—the drug of the nation;"[87] or "Turn off the TV and turn on your brain."[88] Another placard mimicked tabloid headlines in order to mock the state newspaper *Politika*, which dis-torted the actual electoral results: "Because of the enormous interest in holding the election for the sixth, seventh, eighth, and ninth round, ballots are on sale at the newsstands of *Politika*."

In response to police crackdowns, students toned down the imminent threat by inventing numerous funny slogans. On one of their placards, a student suggested to the police an effective way to deal with the pro-tests. It bore the message; "*Creativity* is the only way to fight. Signed, the Federal Police." Other slogans, which symbolized the police as being the regime's "gear" for suppressing protesters, included: "Students against the machine!;" "Enjoy students' protest! You can't *beat* the students' feel-ing!;" "The police directed the students' choir with their baton?!?"[89]

Numerous jokes on protest banners were based on the government's allegation of students being manipulated, or being fascists. When Dragan Tomić, then spokesperson for the Serbian Assembly, claimed that around 30,000 to 60,000 students who took to the street were just a "handful" of manipulated fascists, slogans were immediately created to highlight the absurdity of the accusation. A popular one read, "I have an under-aged, retarded, impressionable, reduced, manipulated, pro-fascist tem-perament."[90] Some placards mocked the regime's hypocrisy underlying its allegation that students were associated with Nazi ideology. This allegation was launched despite the Serbian economy's dependence on the German currency. A placard read, "I swear I hate everything German, so help me Deutschemark!"[91] To poke fun at the regime's xenophobic propaganda promulgated against students, a protester advised, "We shall ban the Danube, it interferes in our internal matters!"[92] Some geographical knowledge is needed to grasp the humor of this joke. The Danube River cuts across five countries in Europe, one of which is Serbia. In Belgrade the river merges with the Sava River, which makes it look like the invasion of a "foreign" river. The slogan thus used the Danube River as a metaphor for the international meddling into Serbian domestic affairs, a common excuse of the regime for bypassing criticisms from the international community.

Socialist mottos and traditional phrases that were "Serb nationalist mantras" were also twisted by protesters. In the wake of a nationalist mobilization during the late 1980s, Milošević launched the slogan, "Serbia's woken up!" In response to the call, a 1996–97 demonstrator recommended: "Serbia's woken up. Somebody make the coffee!"[93] When Bulatović, the creator of a Milošević effigy, was beaten up by the police, students came up with the message; "No one will dare beat you." This satire should be interpreted in the context of the 1989 "anti-bureaucratic" revolution, in which Milošević addressed Kosovar Serbs—then repressed by Albanian officials—with the exact same message.[94] Based on the regime's utilization of heroic poems, songs, and epics, a student twisted the popular citation "Only unity saves the Serbs" to "Only a walk can save the Serbs" (referring to the daily protest walks).[95]

Some vulgar and obscene slogans also performed a subversive function, but others were created without any political reference. For instance, toilet rolls were found inscribed, "we've had enough shit."[96] Others include: "When the ruler is impotent, only the people *arise*,"[97] or "fifty years of sex is enough. We are in climax now" (referring to the fifty years of despair people had been experiencing under communist—and later socialist—rule).[98] Another slogan was based on the double-meanings of the word "egg." For Serbians, "eggs" also imply an obscene reference to testicles. And eggs, in a literal sense, were thrown at state buildings during the protest. This wordplay was apparent in slogans such as, "Why are only eggs [being hurled at state buildings]? Give them [officers] what's in between."[99]

Satirical Street Theater

The 1996–97 protests saw the use of satirical street theater on two different scales: that of the opposition-coalition-coordinated events, and those that were initiated and staged by students. The opposition's "happenings" were intended to draw mass participation in order to interrupt public order. The students' skits were staged by a smaller numbers of protesters, but their sophisticated level of dramaturgy and sarcasm also tended to attracted media attention.

Citizens' staged satirical events, such as the "Traffic Gridlock" and the "Arrest at the Traffic Light" actions created traffic chaos, while allowing people to express their own symbolic form of rebellion. In the "Traffic Gridlock" event, the opposition coalition encouraged car drivers to drive slowly so as to congest the traffic. At some point, they pretended that their cars had broken down and that they were unable to fix them. Then these commuters decided to leave their vehicles in the middle of busy intersections and continued their journey by foot to the city center to join the protest walk. Even children acted as if their "toy cars" were broken, and left them on the street together with adults' cars. When asked by a reporter what happened to his car, one traffic-jammer replied; "Its soul has broken down. It has been broken for a long, long time." In such an incident, the police might have easily arrested "troublemakers," had there been only a few of them. But the coincidence of car breakdowns by 100,000 people could only overwhelm authorities. Despite the actions' absurdity, the symbolism was politically serious. That is, if citizens armed only with their collective will to resist illegitimate authority could overwhelm the basic state function of maintaining order on the roads, what else could these citizens dismantle?[100]

In a similar vein, the "Arrest at the Traffic Light" action enabled the civic subversion of state order. This action took place in the context of the government's ban on any obstruction of streets or main roads, which was issued after a month of protest. In an attempt to appear benign, the government claimed that the ban was aimed at restoring traffic convenience for city commuters, and that it was not purposely aimed at hindering civic rights. In response to this ban, a group of protesters improvised an alternative street action. They "followed" the traffic regulation by "jumping and dancing" when the traffic light was green. While bouncing up and down, they screamed: "It's green, look at the traffic light!" When the light turned red, they went back to the pavement, crying: "Arrest the traffic light!" or "Red bandits, give us our traffic lights back!" This action invited the police to arrest the "red" light, an analogy for the ruling Left Coalition, because it "obstructed" the traffic by stopping all the cars. Based on the imposed ban, moving, jumping, and dancing at the green light should be legal. And the "red" light, which actually created obstacles for commuters, should be considered illegal. Therefore, the police should apprehend the "red" light. Obviously, the rhetorical logic of the action was absurd, which successfully confused the police.[101]

Compared with the larger extent of citizen protest events, students' street skits were carried out on a smaller scale, but their underlying messages could be symbolic and sarcastic to an even greater degree. Themes of these actions revolved around the cleansing of dirtiness and "evil" spirits (often with rituals), mocking regime proxies, and subverting the regime's own propaganda against the student protests.

Numerous student street events were created to "cleanse" sites, such as buildings or public squares. By tidying up these official sites, students implied that the "moral" dirtiness was being wiped away. A foremost target of these actions was the pro-regime rector of Belgrade University, who had strongly opposed student protests. Exhibiting very poor judgment, he broadcast the suggestion that "the protesting students were a handful of seduced and manipulated people," which only served to motivate a response showing how misguided this was. In response to the rector's political stance, students cleaned his office building so that the only remaining "dirtiness" was the rector himself. In a student newspaper they moved to proclaim a "new" definition of "a handful," deduced from the rector's statement: "A 'handful' is a unit of measure for a quantity of living creatures of the same kind. One 'handful' is approximately equivalent to the quantity of some 20,000 of the above-mentioned creatures."[102]

Other similar skits were carried out as rituals either to chase away evil spirits, or to remove "political bugs." When university staff were dismissed from the university council for supporting student protests, students stepped up their actions from merely cleaning the rector's office to conducting a ritual to exorcise "the Devil." They prayed and used candles and garlic to expel the bad spirits, referring directly to university executives.[103] At one point, Parliament postponed its session regarding the falsified election results, claiming that there would be vermin extermination inside Parliament House. Finding this excuse unpersuasive, the students decided that they would provide the service of "disinfecting" the building for parliamentary members. Students sprayed insecticide outside Parliament House, and subsequently carried out a ritual purge of the "political insects" residing in the Parliament.[104]

Some street performances by the students underlined the moral degradation of the regime apparatus that served to falsify the election results. Actions often involved the act of leaving symbolic items in front of buildings of targeted institutions. One of the targets was the Supreme Court, which often failed to deliver justice. On international AIDS day, students encouraged people to bring "condoms" to the demonstration. As protesters walked past the Supreme Court building, they left condoms at the building gate. Simultaneously, protesters shouted; "Condoms for cowards, so they don't catch something while they're *inside*!" In this context, condoms were metaphors for protection from injustice needed by those entering the court building.[105] Another sarcastic skit directed at the court involved 30,000 students leaving copies of the Constitution in front of the Supreme Court building. These copies were gifts from students who thought the court might not have read or even seen the document.[106]

Numerous satirical skits targeted the Electoral Commission. For instance, students hurled rolls of toilet paper at the Electoral Commission building during the daily walk at the end of November. The offer of toilet paper was a metaphor for the students' proposal, put forward to the Committee, to "clear up" their involvement in stealing the opposition's victories. Such involvement was implied to be the grotesque equivalent of excrement and its unpleasant nature. The action was therefore titled, "We've Had Enough of Your Shit."[107]

Several sarcastic actions by students were devoted to countering the regime's propaganda, which had belittled the protesters. The action "Blood Transfusion" epitomized this approach. In January, Mirjana Marković, the leader of the Yugoslav Left Party, had threatened to use violence against protesters. She declared that "a lot of blood had been shed for the introduction of communism into Yugoslavia and that it [the Communist Party] would never go without blood."[108] This rhetoric was a rich source of ideas for an absurd counter-action. After the announcement, a group of student protesters ingeniously set up a blood donation campaign to collect real human blood. Then they went to the JUL headquarters with the collected blood and mockingly asked if the party could please go now that they have their blood.[109]

At times, satirical street events were engineered to counter the regime's attempts to hinder the protest walks. A few days prior to New Year's Eve, cordons of police blocked the pedestrian street Knez Mihajlova, which was the main walking route. Students responded to the regime's ploy by sarcastically acting as if they were held hostage in their own city. They wore prisoner suits, forming a prison circle and walking around with their hands behind their heads. This action was later joined by another 10,000 protesters.[110] To clarify the civic and human rights situation in Serbia, where citizens could be "imprisoned" in their own city, the Students' Initiatives Committee of the Mathematics Faculty published an updated Universal Declaration of Human Rights, subtitled "The Latest Version for the Serbian-Speaking and Territorial Area." The declaration guaranteed Serbian citizens the equal right to "a jail sentence, clubbing, molestation, repression, and all kinds of battery from the persons in charge of this." Also, citizens were assured of "the right to death, captivity, social insecurity and lack of opinion or conscience; the right to be punished for no particular reason, to be innocent until forced to plead guilty, to be restricted in movement and residence within the boundaries of the country, and to be uninformed or misinformed."[111] Students emphasized that Serbian people were obliged to exercise these rights annually.

Other actions dealing with the police prohibition on protesters entering into certain areas included "The Forbidden City," "Mira, Let's Go for a Coffee," and "The Movement in an Inhabited Land." As with the action

4. "Prisoners' Circle" skit, 1997. (Photographer unknown. Courtesy of *Vreme* magazine, Belgrade.)

"Five O'Clock Coffee," executed in the 1992 student protest, these skits represented an attempt by students to reach the house of the Milošević family in the Dedinje suburb. The skit "The Forbidden City" was staged after police had prevented walkers from entering the elite suburb of Dedinje. Students then erected a border cairn made of cardboard and emblazoned with "Dedinje—the Forbidden City." The reference point was that Dedinje had once again become an elitist territory where "commoners" were not granted entrance.[112]

Further attempts to trespass onto the prohibited "territory" of Dedinje were made in the action "Mira, Let's Go for a Coffee." This time, students invited themselves over for a friendly cup of coffee with Marković, at her place.[113] According to Predrag Lečić, then a student protester, the action was conceived by students from the Sociology Department in which Marković was a professor but had rarely conducted a class. Aside from inviting her to have coffee, a female student also offered her a flower "because Mira always had this kind of flower around her ears."[114] However, the attempt to reach her house in Dedinje was, again, unsuccessful.

Showing persistence, students then decided to organize a competition in which more than ten small groups would try to reach Milošević's house, coming from different directions. Whoever could get the closest to the house (usually by means of fooling the police and security guards) would be the winner. The competition went on for several days. Milan Milutinović recalls, "Each group would compete to reach the building [in Dedinje] that was close to Milosevic's house. One of them would say, 'I came closer!' And on the following day, another group tried to beat the winner of the previous day."[115] A group of students finally got to the front gate of Milošević's house, but their entrance was blocked by fully armed security guards.[116]

It was the skit "The Search for the Rector" that was remembered as the most brilliant, contemptuous, and "*Monty Python*-like." The action was engineered and executed by students from the Mechanical Engineering Faculty, and lasted for seven days. The context of this street skit was the absence of the Belgrade University rector after students had demanded his resignation. A team of ten to fifteen students then decided to seek the rector in places they thought he might have hidden. The first stop, made on February 19, was the zoo where the rector was possibly visiting his fellow monkeys. After failing to find him, students moved on to search for the rector in the Danube River, bringing with them fishing rods in case the rector was hiding with other fish in the river. Then they visited the Belgrade Observatory to see if he had found asylum in outer space. The next search, however, was blocked by a police cordon. Students decided to take a break in a nearby park. Meanwhile, they held a biology class in which they discussed the rare species: "*rector impudicus*" and "*sloba vulgaris*." Somebody added that although it was hard to find "*rector impudicus*," species such as "*policus policus* and *militaris agressiva*" were unlikely to become extinct. After a search of the underground (with the help of students from the Mining Faculty), the market, pubs, and restaurants, the rector remained missing. Students, in a final desperate effort, opted for fortune telling, particularly popular in times of hardship in Serbia in the 1990s. The psychic "Branka" told them the rector would be dismissed in ten days. And he was.[117]

5. "The Search for the Rector" skit, 1997. (Photographer unknown. Courtesy of *Vreme* magazine, Belgrade.)

Marović, an architect of the action, notes that students intentionally carried out the skit in the presence of journalists so as to get media coverage. In this way the pressure exerted on the rector did not come so much from the actual student protesters, but more so from the wider public.[118] This awareness of humor's advantages constituted a stepping stone for tactical development by the subsequent movement, Otpor. Moreover, the 1996–97 protests illustrated the discursive and transformative power of humor, creating a subversive space for those who sought political change in Serbia.

Excorporation as a Mechanism of Change: The 1996–1997 Protests' Humorous Slogans and Satirical Performances

In the 1996–97 protests, witty slogans and satirical street performances demonstrated the mode of protest through excorporation, subverting the Milošević regime's propaganda in the process. The protesters mimicked the tone of the regime's justification of electoral falsification, but they distorted or exaggerated the core content to expose the absurdity of such rhetoric. The claims of the regime were contested through the satirical tone underlying the slogans that mocked the endless repetition of election rounds, the Electoral Commission's falsification of the opposition coalition's victories, the court's judgment that legalized the regime's vote rigging, and the media's reproduction of the regime's lies. In a similar vein, some of the students satirical performances were subversive because they were created based directly on the regime's rhetoric, but worked to undermine it. For instance, students' offer of copies of the Serbian Constitution to the court was based on the court's legalization of the regime's unlawful vote rigging. By giving the court copies of the Constitution, the general assumption that the court held the highest authority in implementing constitutional law was questioned.

Many slogans and satirical performances mocked regime figures by utilizing material actually provided by them, thereby bringing the absurdity of the regime's propaganda to the fore. Examples include slogans that mocked the parallel meanings of the names of Mirjana Marković and Slobodan Milošević. They emphasized the contradiction between root word meanings and the destructive consequences of the couple's leadership. In other cases, slogans poked fun at personalities among the ruling elites by using an allegory known for its symbolic offense in Serbia so their indecent manipulative personality was highlighted. One satirical street skit that relied on this strategy was the Mechanical Engineering students' action "The Search for the Rector." The rector's academic background in agriculture, his attempts to downplay the importance of student protests, and his absence at the end of the protest became a terrific pretext for a week-long hilarious search for him. But the twist was the students' visit to a palm reader who predicted the dismissal of the rector within ten days. In this sense, while the Rector's own narratives gave meanings to the students' actions, the students' twist in the end led to the destruction of the narratives' source.

By imitating the tone of the regime's defamation of protesters, various slogans and satirical street performances were created to counter the allegations against them. Countless slogans reflected protesters' use of self-deprecating humor to make absurd the regime's denunciation of them. Satirical performances such as "The Prisoners' Walk," "Blood Donation," and "The Forbidden City" demonstrated how protesters utilized the regime's defamation of them to unveil the invalidity of the claims. In these actions, the regime's propaganda was distorted or exaggerated to the level of the absurd. "The Prisoners' Walk" showed the regime's restriction of civil rights by using the analogy of the prison. In the action "Blood Transfusion," students twisted Marković's threat of a protest crackdown by taking her reference to blood literally. Subsequently, they donated their blood to fulfill the first lady's wish and to enable her party to then step down from power.

The process of excorporation—as detected in the 1996–97 protests—paves the way to refine power theory underpinning nonviolent activism. The conventional wisdom indicates that nonviolent actions work to undermine the opponent by removing the resources that support their power. And as obedience underpins all these resources, nonviolent activists are encouraged from the outset to cease to obey those that rule them. The fundamental assumption is that obedience is voluntary and thereby consent-based. This implies that the people can give and also withdraw their consent from ruling elites, presumably because they are equipped with a sufficient degree of free will to be able to do so.

In light of discursive domination, consent withdrawal is virtually impossible because the individual is governed by discourses that influence his or her behaviors and perception of truth. Nevertheless, where there is power, there is also resistance. Humor constitutes a site of this nexus between domination and resistance. Satire and parody, in particular, enable subordinates to engage with the rhetoric and symbolism underpinning the authority of those in power, and in the process, this rhetoric and symbolism is altered and distorted to absurdity. The 1996–97 protests demonstrated ways in which a discursive power that has led people to believe in a regime's propaganda can be weakened by the process of excorporation. In this sense, changes did not result from activists' demands being met due to substantial pressure put on the opponent—as suggested by nonviolent action theory. Rather, they took place at the level of popular perception that desecrated the image of the regime's invincibility.

Emotion and Imagination in Nonviolent Conflicts: The Carnivalesque

The carnivalesque features of the 1996–97 protests suggest the power of humor to transform the antagonism of street protests to cheerfulness. Episodes of carnivalesque behavior included activities such as food throwing (e.g., eggs), noise-making (e.g., whistling, banging of pots and pans, and car horn honking), festive parades, game playing, and theatrical performances. There were also a diverse range of flags and commercial banners used to replace the usual display of national flags, reviving the "cosmopolitan" atmosphere of Belgrade. The regime's slogans—with their dull and hostile messages—were substituted with witty slogans to express creativity and playfulness amongst the protesters. The carnivalesque protests reached their apogee in the standoff students named as the "Cordon against Cordon" action. The action was a carnivalesque response to the police blockade of Belgrade's main walking route. During the standoff, the Students' Main Board spearheaded the organization of carnivalesque activities, ranging from an all-night discotheque, parties, to beauty contests. The crowd danced, drummed, sang, and hugged one another, forcing the police to deal with festive emotions unfamiliar in their experiences of crowd control.

The joyfulness generated by the carnivalesque activities largely transformed the atmosphere of hostility between the authorities and protesters. As with other protest movements, anger and frustration toward the regime's rigging of votes and its policies generally drove people to take to the street in 1996–97.[119] The escalation of mass outrage had positive and negative effects. On the one hand, it kept alive the sense of urgency among protesters. On the other hand, it heightened antagonism between the protesters and those they perceived as representatives of the regime. The clash that occurred between Belgrade-based protesters and Milošević's supporters—bused in from the Serbian provinces on December 24, 1996—reflected how hostility could undermine the nonviolent discipline of protesters. The generation of outrage as a dominant emotion at a protest could turn it from one of nonviolence into a riot. Because of this, there were attempts to mitigate feelings of anger through the promotion of carnivalesque activities. Protest organizers, especially students, learned that had the protest participants been incited to provoke police officers, the regime would have conveniently justified a crackdown. The majority of carnivalesque activities were organized precisely to avoid this outcome. But importantly, once a carnivalesque atmosphere was established and felt, protest participants were even inspired to improvise festive activities themselves without further organization. Enjoying fun activities on the street came to dominate the 1996–97 protests and eventually marginalized the collective rage that had initially motivated protesters.[120]

The impact of nonviolent action on the emotions of a movement's participants has been little addressed. In pragmatic nonviolence, existing analyses place the emphasis on the effectiveness of nonviolent strategies and tactics in achieving the goals of a movement. Methods that are considered powerful tools should result in putting pressure on an opponent to eventually grant activists their demands. However, these methods potentially generate hostility among grievance groups toward the parties they oppose.[121] Similarly, anger-laden speeches often dominate the protest scene. They work to sharpen the grievance group's resentment toward the opponent, i.e., toward a person or a people rather than a corrupt system.[122] As a result, an atmosphere of threat and distrust is established, providing grounds that enable nonviolent discipline to be dismissed by protesters.[123] At the other end of this position spectrum stands the suggestion by principled nonviolence that nonviolent activists should remain altruistic, trustful, and compassionate when encountering an opposing party. There is a common assumption that "love" will work its magic to change the heart of the opponent.[124] For those employing nonviolence because of its strategic superiority to armed tactics, this emotional obligation can appear unrealistic and too demanding.[125]

In a nonviolent conflict, carnivalesque humor constitutes an alternative means of expressing emotion that overcomes the dilemma of choosing between getting angry at those responsible for the oppression being resisted, or loving them in spite of it. For those regarding nonviolence as a technique of struggle, the influence of methods selected can alter the atmosphere of the struggle and therefore should be of concern. Allowing hostility-filled methods to dominate the protest scene can heighten tension between the authorities and protesters. And hostility can translate into a protester's provocatively dangerous reaction to the security forces.

A lack of nonviolent discipline induces at least two negative impacts for a protest movement: (1) it may result in a decline in the leverage the movement can exercise among third parties and thus diminishing chances for the campaign's success; (2) it may provide the regime with a justification for a crackdown, which can cause a large number of casualties and discourage prospective participants from joining the campaign.[126] Carnivalesque activities can prevent these drawbacks by generating cheerfulness and amity so as to tone down collective rage. This can help activists refrain from provocative behavior, and thus avoid clashes with security forces. But this is not a case of activists refraining from provocation due to their altruism and compassion toward the opposing regime's apparatus. What carnivalesque protests do is to construct a climate of cheerfulness, which influences demonstrators to forget their antagonism toward representatives of the regime. Carnivalesque humor can displace anger from the emotive space of a street demonstration.

Another potential benefit of carnivalesque humor manifests at the level of perspective. Carnivals provide a space, albeit temporary, for imagining the alternatives to the seeming fixed reality one is facing. The humor generated in the atmosphere of a carnival brings into existence a cosmology within which official seriousness is transgressed by playfulness, and the indulgence of pleasure and imaginative use of words in conversation. Social roles can be reversed. The invincible is reduced to the vulnerable. Dance, music, and singing are performed in the gloomiest place. People laugh to cast aside the seeming miserable reality imposed upon them.

The spirit of the carnivalesque is vivid because of its emergence from the most unlikely site: a state of pessimism and sorrow. The contrast between carnivals and their background setting reflects the force of life's struggle against the cult of death. This contrast was discernible in the 1996–97 protests which emerged in the context of Serbia's turbulence in the 1990s. Regular protesters and those from the civil sector provided testimonies that the hardship widely experienced at the time strangely enabled the carnivalesque protest to be an escape from the everyday struggle for survival.[127]

The depressing backdrop allowed the 1996–97 protests to represent an alternative world envisioned by the protesters. Dragićević-Šešić notes that the 1996–97 carnivalesque protests were equivalent to "a festival of freedom." They embodied "the *vision* of abolishing certain relations and privileges of power, of finding a more adequate political expression."[128] Laughter, joking interactions among protesters, smiling, the cosmopolitan flags, rock 'n' roll concerts, theater performances, and other carnivalesque occurrences improvised by the protesters depicted the image of "another Serbia."[129] Carnivals provided a space for Serbians to imagine this reality in parallel with the popular perception of Serbia being a war-mongering, nationalist and xenophobic country. The carnivalesque protests did more than just turn the world experienced by most Serbians at the time upside down. They also transcended cognitive limits to enable hope and a view of the possibility of changes to come. Despite disillusionment consequent to the 1996–97 protesters' failure to achieve substantial change, the carnivalesque spirit persisted. The image of reality transformation presented in the 1996–97 carnivalesque actions would be actually realized by Otpor activists' campaigns, which strategically directed humor at the regime so as to sabotage its legitimacy among Serbian populace.

Conclusion

The 1996–97 protests provided a platform for demonstrators, especially students, to develop three types of humorous protest actions: carnivalesque rallies, witty slogans, and satirical street theater. The satirical street theater and carnivalesque rallies, in particular, reflected the discursive, emotive, and cognitive effects of humor. Satirical street actions were designed based on Milošević's rhetoric and policies, and his cronies' personalities. Their original contents were distorted to the absurd, and thereby their discursive undertone became less convincing. In contrast to this subversive effect, carnivalesque actions principally generated the cheerful atmosphere that helped tone down protesters' anger, and thereby prevented provocation of the security forces. Nonviolent discipline was sustained, challenging the regime's justification for a violent crackdown. Emerging was the impact humor could have on the overcoming of a cognitive blockage among many Serbians, which enabled the regime's consolidated authority. This impact would be further developed in Otpor's campaigns.

PART TWO

Otpor and Its Subversive Humor

4

Fighting Milošević
with Otpor's Clenched Fist

The Campaigns

The outcome of the 1996–97 protests, which failed to topple the Milošević regime, was to propel a group of student activists to found the Otpor ("resistance") movement. They put forward the goal of democratic change, shifted the earlier protest methodology from taking to the street to staging media campaigns, and reached out to the young in the regime's stronghold towns. Humorous street actions were schematically designed and executed, and encapsulated coherent messages that aimed to convince the Serbian public to vote against Slobodan Milošević. These changes would set the stage for enhancing the strategic advantages of humor, making the speed and scale of the effects of the excorporation process and carnivalesque imagination greater than humor used in the 1996–97 protests.

The Context of Otpor's Emergence:
Political Setbacks after the 1996–1997 Protests

Political setbacks after the 1996–97 protests prompted leading student activists to develop a new movement that would uncompromisingly pursue regime change. Three aspects of these setbacks deserve particular attention: popular disillusionment with the outcome of the 1996–97 protests, the regime's enactment of draconian laws, and the North Atlantic Treaty Organization's (NATO) 1999 military intervention in Kosovo.

First, Serbians in general were disappointed with the outcome of the 1996–97 protests, which did little to challenge the regime's power.

In February 1997, the ruling parties implemented the *lex specialis* law to recognize the opposition coalition's electoral victories in forty-one municipalities. The demands of the opposition parties were met, and the demonstrations were called off. Soon afterward, however, Milošević moved to install himself as the Yugoslav president on July 23, 1997.[1] To further secure his presidency, Milošević granted his close political technocrats positions at the federal level.[2]

The existing divisions among opposition politicians facilitated the consolidation of Milošević's power. After Milošević became the Yugoslav president, the election for the Serbian president was organized. Opposition leaders began to discuss whether they should nominate Zoran Đinđić of the Democratic Party (DS) or Vuk Drašković of the Serbian Renewal Movement (SPO) as the opposition coalition's candidate. Eventually, the decision came down to Drašković largely because of his popularity among conservatives. Đinđić, who was then the mayor of Belgrade, publicly announced his disagreement with this decision.[3] Tensions arose and shortly before the Serbian presidential election on September 21, 1997, Drašković proclaimed—in the third Congress of the SPO—that his party "could achieve victory for 'new Serbia' on its own without help from its former coalition partners." The opposition coalition then broke up along the lines of Đinđić's DS, which was allied to Vesna Pešić's Civic Alliance of Serbia (GSS), and Drašković's SPO.[4]

Milošević was aware of the opposition's infighting and knew how to turn it to his advantage. After the breakup, Đinđić prepared to lead his party and the GSS in boycotting Serbia's presidential election.[5] Meanwhile, in a meeting, Milošević promised Drašković "political liberalization" if he represented the opposition parties and joined the elections. Drašković interpreted this move as a recognition by Milošević that he was the legitimate opposition leader, which eventually convinced him to distance the SPO from the opposition coalition and participate in the elections.[6]

The continual turmoil within the opposition parties diminished Serbian trust in politicians. The Milošević-nominated candidate, Milan Milutinović, eventually won Serbia's presidential election. Drašković accused Đinđić of causing this defeat by leading and encouraging key opposition parties to boycott the election. On September 30, 1997, together with other SPO, SPS, and SRS representatives, Drašković called for an urgent meeting of the Belgrade City Assembly to dismiss Đinđić from the position of Belgrade mayor.[7] Đinđić responded to being purged from office by organizing a mass protest in Belgrade, which was attended by 15,000 people, but the protest was met with a harsh police crackdown.[8] This all led to an increasing sense of disappointment and hopelessness among Serbians. Subsequent to a police beating for participating in the protest, the singer Aleksandra Kovač bitterly stated her reason for participation, which had nothing to do with Đinđić or his party. Rather, she was "sick and tired of the whole lot of them, sick and tired of their lies, because many of [her] contemporaries had left the city, and because they had turned Belgrade into a village."[9]

Popular disillusionment with the outcome of the 1996–97 protests posed a strategic challenge for any subsequent anti-regime movement. On the one hand, the opposition coalition remained an essential mechanism for toppling the regime by means of election. Inevitably, the movement that called for the electoral overthrow of the regime in power would need to present a more desirable political option to the voting populace. And because the protest movement did not serve as a political party, the only remaining alternative was the opposition parties. On the other hand, the opposition politicians had disappointed the public with their political rivalry. This fragmentation allowed Milošević to remain in power fundamentally because his party represented the only political stability in Serbia. The public may have continued to vote for him simply because the disunited opposition parties were seen as a worse choice. Alternatively, the disillusionment of many may have meant they decided to ignore the whole election, which may account for the low turnout of the 1997 presidential election.[10] Political apathy seemed to be prevalent. This situation impressed upon any future protest movement the need to overcome the political deadlock, foremost by fostering unity among the opposition parties. This would be the surest way of establishing widespread confidence in democratic elections as the way to bring about regime change.

The second setback that needed to be addressed was the regime's imposition of the university and media acts in an attempt to curb freedom of expression. On May 26, 1998, the regime imposed the University Act to hinder the rise of student activism growing out of the 1996–97 protests. The act empowered the regime to replace university chancellors and deans of faculties with elites from the Left Coalition.[11] In addition to this measure, the draconian law required academic staff to sign new contracts regardless of the terms of their existing contracts and guarantees of tenure. To many, this was equivalent to "loyalty oaths."[12] Those who refused to sign the contract paid the price by being dismissed.[13]

On October 20, 1998, the National Assembly enforced the public information law, which made it illegal to spread information that caused "anxiety, panic, and defeatism" among the public.[14] Through implementing the new law, the government could impose heavy fines on individual journalists or news agencies criticizing its violation of civil rights and its incitement of the Kosovo war. This practice nearly caused the bankruptcy of the independent media industry. For instance, in December 1999, *Blic* and *Danas* were fined up to DM 54,000 each for publishing a statement that accused the regime of engaging in "state terrorism."[15] Other local radio stations, under the Association of Independent Electronic Media (ANEM), had their licenses revoked or their cable lines were simply cut.[16]

The regime's draconian laws generated the feeling that the overthrow of Milošević was the only path that could lead to democratic change in Serbia. A series of civic protests were held, but failed to bring about substantial political reforms. Moreover, for each protest that was staged, the regime stepped up its campaigns to suppress media and university freedom. The background of this ongoing strife led a group of student veterans from the 1996–97 protests to believe that the past protests had ultimately failed because of their "flawed strategies" and goals that were too conservative. For the prospect of a democratic transition to be realized, these students determined that Milošević must be removed from power.[17]

The third setback was due to the 1999 NATO bombings, which strengthened the regime's rhetoric of a foreign conspiracy against Serbia, and this rhetoric was repeatedly employed to justify crackdowns on domestic dissident movements. In early August 1998, the fighting between Yugoslav forces and the Kosovo Liberation Army (KLA) was "escalating to dangerous levels."[18] Western powers attempted to strike a deal with Milošević and the KLA, demanding a cease-fire in Kosovo from both sides.[19] However, as Milošević refused to sign the agreement, NATO decided to carry out aerial strikes in Serbia commencing on March 24, 1999. The air raids, which lasted for seventy-eight days in Belgrade and another nineteen towns in Serbia, caused between 489 and 528 deaths.[20]

Throughout his political career, Milošević derived his popularity, at least in part, from his xenophobic rhetoric, and the NATO air strikes helped to amplify its appeal. Generally, a fear of foreign conspiracy against Serbia prevailed in the nationalist discourse.[21] Milošević had successfully manipulated this discourse, thereby securing for himself the ruling position in Serbian politics for a decade.[22] During the NATO attacks on Serbia, ruling elites did not hesitate to amplify their xenophobic rhetoric by linking the bombings to a planned conspiracy between the Kosovar Albanians and Western powers.[23]

The NATO strikes provided the regime with a propaganda resource to portray dissidents as "traitors" who facilitated the West's conspiracy against Serbia. Foremost on the list of targets were nongovernmental organizations and the independent media. For instance, when NATO's threat of air strikes was imminent, Vojislav Šešelj, the leader of the Serbian Radical Party, proclaimed in a Serbian parliamentary session: "If we cannot grab all their [NATO] planes, we can grab those within our reach, like various Helsinki committees, and Quisling groups."[24] During the NATO bombing, the regime enacted the war decree. It was used to ban a host of independent media organizations that were accused of broadcasting information that conflicted with the regime's propaganda against NATO. These independent media groups were denounced as propagating foreign lies and being servants of the West aiding them in inflicting damage on Serbia.[25] In a similar vein, human rights organizations were blamed for participating in "the service of foreign propaganda."[26]

The most deadly case labeling a dissident as a "national traitor," in an attempt to suppress their outspoken anti-regime behavior, was the murder of journalist Slavko Ćuruvija. In October 1998, Ćuruvija and his colleagues published an open letter in the independent weekly magazine *Evropljanin*. The letter strongly condemned the regime for inciting the Kosovo war and for causing "Serbian society's decline."[27] In March 1999, during the

NATO air strikes, a state newspaper then referred to him as a "national traitor who supported NATO aggression," and threatened that "his treason would not be forgotten."[28] Soon after, Ćuruvija received a warning to leave the country because his life was in danger. Before he had made any decision about leaving, on April 11, 1999, Ćuruvija was assassinated on the doorstep of his home in broad daylight.

Media suppression and the murder of Ćuruvija were warning signs to dissidents that the rhetoric of national treason was becoming a lethal weapon for the regime to justify its harsh repression. Any anti-regime campaigns launched in this period could easily be associated with "foreign meddling," and could therefore incur severe punishment. The presence of these life-threatening dangers shaped the protest movement's repertoires to protect their activists from experiencing harsher repression. But in the event these more extreme repressive measures were encountered by the protest movement, the repertoires they were developing were intended to enable them to exploit the repression as a cry for further public support.

The Emergence of Otpor

Subsequent to the 1996–97 protests, dissatisfaction with student activism and professional politics shaped the founding of Otpor. In the autumn of 1998, these student leaders gathered and discussed the establishment of a new protest movement that could bring about substantial democratic change. The "clenched fist" was adopted as the logo of this new student movement, which was named for the Serbian term for "resistance" (otpor)[29] Prominent figures included Srđa Popović, Ivan Marović, Slobodan Homen, Nenad Konstantinović, Vukašin Petrović, Ivan Andrić, Slobodan Đinović, Jovan Ratković, Andreja Stamenković, Dejan Ranđić, Milja Jovanović, Branko Ilić, Siniša Šikman, Pedrag Lečić, Vladimir Pavlov, Stanko Lazendić, Miloš Gagić, Srđan Milivojević, Jelena Urošević, and Zoran Matović.[30]

Otpor's initial activities commenced in the second week of November and continued through December 1998. In mid-November 1998, high-profile politicians attended a ceremony for the sixty-first anniversary of the Faculty of Economics at Belgrade University. Otpor activists Srđa Popović, Branko Ilić, and Ivan Andrić interrupted the national

6. Otpor's clenched fist graffito in Novi Sad. (Photograph by and courtesy of Aleksandar Pavlović.)

anthem being played during the ceremony by whistling, a reminder of the 1996–97 protests. They also hung a banner bearing the message "Live the Resistance," from the second floor of the faculty building.[31] In Novi Sad, activists raised the flag with the fist symbol in front of the building of the regional administration.[32]

From March to July 1999, Otpor suspended its activities due to the NATO bombings, and resumed its operations in August shortly after the air strikes ceased. Activists kicked off their "Declaration for the Future of Serbia" campaign as Otpor's first official action. The campaign collected signatures of support from all the important student organizations and many prominent figures in Serbia. According to Nenad Konstantinović, the declaration "became Otpor's strategic document defining the main problems and objectives of the movement, as well as the methods used."[33]

Goals and Motivations

Bringing down Milošević was Otpor's primary goal. In the period of initial discussions, there was a proposal that the goal of the movement should be the abolition of the University and Media Acts.[34] However, later on, leading activists agreed that such a demand would not cause much change because the regime would still exist. They considered that any goal allowing the continued existence of the regime would be to repeat the mistake made by the opposition parties and protesters in 1996–97. At the end of the day, Milošević's authority was consolidated through the co-option of the disintegrated opposition parties and student leaders. The movement's goal, then, had to be radical in the sense that the "real" democratic transition in Serbia would only be possible after Milošević had been toppled. As Ivan Marović strongly states, this is "because he was the obstacle for everything."[35]

Despite the seemingly single goal of Otpor, the statement that Milošević was the obstacle to "everything" reflects the heterogeneous motivations of rank-and-file activists. The outrage toward the Milošević regime was personal.[36] According to a demographic survey of Otpor members, poverty and joblessness was a common characteristic of activists. They were drawn to Otpor because of their awareness that Milošević and his policies were the cause of their impoverishment.[37] Others despised the regime because they—the young men who made up at least 60 percent of Otpor's members—were being drafted to the front line and had to sacrifice the best years of their lives.[38] There were a number of activists who wanted to see Serbia become a "real" democracy, whereby elections constituted the civic means of changing the government. They also hoped to live in a society where civil as well as minority rights were respected.[39] "High politics" aside, Serbian youths in general desired to live a "normal" life, to be able to travel, to attend concerts in other countries, and to afford their children's education.[40] There were also young people who joined Otpor just because they wanted leisure, a social life, and to gain recognition among their peers.[41]

Activists' diverse motivations made Otpor a movement without a strict political ideology. The clear, singular goal—"Milošević must go"—was the reason the movement could include dissidents from diverse walks of life, be they socialist, monarchist, democrat, feminist, pacifist, nationalist, anti-fascist, religious, atheist, or merely rock fans.[42] Put differently, as a movement, Otpor was both homogeneous and heterogeneous. Its single goal made it possible to embrace the diverse motivations of the individuals and groups involved, turning them into a united front of resistance.

Strategies

Otpor sought to bring down Milošević by means of election and through the employment of nonviolent methods. Leading activists hoped to defeat him at the federal election. To achieve this mission, they would need "one candidate against Milošević," popular votes for this candidate, and "some mechanisms that could prevent Milošević from stealing the election."[43]

Otpor planned for Milošević's electoral defeat by mobilizing support from three groups: the international community, the opposition parties, and the Serbian public. International support came in the form of recognition of Otpor as a major force of civil society working against the Milošević regime.[44] Organizations such as the United States-based International Republican Institute (IRI) provided a training workshop on monitoring voting, while the United States Agency for International Development (USAID) granted funding to produce campaign material from October 1999.[45] Otpor's leading activists achieved this series of international endorsements largely because of their deliberate attempt to persuade Western powers that the movement's approach to the overthrow of Milošević would be more effective than military intervention.[46]

But it was only the opposition parties and the Serbian public that could bring Milošević to electoral defeat. In September 1999, eighteen opposition parties formed a coalition under the name Democratic Opposition of Serbia (Demokratska opozicija Srbije or "DOS"). However, there was deep fear of infighting and a coalition breakup.[47] Otpor's plan was to apply public pressure on the opposition parties to maintain an integrated coalition. Public pressure was also needed to push DOS to nominate a single presidential candidate, for whom Otpor could rally popular support.[48] Votes for this candidate would be obtained through continuous campaigns that would work in two directions. First, they would demonstrate Milošević's deficient legitimacy to the Serbian populace. Second, the campaigns would serve to popularize the idea of Otpor—"resistance"—which would be associated with a vote for the opposition's candidate.[49] There were three strategic pillars conducive to implementing these plans: nonviolence, campaigning and public relations, and marketing techniques. These strategies reflected Otpor's refined approach to subverting the regime and, to a great extent, shaped the movement's tactical use of humor.

Nonviolence

Nonviolence governed Otpor's principles for executing protest actions. The movement prohibited its members from inflicting physical harm or threatening the authorities or civilians. Otpor's decision to use non-violence stemmed from its strategic awareness and intuition. Leading activists had learned the downside of protesters' hooliganism in the 1991 protest. For instance, Milivojević notes that he participated in that protest and saw protesters throwing stones at security forces. This act, however, only gave the regime justification for a military crackdown on protesters. More importantly, the riot-like nature of the protest discouraged potential participants.[50]

And to the contrary, activists had experienced advantages from the protests in 1996–97 when the regime was without instruments to deal with nonviolent demonstrators. The Milošević regime had gained the reputation of being the "butcher of the Balkans" when it came to battles with neighboring countries, and in the 1991 protest, it did not hesitate to bring out the tanks and crush rioters on their own soil. However, the regime held back from the use of force against the 1996–97 demonstrators mainly because it "did not know how to respond to nonviolent resistance."[51] Nonviolence constituted a battleground unfamiliar to the Milošević regime.

Because nonviolence was politically advantageous, Otpor perceived it as effective. Otpor's early days saw the continuous debates on whether or not activists should resort to violent tactics. There were those proposing the employment of armed methods in order to radicalize the protest. A few others suggested retaliation as a response to police repression.[52] Eventually, most activists agreed to commit to nonviolent resistance. Marović concludes that the movement's decision to deploy nonviolent or armed tactics depended on its capacity to build a coalition consisting of a wide range of sectors in society. In the case of Otpor, nonviolent methods helped it achieve the construction of this coalition. The majority of people tended to participate in nonviolent protest campaigns. At the same time, the nonviolent image of Otpor generally persuaded the regime's allies to shift their loyalty to the movement. As long as this coalition was extensive enough to cover the social base of the regime, "even if there was violence, it'd play a very marginal role in our struggle."[53]

Campaigning and Public Relations

Otpor's nonviolent resistance campaigns were based on a public relations framework. The movement attempted to mobilize support from the Serbian public and opposition parties. This mission required long-term campaigns, which necessitated establishing a communication channel with the public to help them overcome any fear associating Milošević with the survival of Serbia.[54] At the same time, the campaigns needed to expose to the populace Milošević's deficient legitimacy, while eliciting their trust in the opposition parties. Otpor's leading activists realized that achieving these aims would require establishing a process whereby persuasive messages could be transmitted to the public.[55]

Otpor shifted its central method of protest from gathering masses of people onto the street to public relations campaigns in the media. According to Milja Jovanović, the experience of the 1996–97 protests taught key activists that the success of street demonstrations was limited by the number of people who participated. When the numbers declined, the protest tended to lose its political momentum. Further, street protests could at best only last for a few months, which was insufficient for activists to convince many people to get on board with them. This was the reason utilizing the media was critical in providing the movement constant visibility in the public mind.[56]

To gain their desired publicity, Otpor paid enormous attention to opportunities for publicizing protest events in the media, and the regime's repressive responses to them. There were three ways activists sought media coverage of their campaigns. First, shortly before Otpor's street actions, the press team would leak information to only one newspaper, giving that publication an exclusive story that it would be motivated to publish. In the following week, they would repeat the process, providing exclusive information to a journalist from another newspaper. Second, Otpor's actions were designed to be "photogenic" so they would be published on the front page. By being on the front page, despite the absence of details about the action, Otpor and its momentum were visible. Those walking past newsstands would see Otpor regardless of whether they purchased the newspaper. In this way, Otpor's visibility and reputation would increase. Lastly, in cases where actions provoked arrests, activists organized a press conference as a follow-up. In this way, the movement could exploit the regime's repressive mechanism by turning it into its own propaganda tool. In the press conference, Otpor often emphasized the illegitimate and excessive reaction of the regime to the activists' (typically funny) street theater. This tactic was in line with the movement's strategy of the public disclosure of Milošević's ruthlessness.[57]

Marketing Techniques

Otpor's marketing techniques were also aligned with its public relations framework, which enabled Otpor's campaigns to resonate with a mass audience. Otpor activists relied heavily on different forms of pop culture, including humor, to turn the movement into the "brand" of national opposition.[58] To persuade the "customers" to purchase their political product, Otpor activists engaged in three processes: the identification of public opinion, the creation of brand, and the outsourcing of brand creators. In the first process, Ivan Andrić points out that messages conveyed in Otpor's campaigns were always designed based on public opinion regarding the Milošević regime and the future of Serbia. In this way, "[Otpor was] just saying what most of the people were thinking."[59] Charged with realizing this mission was Otpor's marketing team, consisting of ten to fifteen activists who received occasional advice and logistical assistance from friends at the Strategic Marketing and Media Research Institute. Prior to launching campaigns, this team distributed surveys asking people for their opinion about the campaign's messages and poster layouts. After the campaigns were launched, the marketing team also facilitated focus groups to obtain feedback on the campaigns.[60]

Second, in the process of brand production, Otpor co-opted iconographies popular within society. In this way, people could easily recognize the movement's messages. This methodology was employed in the creation of many promotional posters throughout Otpor's campaigns. For instance, activists found that when Milošević gave a speech for the

Communist Party when in his thirties, he had used the clenched fist symbol as the background on the stage. An Otpor activist happened to have this image. In one Otpor poster, the photo was cropped and redone, bearing the message, "Otpor before Otpor." The sarcastic title suggested, tongue in cheek, that Milošević was in fact an Otpor activist who had been working for its cause before Otpor even existed.[61]

Mass production underpinned Otpor's ubiquity as the label of resistance. Promotional materials such as posters, stickers, and T-shirts contained catchy themes from Otpor's campaigns. Millions of these items were produced and distributed to Otpor branches across Serbia. These promotional materials enabled the repeated transmission of Otpor's messages to the Serbian public. This advertising approach contributed to the cultivation of a popular consciousness about resisting Milošević.[62]

Lastly, the mass production of campaign paraphernalia accorded with the idea of outsourcing the Otpor brand. The movement encouraged individuals' adoption of resistance as a concept. One did not need to be a formal member of Otpor in order to undertake protest action. This approach was translated into numerous "small acts of resistance" to spread Otpor's message, ranging from spraying graffiti, putting up posters, pasting Otpor stickers, to wearing badges and T-shirts. With these small acts of resistance, individuals could exercise a certain extent of autonomy while retaining their symbolic association with Otpor.[63]

This notion of individual resistance proved advantageous for Otpor's expansion of support. As we shall see, in remote areas where Milošević's SPS exerted control in local government, being an official member of Otpor was too dangerous for town inhabitants. Therefore, the "small acts of resistance" constituted an option for their participation in Otpor's activities, without running the risk of repression. In turn, this method enabled Otpor's recruitment of "anonymous" supporters whose votes eventually brought Milošević to electoral defeat.

Organization

A collective leadership and autonomous local branches formed the base of Otpor's organization. The leadership consisted of a circle of original members who decided upon issues such as funding and external relationships, marketing and press, material production and distribution, and "human resources" (i.e., recruitment and supervision of training sessions).[64] Tasks were assigned to participants on a rotational basis in Otpor's early days, but after the transformation of Otpor from a student movement into a people's movement in February 2000, roles were assigned on a more fixed and permanent basis, providing a more efficient and professional division of labor.

Having a decentralized leadership structure proved advantageous for Otpor, especially when the regime stepped up its repressive measures. In May 2000, after the regime outlawed Otpor as a terrorist organization, authorities began to make sweeping arrests of activists.[65] However, when the head of one team was detained, the collective leadership ensured the replacement of this activist with other Otpor activists. Consequently, the regime could not entirely halt Otpor's activities because "[i]t was impossible to arrest all of these leaders."[66]

It was the Otpor's cell-based organizational structure that enabled the movement to mobilize votes from the grassroots, especially in the regime's stronghold towns. Out of twenty-four cities and 150 municipalities in Serbia, there were approximately 130 branches of Otpor, with between 30,000 and 60,000 supporters and activists.[67]

There were three channels through which Otpor established its local branches: networks of university friends, individual requests, and local leadership. The first developed from the 1996–97 protests where like-minded student activists gathered and became friends. The networks emerged within and across universities. Consider as an example the network of friends from Novi Sad University. The 1996–97 protest there was spearheaded by around ten philosophy students. Out of this number, Vladimir Pavlov, Stanko Lazendić, and Miloš Gagić founded an Otpor branch in Novi Sad in 1998. They invited university friends whose hometowns were scattered across Vojvodina province (of which Novi Sad is the capital city) to join them.[68] Later, these activists established Otpor branches in their home towns.

The second channel was through individuals who approached Belgrade activists to launch and set up branches in their towns. Successful applicants were invited to the "introductory meeting," where they were informed of Otpor's basic principles. These principles included "doing things in a nonviolent way" under the label of Otpor, conveying coherent messages consistent with the movement's goals in protest actions, and the use of humor in these actions.[69] The recruitment process was a filter for Otpor to only allow those committed to the idea of nonviolent struggle on board. And throughout the campaigns, leading activists fostered the "organization culture" that prohibited vandalism, retaliation against the authorities, and "aggressive humor."[70]

Once the branch was set up with around ten to fifteen members, teams from Belgrade or from regional offices would provide training sessions for new members.[71] Afterward, headquarters would leave it up to local branches to disseminate tasks in their teams. In this sense, each branch could exercise a degree of autonomy in creating actions and running campaigns according to local contexts.[72]

The third channel Otpor used to establish branches was through local leadership contacts. According to Marović and Siniša Šikman, there were some areas where anti-regime figures had led civic protests before Otpor branches were founded. In this case, activists from Belgrade would try to persuade these local leaders to join the movement and run an Otpor branch in their towns. The local figures came from diverse walks of life—they could be painters, trade union leaders, journalists, and in few cases, local opposition politicians. Nevertheless, for them to run an Otpor branch, these leaders had to be respected by the locals enabling them to exercise a certain extent of influence.[73]

In sum, Otpor committed itself to toppling Milošević through electoral defeat. It pursued this goal through campaigns that exposed the regime's illegitimacy to the Serbian public, promoted Otpor as the force of popular resistance, and pressured the opposition coalition to maintain its unity. They anticipated that Serbians would be convinced to vote against Milošević. "Doing things in a nonviolent way" constituted the protocol of campaign conduct: activists excluded acts of sabotage from their street actions while making use of nonviolent discipline to counter regime repression, as we shall further see. Otpor's organizational structure

enabled grassroots involvement in the protest campaigns, which accelerated anti-regime sentiment. The nature of the organizational structure
also allowed humorous protest actions to proliferate across Serbia.

Altered Characteristics of Humorous Street Actions:
From the 1996–1997 Protests to Otpor's Campaigns

Otpor's humorous protest tactics were developed from the 1996–97 protests to correspond with the movement's goals, strategies and organizational structure. Due to Otpor's goal to bring down the regime, humorous
protest tactics were generally designed to convey a message that convinced the Serbian populace of the regime's illegitimacy. To achieve the
stated goal, Otpor carried out anti-regime campaigns, heavily relying on
public relations techniques. As a result, satirical street theater constituted
the form of humor helpful for attracting media attention, and eventually helped Otpor gain increasing publicity. The movement's growing
network of local branches enabled the proliferation and coordination of
humorous protest tactics. Local activists were encouraged to infuse their
protest actions with humor. Humorous protest actions flourished in line
with the growing number of Otpor's local branches.

From Spontaneous Humor to Goal-Oriented Humor

Otpor's revolutionary goals fostered a reorientation of humorous actions,
which became less spontaneous and more purposeful than the 1996–97
protests. The earlier campaign had sprung up as a reaction to vote rigging.
Although the protesters' demand was clearly the recognition of the original election outcome, the role that humor played in achieving their goal
was minimal. Rather, witty slogans and carnivalesque rallies constituted
an expression of individuals' defiance and, more likely, an outlet for having fun. As a result, the political message conveyed in humorous protest
actions was eclectic. There was no agreement among protesters regarding
the target of these actions. Nor was there an elaborate discussion on the
purpose of using humor, at least at the beginning of the protests.[74]

In contrast, Otpor's use of humor was relatively purposeful in supporting its goal of creating a crisis of legitimacy for the regime. According to Marović, compared to the 1996–97 protesters, Otpor activists "were

much more aware of why [they] needed humor and what kind of humor would be conducive to the removal of Milošević."[75] In Otpor's campaigns, humorous protest actions were planned to unveil the absurd role played by bureaucrats and security forces in serving the regime. In helping regime supporters to better understand the errors of their ways, Otpor activists expected that regime loyalty would diminish.[76]

In addition, Otpor activists realized they could "channel" the spirit of humor felt in the 1996–97 protests to help achieve the goal of regime change. Put differently, the positive energy of humor was utilized as a method to counter the atmosphere of fear and hopelessness that had helped the regime remain in power.[77]

Otpor's goal of regime change was conveyed through messages of humorous street actions. These messages aimed to unveil the regime's absurdity and illegitimacy to its allies, to its own security apparatus, and to the general public. Moreover, humorous protest actions were invented to deal with popular despair and political apathy that allowed the regime's maintenance of power.

From Carnivalesque Rallies to Satirical Street Theater

The strategic shift from using street gatherings to media campaigns influenced Otpor activists' preference for satirical street skits rather than carnivalesque rallies. Carnivalesque rallies dominated the 1996–97 protests fundamentally because the site of the protests was the street. Festive activities such as street parties, costume-parades, games, and plays were initially organized to entertain street demonstrators, encouraging their continuous participation in protests despite the winter cold. Later, student protesters might have become aware of other functions of carnivalesque events, such as preventing clashes with the police or maintaining media coverage of the protests. However, street entertainment was the foremost reason for the organization of these events.[78]

For Otpor, satirical street theater proved most effective as the *stimulus* for media attention. Some founding activists learned from the 1996–97 protests that street demonstrations could accomplish a protest's goal only if the number who turned out was large enough to capture media attention. However, maintaining these large numbers was difficult when the protests became prolonged. If Milošević had not accepted the opposition's victories when he did, and if protests had needed to last for more than four months, the number of participants would likely have dropped off. This decrease would just as likely have meant the protest's failure. Otpor saw such reliance on protester turnout as a major drawback of this method of protest—through public assembly.

This lesson led to Otpor's strategic shift. The movement aimed to carry out a two-year campaign as the means of changing the popular mentality, and eventually transferring popular votes from Milošević to the opposition parties. For this approach to be effective, activists opted for the media as the site for protest campaigns, rather than the street. Constant news coverage of the movement allowed Otpor's presence to remain in the public mind. And leading activists were aware that satirical street theater could trigger media interest sufficient to publish stories about the movement.[79]

Satirical street theater facilitated Otpor's strategy of spreading the message of resistance to the Serbian populace, without having to mobilize large numbers of protesters onto the street. Unlike mass demonstrations, satirical street skits could be staged by a small group of activists equipped with just their creativity and a clear political message. And due to the absurd and theatrical elements they employed, the media tended to publish photos of the actions on the front page.[80] With media coverage of the skits, the general public could participate in Otpor's activities just by glancing and chuckling at the published photos. Expressed differently, the true measure of the number of participants in these satirical protest actions, as covered by the newspapers, included millions in the anonymous media audience.

From Urban-Confined to Nationally Coordinated Humor

Otpor's diffuse organizational structure enabled the extensive scale on which humorous protest actions were executed. In the 1996–97 protests, the staging of humorous protest actions was confined to Belgrade and a few other urban cities where the opposition coalition had victories. The urban confinement of these actions was largely due to the ad hoc nature of student organization. In Belgrade, students' humorous protest actions proliferated and they inspired students in other major cities. However, there was no substantial attempt to coordinate the actions between Belgrade and other areas.[81] As a consequence, humorous protest actions flourished in only a few cities; their advantages could not be maximized. The regime was forced to face collective ridicule only in the major cities, and not across all of Serbia.

In contrast, the expansion of Otpor's branches across Serbia enabled the nationwide lampooning of the regime. Otpor activists from its Belgrade headquarters encouraged the tactical use of humor throughout the cell-based organizational structure. Accordingly, during the period of Otpor's campaigns, humorous street skits, as staged in Belgrade's 1996–97 protests, could be seen even in small towns. Activists exercised a degree of freedom in creating humorous protest actions based on local contexts and history. According to Šikman, localizing humorous street actions allowed activists to take into consideration what was regarded as funny in the areas under their supervision. What constituted the local sense of humor could not always be identified by the urbanites from Belgrade because "what's funny for people in Belgrade maybe not be funny for those in Leskovac [a town in sourthern Serbia]."[82]

The extensive branch network provided solid ground for the proliferation of Otpor's humorous protest actions. If a local Otpor local branch were to carry out just one street skit per week,[83] that branch could invent over thirty actions in 2000 alone. If there were approximately 130 branches of Otpor in September 2000,[84] by extrapolation, those branches could have executed at least a few thousand humorous protest actions that year. The multiplicity of humorous protest actions enabled by the organizational structure could maximize the effects of humor. If activists expected that humorous protest actions could facilitate the strategy of maintaining Otpor's public recognition, then the extensive branches allowed this strategy to be effective nationally. The regime was propelled to counter the ridicule, not only in Belgrade, but throughout Serbia.

These changes corresponding with the development of Otpor as an organized movement contributed to intensifying the processes and effects of excorporation and carnivalesque imagination. These processes and effects of humor can take place in the everyday conduct of making jokes about authorities—as discussed in previous chapters. The nascent humorous protests in Serbia's early 1990s and 1996–97 reflected the changing site of humor's operation, from private to public space, from circles of family members and friends to the street. However, these protests remained spontaneous and to a large degree uncoordinated. Otpor showed the purposive use of humor in accordance with its overarching strategy and organizational structure. As a result, the processes of excorporation and carnivalesque imagination potentially intensified. The ruling elites' rhetorical subversion was coordinated nationwide. The regime's loss of rhetorical and symbolic bases of power proceeded rapidly in periods when Otpor's campaigns were launched. Meanwhile, activists encouraged young people to reimagine Serbia as a place where they could live a meaningful life and raise their families through national festivals, concerts, and parties. These carnivalesque activities not only allowed young Serbians to "exit" the regime's domination, but also prompted them to pursue the construction of a free and fair society. In other words, the development of Otpor, followed by strategic planning and purpose, rendered the speed and scale of the effects of excorporation and carnivalesque imagination to be greater than those resulting from the 1996–97 protests.

Conclusion

The goal of toppling Milošević, reliance on public relations and marketing techniques, and a branch-based organization shaped the development of Otpor's humorous protest actions. Drawing lessons from the earlier protests, especially setbacks subsequent to the 1996–97 demonstrations, Otpor's founding members put forward regime change as their principal goal. Instead of taking to the streets, activists employed public relations and marketing techniques to popularize their anti-regime campaigns. Moreover, the campaigns were effective nationwide largely due to Otpor's regional branches, which enabled the movement's influence even in the regime's stronghold towns. These aspects of Otpor's development shaped the changing nature of humorous protest actions. The messages conveyed in the actions were designed to expose the regime's absurdity. And the extensive branch network enabled a proliferation of humorous protest actions, guaranteeing their effect at the national level.

5

Strategic Humor

Satirical Street Theater, Parodic Protest Actions, and Carnivalesque Events

Throughout the two years of campaigns by Otpor, humor was used as a crucial tool to get media coverage of the movement's actions, and thereby increase its publicity. Activists from hundreds of Otpor branches were encouraged to combine their protest actions with humor to achieve this goal. They created innovative satirical street theater to mock the regime's propaganda and organized a broad array of concerts and parties to promote their resistance campaigns. Parody emerged as a key form of humor utilized by activists to co-opt national symbols and historical narratives, once manipulated by the regime to consolidate its own power. While Otpor's strategic innovation improved the effects of excorporation induced by satirical and parodic actions, carnivalesque events created an alternative image of Serbian society. These provided crucial insights into the impact of imagination on a nonviolent revolution.

Satirical Street Theater

Typically, Otpor's satirical street theater highlighted the absurdity of the regime's propaganda and the economic hardship it had precipitated. It also personally attacked regime figures. Numerous protest actions were created specifically to counter unfounded allegations by the regime about activists being terrorists, and in response to repression by the police. Cheerful and symbolic actions were created to empower town dwellers to join the forces of resistance.

The Regime's Propaganda

One of Otpor's earliest and most famous skits was "Dinar for a Change" (*Dinar za smenu*). It played on the propaganda that accompanied the regime's new agricultural policy, which was titled "Dinar for Sowing" (*Dinar za setvu*). The policy extorted already impoverished Serbians to donate some *dinars* (Serbian currency) for agricultural improvement. Taking words from the policy's title, Otpor activists announced a parallel policy named "Dinar for a Change."[1] At the entrance to the pedestrian street Knez Mihajlova, they placed an empty petrol barrel with an image of Milošević pasted on it surrounded by a target symbol. Next to the barrel was a stick and instructions: "If you put dinars inside [the barrel], you can use the provided stick to beat Milošević's picture."[2] The instructions also suggested that "If you don't have any coins because of Milošević, hit [the barrel] harder."[3] According to Siniša Šikman, this action was very popular. People lined up to batter the barrel, as it was a channel to express their anger and dissatisfaction with the regime. Passersby who did not participate still "heard the noise," so they stopped and watched other people beating the barrel and laughed.[4] Most of the time during these activities, no activist was present. Hence, the organizers of this action could get away with ridiculing Milošević.[5] Even more painful for the regime, this public mockery was reported by the national press such as *Danas*.[6]

The regime propaganda of "reconstructing the country" from "NATO aggression" provided ammunition for numerous Otpor skits. In Novi Sad, the biggest bridge near the "Petrovaradin" fortress was destroyed during a NATO air raid.[7] Milošević managed to build a new bridge, but for the locals, it was poorly constructed and not very safe. Milošević and his entourage organized a grand opening of the new bridge in Novi Sad anyway. He delivered a dramatic speech and presented awards to loyal citizens and military heroes for their contribution to the "reconstruction" of the nation. For Otpor activists, the absurdity was obvious. In no way did the cheap bridge compensate for the aftermath of the bombing. To highlight the absurdity, activists built a "toy bridge" in a park in the city's center, and mimicked Milošević's speech. The message conveyed in the skit pointed to the shallowness of the government's reconstruction plan. The bridge was doomed to collapse because it was poorly built. The quality was as if it was a child's toy.[8] The action was reported in the independent newspaper *Danas*.[9]

Similarly, in the northern border town of Subotica, activists lampooned the slowness of government response in realizing its "reconstruction" projects. One day the activists gathered in the downtown area, inviting people to write a reminder letter to the president, before tying the letters around the legs of pigeons. Because using pigeons symbolized an ancient method of communication, this protest action was depicting metaphorically the slowness of bureaucratic red tape, and the delays it was causing to the government's reconstruction plans. As with the pigeons, which could take forever to reach Belgrade or even fail to deliver people's mail, the performance suggested the regime's administration was ineffective at completing its tasks. The real need for reconstruction was incongruous with the capabilities of this regime.[10]

In Kragujevac, the regime had promised to "reconstruct" the damaged railway, replacing the old one with a French TGV fast train. For activists, the promise was but another joke. One day activists declared that Serbians did not need to wait for the fast train as they already have a "fast river." To prove their claim, activists floated a Styrofoam bottle in the river "Lepenica" with a letter to the government inside it. They invited passersby to join their protest action by also writing a letter to the government and putting it in a plastic bottle to let the river carry it to the capital city. If the river was the fastest means of transportation, the letter would reach Belgrade in less than an hour. But everyone knew that it was absurd, as was the government's promise.[11] This action was reported in the tabloid *Blic*.[12]

In the central city of Kraljevo, the regime boasted it would build the biggest port in the region. But it was obvious that the local government was short of finances, and neither did the medium-sized city of Kraljevo have the required geographical capacity to become a "regional port." The absurd claims of the regime were mocked by Otpor through staging an event in which activists floated a large assortment of ships made of paper on the river. The action demonstrated to people that the river bank could only accommodate paper ships. Activists informed journalists, who witnessed and reported this satirical action.[13]

In the western city of Valjevo, the regime had long bragged about its railway construction efforts. However, their main project had never been completed. So Otpor activists went to the site where the train track was supposed to be built. They painted a cardboard sign to indicate a "new" train station with the image of a train tunnel on it, and erected their sign on this railway construction site. Activists wanted to show that the government was unable to fulfill its promise, and therefore citizens needed to take matters into their own hands by at least building an imitation train tunnel.[14]

Otpor activists from the southern city of Leskovac poked fun at an unfinished swimming pool, which had been under construction for four decades in the city center. They decided to take over the government project by making a clay model of the pool and putting it on display at the construction site. Afterwards, activists in swimming suits and goggles performed an opening ceremony for their "pool" made of clay. The absurd scene of the actually unfinished real swimming pool beside the fake pool made of clay, along with an Otpor crew fully equipped in diving gear, drew attention from passersby. It reminded them of the disconnection between the regime's propaganda and reality.[15]

Satirical theater organized by Otpor presented criticism of the regime's media monopoly and suppression of outspoken journalists. A prime example took the form of the action "The Eclipse of the Media" (*Pomračenje medija*) initiated by activists in Novi Sad. In June 1999, the state-controlled news media warned people against going outside their houses to watch the eclipse of the sun. This warning exemplified the state's practice of generating fear through the media. A few days before the eclipse, a group of Otpor activists and local journalists set up a television screen—made of paper—on a pedestrian street in downtown Novi Sad. Sitting in front of the paper TV were Otpor activists wearing 3-D glasses, sunglasses, and even goggles. With stern faces they watched daily news reports and all the state-promoted kitsch TV shows. Onlookers were given flyers explaining that the action showed the "eclipse" of the media, with the obscuring and "darkening" of information. This was what they should be afraid of, not the eclipse of the sun.[16]

In small towns such as Aleksandrovac and Zrenjanin, activists came up with different creative ideas to address the issue of the public's restricted media freedoms. In the action titled "Brain Washing," Otpor activists in Aleksandrovac acquired a TV set and placed a drawing of a bone and the logo of the state television station on the screen. They set up this equipment downtown and pretended to turn on the state TV program, but the original audio from the state news report was replaced with recordings of absurd statements about economic development from Milošević's speeches mixed with Serbian brass bands and psychedelic music. Next to the TV set were activists washing a plastic model of the human brain with water from a jug. The metaphor of the performance suggested that people had been "brainwashed" by the absurd speeches of their country's leader and by nonsensical, ridiculous news. All this was represented by a bizarre mixture of noises from state news broadcasts, speech excerpts, and a techno soundtrack. In addition, Otpor activists wanted the bone image on the TV screen to express the idea that the Serbian populace had become submissive, just like a pet dog that was fed and domesticated by its master.[17] This satirical protest was covered by the independent newspaper *Danas*.[18]

7. "Brain Washing" skit. (Photograph by and courtesy of Dalibor Glišović.)

Zrenjanin activists were concerned about the 1998 Media Act, which imposed a large fine on outspoken journalists. To raise public awareness about the regime's harassment of reporters, activists produced a sarcastic "fine certificate": "Citizens of Zrenjanin fine the office of the Radio Television of Serbia (RTS) because of its biased and unilateral news report, because of its negligence of poor citizens who are short of basic goods such as sugar and milk, because of its broadcast of Belgrade RTS's lies and deceptions, because of its promotion of kitschy and trashy values. . . . For these reasons, the RTS is obliged to pay the fine of 750,000 dinars. This sum of money should be deposited in the accounts of pensioners as soon as possible."[19]

The certificates were distributed to journalists of the state-run media. Petar Lacmanović, an architect of the action, explained that the aim of this action was to create a dilemma for the regime media. Accepting the certificate would imply their acceptance of the accusation written on the certificate. However, if the journalists declined the offer of a certificate, "they would show bad manners and the lack of a sense of humor. In both cases, they looked ridiculous."[20]

8. "Fine Certificate" skit. (Photograph by and courtesy of Petar Lacmanović.)

Economic Hardship

Otpor invented brilliant satirical events in an attempt to expose to the public the economic damage inflicted by the Milošević regime. In Čačak, Otpor activists organized the action "JULasik Park" in the town park, the title of which mockingly compared Mirjana Marković's communist party (JUL) to the backwardness symbolized by dinosaurs from the Hollywood blockbuster, *Jurassic Park*. The action depicted different scenes that showed the everyday hardships that people faced. For instance, a group of activists lined up in a long queue just to buy some food. Another group gathered in front of the US and Canadian embassies, applying for visas to flee Serbia. Another group performed a scene showing the regular beatings dished out to citizens by the police. In another event also held in the same park, fifty or so activists were playing children's games such as "Monopoly" and "Risk" (a strategic war planning game). These games represented the economic recession and the destruction caused by the Yugoslav wars instigated by the regime. Afterward, they went to the city hall to give these games to the authorities, notifying them that now that they had "real games" to play, they should stop playing around with the real lives of people.[21] This satirical event made it onto the front page of the tabloid *Blic*.[22]

In the western city of Užice and northern town of Zrenjanin, the lack of goods necessary for everyday survival inspired the street skits activists staged. The Užice branch of Otpor highlighted the endless wait that people endured for delivery of basic cooking oil to shops. A few dozen activists acted as if they were in a line for something. Out of curiosity, passersby asked the Otpor crew what they were waiting for. After replying they were expecting "the arrival of cooking oil," the rumor spread. Soon after, the line grew to include hundreds of people. Then a car arrived, but the driver (an Otpor activist in disguise) brought only one small container of the oil. He poured a tiny amount of the oil into a tea spoon to distribute to each of those who had been waiting in the line for hours. Marko Simić pointed out that the action purposely "put a spotlight on this reality [the lack of access to basic goods in everyday life], which wasn't seen clearly by people."[23]

In Zrenjanin, "honey and milk" was a theme used to mock poor living conditions and the regime's efforts to conceal this fact. According to Lacmanović, the skit was based on a Serbian idiom, "honey and milk," which means "everything is fine." It was a phrase that summed up official propaganda, which always portrayed the Serbian economic situation as prosperous. This propaganda contrasted so obviously with the daily struggle of ordinary Serbs to make ends meet, even to afford "honey and milk" (literally). To unravel this reality, the Otpor team announced that honey and milk would be given away for free. When locals arrived at the announced distribution point, activists poured milk from empty bottles and honey from empty containers. They told the town dwellers that this scenario represented the reality of lacking basic goods, in contrast to the regime's forged lies about Serbia's wealth. In this scenario, neither the poverty nor the lies were "fine."[24]

Regime Leadership

A host of Otpor's street pranks targeted leading figures in the regime, either by predicting their downfall or mocking their personalities. For example, in October 1999, Belgrade activists carried out the action "It's Rotten; It's Going to Fall," which targeted and mocked Milošević and his wife. Activists decorated two pumpkins to personify the couple and placed them in a tree. Then, they shook the tree so the pumpkins fell. Activists were subtly saying that the rotten pumpkins (allegorically representing the country's leader and the first lady) were something bad that should be removed from the tree (a metaphor for Serbia as a country).[25]

During the eclipse of the sun in 1999, Belgrade activists put together the action "It Is Not the End of the World, Only the Fall of the Regime" (*To nije smak sveta, samo režim pada*). They erected a telescope on a pedestrian street in central Belgrade, and replaced the actual lens of the telescope with Milošević's image mockingly represented as a falling comet. The telescope was turned to the direction of the residential area of Milošević and his family. Passersby were invited to look through the lens so they could see the "fall" of the Milošević comet.[26] This action was repeated in the southern city of Niš on the same date, and covered in the independent media by B92.[27]

The Hague's indictment of Milošević in May 1999 for war crimes in the former Yugoslavia provided further ammunition for Otpor's satirical performances. For instance, on August 20, 1999, Milošević's birthday, activists in Niš and Belgrade threw birthday parties for the president. They invited thousands of the towns' residents to attend the parties and wrote their wishes on birthday cards for Milošević. Other gifts included a one-way ticket to the war crime tribunal in The Hague, a prison uniform, books authored by his wife, and a pair of handcuffs. The papier-mâché birthday cake was also made in the shape of a five-pointed star, the symbol of the former Yugoslavia, but the cake was cut into pieces adorned with small flags of Serbia and Montenegro, Slovenia, Croatia, and Bosnia- Herzegovina.[28] The message was that on the president's birthday, people should remember the disintegration of Yugoslavia instigated by Milošević. [29]

In Užice, through the action "Seeing the President off to the Hague," activists expressed their desire to see Milošević extradited to face a war crimes trial. They made life-size caricatures of Milošević and Marković from cardboard that portrayed the couple carrying suitcases, turning their backs, and walking away. The huge caricature was erected in the pedestrian area of downtown Užice, with a sign inviting passersby to take a photograph with the couple and bid them farewell.[30] The same action was staged in Valjevo but under a twisted title, "The Road to Hell."[31] In Milošević's hometown, Požarevac, activists tied the communist symbol of the five-pointed red star to three balloons filled with helium—they wished that the wind would blow the "star" to The Hague.[32]

Ridicule of the first lady could hardly have been cheekier than demonstrated by the street pranks in Kragujevac. According to one popular anecdote, Mirjana Marković had received awards from the Russian government in the late 1990s. Adopting the model of the protest action "Awarding the Roasted Pig," which had been performed by the same protesters during the 1996–97 campaigns, activists announced that they had an award for Marković, too, as the Russians had before them. But because she could not be present in their neighborhood (of course, the activists did not bother to invite her), they would give the award to a turkey instead. The ceremony was entitled "Awarding the Turkey." Approximately thirty activists went to the city center where the awarding of the turkey would take place, and they taped a plastic flower to the head of the turkey, an allusion to Marković's bizarre fashion sense. Soon afterward, the police arrived. Determined to complete the performance, an activist mimicked the turkey's moves and managed to receive the award briefly before the police took him away and confiscated the real turkey.[33] To add to the hilarity, activists filed a lawsuit against the police, charging them with violating animal rights.[34]

This skit contains three layers of humor. The first layer is cultural. In Serbia, referring to a woman as a turkey is tremendously offensive because it implies that she is stupid. The second layer relates to the Kragujevac activists' teasing of Marković's outmoded fashion by inserting a flower behind the turkey's "ears." And the last layer of ridicule relates to activists accusing the authorities of animal rights violations: launching a bona fide lawsuit in this context made the whole legal system appear absurd.

In Leskovac, due to the control the ruling parties exerted over local government, activists opted for a more subtle form of mockery, rather than in-your-face street pranks. A popular action there was also directed at satirizing Marković. Marković's Yugoslav United Left Party (Jugoslovenska udružena levica) is known by the acronym JUL. According to Vladimir Stojković and Dušan Pešić, there was a common brand of chocolate bar called "Julka." The Julka bar's standard product packaging—which activists did not alter—incorporated the image of a cow with a flower on its head. Otpor's objective was to insult Marković by associating the dominance of JUL—the political party—with the dominant chocolate brand in the Serbian confectionery market at the time. Activists offered bars of Julka to passersby in the city center, and by distributing them, the Otpor team insulted Marković by associating her and JUL with the image of the cow on the chocolate bar's packaging. The police had no grounds for making an arrest since activists were simply giving the locals some chocolate.[35]

Regime Allegations and Police Repression of Otpor

A host of actions were engineered to subvert the regime's allegations that Otpor was a terrorist organization. A well-known example was a skit staged in Niš. In front of the police station, Otpor activists set up a stage. Surrounded by other activists and bystanders, one activist was pointing at another, showing bystanders that this was exactly what a terrorist looked like. He resembled a nerd because he wore glasses. This meant he had read a lot. But because the police accused him of being a terrorist, it implied that being literate was dangerous for Serbia.[36]

This plot line was employed by activists in other cities such as Užice, Kraljevo, and Subotica, but with a twist. To ridicule the implication that Otpor was a youth-based terrorist movement, Užice activists made a mock bridge from cardboard. Under it were placed loads of pens and inkstands. When a large enough crowd of passersby had surrounded them, the crew announced that "landmines had been planted under the bridge."[37] Otpor activists in Kraljevo responded to the terrorist allegation by staging the skit "The Terrorist Act." Donning military uniforms and carrying toy rifles, the crews marched in a militaristic style on a downtown street. Their destination was the police station. Vladimir Marović, the coordinator for the Kraljevo branch, recalled that the group walked through the pedestrian street and ignored the traffic sign. Afterward, they proclaimed, "This is a terrorist act because we didn't obey the traffic sign. This is the kind of terrorists we are."[38] In Subotica, activists did not bother to deny the regime's allegation that they were terrorists. Rather, about sixty of them went to the police station to "collectively surrender."[39]

Street pranks were improvised to strike back at the police confiscation of Otpor's promotional material (e.g., posters, T-shirts, and stickers).[40] In early September 2000, the police raided Otpor's headquarters in Belgrade and confiscated their campaign paraphernalia. Activists responded to this outrageous move, dubbed "Unload 2000," with the action "Load 2000." Days after the raid, they intentionally leaked the information that more material would be "loaded" in the office. The police, of course, heard about this and planned another confiscation raid. The scene began with activists pretending to bring a lot of heavy boxes into their office. As anticipated, the police arrived and took away these boxes. Feeling the unusual lightness, the police open the boxes only to find scraps of newspapers. The images and the news of sober police stunned by the empty boxes even appeared in international news coverage.[41]

Other activists believe that actions such as "Load and Unload 2000" could bring into question the loyalty of rank-and-file officers operating on behalf of the regime. According to Marović, the action actually demonstrated to police officers how the regime was driving them toward encountering such humiliating situations. He explains: officers joined the police force because they wanted to catch criminals, to do serious things for society, not to "be mocked by kids." The "Load and Unload" action possibly made them angry at their superior commanders who ordered them to intervene and prevent the Otpor's playful and harmless activities.[42]

The idea of tricking authorities was also translated into street pranks improvised in different towns. For example, in Požarevac, activists leaked information that promotional material would be sent from Belgrade and left on the river bank close to downtown. When the police came in pursuit, all they could find was a fisherman who had no idea what such a big crowd of police were so frantically searching for.[43] Activists in the central city of Čačak employed this tactic in response to a police plan to confiscate material that was to be sent from Belgrade. It was intended for the material to be disseminated to participants at a mass gathering in mid-2000. Željko Trifunović, the coordinator for Otpor's branch in Čačak, was aware that the police were tapping his phone. So, during a phone conversation, he deliberately informed his friend that he was on the way from Belgrade back to Čačak, bringing with him posters, T-shirts, and stickers in his car. Then, he left the car somewhere on the road, took all the material with him, and continued the trip to Čačak by bus. As expected, the police found the car, but not the material. When Trifunović arrived at the event, he told some 20,000 attendees about how he had fooled the police. "It was such a huge embarrassment for the officers stationed at the protest site."[44]

Empowering Town Residents

Activists in regional cities and towns carried out several street actions that encouraged ordinary people to overcome their fear and sense of powerlessness. For example, in Leskovac, activists distributed the seeds of a flower called *prkos*, which means "defiance" in Serbian. The flower was so named because it can grow in almost any conditions. The flower, in this sense, symbolized perseverance in resisting a ruthless regime. While giving away the seeds, activists told people that they should become "defiant" just like the flower.[45]

In Zrenjanin, activists boosted the morale of locals by opening "The First Resistance Street." In the initial action for the Otpor branch there, activists occupied a small space in the pedestrian area with their clenched-fist flags and banners. Not only did they publicly announce the presence of Otpor in Zrenjanin, but they also wanted to spread the message that establishing "Resistance Street" was only the first step in a long march of projects geared toward acquiring political freedom. In this project, people were encouraged to expand "Resistance Street" to encompass all of Serbia.[46]

Occasionally, absurd street theater was deliberately used as a tool to recruit new members. Take for example the action in Novi Sad dubbed "Otpor Is Looking for a Man" (*Otpor traži čoveka*). This was based on the story of Diogenes, the Greek philosopher who had dwelled in an old barrel because of his determination to live in poverty. He used to stroll about in the Athens Agora in full daylight with a lamp. When asked what he was doing, he cynically replied "I am just looking for an honest man, but haven't found one." Based on this story line, some activists put barrels made from cardboard around their bodies and walked around the city center carrying candles in broad daylight. This motley Otpor crew approached people and asked if they saw any honest man. If they did, Otpor would recruit them, since such people might be able to help Otpor in fighting a corrupt regime. A *Danas* journalist found this action exotic and reported on it.[47]

Parodic Protest Actions

Otpor's parodic protest actions were created to reclaim national symbols and historical narratives that had been manipulated by the regime to strengthen its symbolic authority. This use of parody was in line with Otpor's reliance on marketing techniques to enable the movement to appropriate the regime's emblems, "taking everything belonging to the regime, its supporters and its symbols."[48] Popular events, national commemorations, historical narratives, and famous Serb figures were all targets in Otpor's parodic protest actions.

Popular Events

When the regime organized national celebrations as a part of its populist project, Otpor would mimic the celebrations, but distort their meanings.

Otpor's event for the Orthodox New Year (January 13) in 2000 epitomized this approach. Activists' basic idea was to bring home to the Serbian public the reality that "there was nothing to celebrate in 2000" if the regime's power remained intact. At the start of the action, the Belgrade team spread the rumor about the grandness of the New Year event, claiming that the biggest concert in the region would be held and performed by internationally famous singers and bands such as Madonna, the Red Hot Chili Peppers, the Rolling Stones, and Sting. Even the prominent freedom fighter Nelson Mandela would come to deliver a speech. The rumor attracted tens of thousands to Belgrade, gathering at Republic Square in the city's center. Although big names turned out to be local bands and drummers, the crowds continued enjoying the concert anyway. The festive mood, however, came to a halt at midnight when the lights were turned off. Then, the screen on the stage showed images of wars and the economic hardship in Serbia during the 1990s. Concurrently, Boris Tadić, an opposition politician and a future president of Serbia, read out the names of real war victims and eventually posed a confronting question to the gathered masses: "Do you know who these people were?" He continued, "These were victims of Milošević's wars. Do you have a reason to celebrate anything? Now go home and think what to do so that we have a reason to celebrate the Orthodox New Year next year."[49]

Bringing misery into focus during a celebration and telling people to go home in the middle of a party is certainly an anti-climax, and definitely not part of a conventional New Year's celebration. Otpor activists admitted that initially they were worried about the feedback from the prank—which could have ranged from damaging Otpor's publicity program to assaults on activists themselves. Yet, the consequences turned out to be the ones they had intended. Employing an anticlimax twist to wind up the event enabled Otpor to satirize the mass celebratory euphoria. For activists, this was a metaphor for the popular amnesia of the regime-inflicted destruction of Serbia. Milja Jovanović recalls: "A few people threw bottles, but the majority, after a few minutes of silence, walked home. They really listened to us. There was no one at the square. It was really a strong message, and I think people from Serbia and from abroad really understood that we were serious. People came to the event to celebrate, to have some fun, but you just hit them in the face with the Otpor fist."[50]

Otpor's "First Congress," in February 2000, was a clear act to take symbolic ownership of an event originally belonging to the regime. It was organized as a parody of the Socialist Party's Fourth Congress, being held on the same date to renew Milošević's presidential position in the Party. Otpor activists successfully generated an atmosphere in their own congress similar to the Socialist congress. They dressed up in military-style uniforms, Otpor T-shirts, trench coats, and black leather jackets. The light in the auditorium hall was dimmed. The hall was decorated with black and white items. Standing in front of a line of stern looking activists was Marović sporting a military haircut, and donning a grey trench coat. He gave a speech in the so-called "Leninist revolutionary style," solidly declaring that all arrests and harassment by the regime could only strengthen Otpor as a force against the regime itself.[51] Then, Srđan Milivojević from Kruševac boldly proclaimed: "I was the fifth column [i.e., a traitor], because I am the fifth in the line waiting for bread and milk every day, a hooligan who disturbed public order by pasting posters of Otpor that read, 'Resistance because I love Serbia,' and a drug addict because I am addicted to freedom, and every day I want more of it."[52]

Activists from regional branches of Otpor attended the congress to witness the transformation of Otpor from a student movement to a people's movement. But the significance of the congress can be considered as something beyond just an organizational transformation. Marović points out that staging the parallel congress constituted the opposition's challenge to the Socialist Party. It was a demonstration for the public to see "the battle line between the Socialist Party and Otpor."[53] A painful truth for Milošević, perhaps, was that he once made use of communist symbolism in his populist program, portraying himself as the legitimate heir of Tito. Otpor was following a similar path, but their goal was to use the populist discourse of Milošević to turn his symbolism against him, and undermine his authority.

National Commemoration and Historical Narratives

Otpor parodied national commemorations and historical events, which had originally been instrumentalized by Milošević to construct his own image as a heroic Serbian figure. The Kragujevac branch of Otpor employed this approach to great effect. According to Zoran Matović, activists deliberately picked national holidays and commemoration dates, organizing events and actions accordingly.[54] For instance, on Labor Day (May 1) of 2000, the Otpor team in Kragujevac hosted a nationwide event titled "Proletarians of the World United," which brilliantly took ownership of a symbol held dear by the socialist and communist parties. The activist Marija Mista announced that May 1 "belongs to us, to all honest people who work to make a living, not to the corrupt criminals."[55]

Such a statement should be taken seriously, as Kragujevac has a strong historical association with May Day. The city was one of the first areas in Serbia where Tito's Partisan movement raised the "red flag." Also, it has been the stronghold town of factory workers and trade unionists. Being aware of this background, Otpor activists deliberately launched an application to arrange the event at the city hall where the SPS's annual May Day celebration took place. Eventually, SPS politicians decided to withdraw their application.[56] Otpor's event was attended by approximately 15,000 to 20,000 workers and sixty activists from central and western Serbia.[57]

Tito's train trip throughout Yugoslavia inspired Otpor's farewell party, organized on the occasion of Ivan Marović's departure for military service. Two weeks prior to the elections in September 2000, Marović was drafted to serve in the navy, and would be based in Montenegro. The call up, he believes, was the regime's attempt to create a dilemma for him. If he disobeyed the order, he would confirm the regime's propaganda—that Otpor was traitorous. But if he decided to join the navy, the regime expected that Otpor would be weakened without his contribution. Eventually, Marović accepted the draft call while turning the trap to Otpor's advantage. He traveled from Belgrade to Montenegro by train just as Tito did when he was on tour to visit his supporters throughout Yugoslavia. At every station where the train stopped, local activists and Otpor supporters gathered, waved at Marović, and greeted him with flowers. In some towns, there were even singing performances. No arrest occurred until the train reached the western gateway of Serbia, Užice.[58] Marović managed to arrive in Montenegro, but his trip was not one of an ordinary conscript. Rather, it was a journey to counter the regime's denunciation of Otpor as unpatriotic by demonstrating to the Serbian public the movement's historical acknowledgement of communism's significance.

In areas where the Tito-led Partisan movement remained an ideal of the struggle, Otpor's parodic protest actions often revolved around Tito and dates important for the national remembrance of him. For example, in Užice, there was a Tito monument in the town center. On the twentieth commemoration of Tito's death, Otpor activists went to the monument, gluing Otpor application forms on the monument. Afterwards, they announced that "Tito has changed his mind" and now supports Otpor completely. Activists then swore an oath of allegiance to Tito, "vowing to learn and work diligently, defend the freedom of speech, and keep darkness off the streets. . . ."[59] Afterwards, an activist impersonated Tito, stating that he hoped the citizens of Serbia would not take twenty years to meet these promises.[60] Simić from Otpor Užice adds that the whole scene was absurd because activists imitated the kind of speech Tito had always given. But the twist was the speech's sarcasm being directed at Milošević who brought about darkness in Serbia. The youth were urged to defend the country from this darkness.[61]

In a similar vein, the Otpor crew from Valjevo held a Youth Day event, which was celebrated on Tito's birthday (May 25) in the heyday of Yugoslav communism. Activists organized the same kind of relay race as had been staged in Tito's time, but they ended the race at Tito's monument, to which they presented a baton as a gift for his birthday.[62] The practice was sarcastic because the Relay of Youth was actually cancelled in 1988, the year when Milošević was emerging on the political scene in Yugoslavia. In many ways, the parody of the race denotes nostalgia for a glorious Yugoslavia of the past destroyed by the Milošević regime.

At the end of July 2000, Otpor carried out an action synchronized across dozens of towns, using the word JUL as a pun. The pronunciation of the acronym JUL, that stands for Mirjana Marković's Yugoslav United Left Party, is the same as for the Serbian term for the month of July (*Jul*).

Otpor declared the nationwide action "The End of JULy 2000" to mark the countdown to the removal of JUL from the Serbian political landscape. Ideas for actions staged under this theme varied from town to town. For instance, in Kraljevo, activists flushed the calendar page for July 31 down their toilets in their offices. In Kragujevac, the Otpor team invited passersby in the city center to wrap a cube of sugar with toilet paper inscribed with the letters JUL. Then, they were asked flush it down a toilet bowl painted with an Otpor clenched fist. In Kruševac, activists threw an ice sculpture in the shape of the communist five-pointed star from the downtown bridge into the river.[63] In Niš, the crew there got rid of weeds in a public park, announcing that these weeds were analogous to JUL.[64]

Famous Serb Figures

Famous Serb figures were a reference point of the regime's nationalist propaganda. To subvert this propaganda, activists "registered" the monuments of these figures as Otpor members. One way to do this was to cover the monuments with Otpor T-shirts and flags. In Valjevo, monuments of politicians and academicians situated in the downtown area were found wearing enormous Otpor T-shirts.[65] In Novi Sad, activists recruited the monument of the poet, Jovan Jovanović Zmaj, located in the city square, by wrapping it in Otpor's clenched fist flag.[66] Belgrade activists targeted the monument of the scientist "Nikola Tesla," which was also draped in an Otpor fist flag.[67] However, in Kraljevo, according to Matović, there was no monuments of persons, but only an armored vehicle. So, the crew there decided to wrap it with the Otpor flag.[68]

Another method of recruiting prominent figures was through registering them on an Otpor membership form. Šikman notes that at some point in 2000, application forms with names and (counterfeit) signatures of famous figures were printed and publicly shown. It was to indicate that even historical figures had decided to take part in Otpor's campaigns.[69] Recruited figures included Nikola Tesla, Vuk Karadžić (the great nineteenth-century linguist and literary figure), and Stanoje Glavaš (a freedom fighter and a Serb hero during the First Serbian Uprising against the Ottoman Empire in 1790).[70]

9. "Dressing Up the Monument" action. (Photograph by and courtesy of Aleksandar Pavlović.)

At times, instead of co-opting pillars of the regime, Otpor activists satirically "integrated" themselves into the regime. For instance, in Kraljevo and Smederevo, Otpor teams gathered at Socialist Party offices and requested applications for party membership. Unsure how to respond, the staff asked them to leave and then closed the offices.[71] In Niš, the SPS announced Milošević as the national hero. Sarcastically, activists wanted to express their complete agreement. They titled the action "Slobodan Milošević, Ostensible Hero" and visited the SPS office in their city to award the president with a hero medal.[72]

Carnivalesque Events

The organization of concerts, festivals, parties, and feasts constituted key elements of Otpor's carnivalesque humor. The movement deliberately utilized these kinds of festive events to publicize the election campaigns. Moreover, activists were aware that urban culture and its rebellious characteristics were not a realm within which the regime practiced effective manipulation. Popović notes, "Since [the authorities] were not giving a dime to [support] drama, music, theater, or cultural events, generally, we produced more and more public events in that way because we knew that we could defeat them on that ground—this is our ground. So, [Otpor] became an organization capable of organizing these kinds of public events."[73]

In contrast to the 1996–97 protests where carnivalesque activities merged with street protests, Otpor's carnivalesque events constituted the protests in and of themselves. The events were held off the street and scattered across different places such as local city halls, sports stadiums, main roads, hospitals, and police stations. In other words, these sites were diverted from their original purposes and converted into stages of protest against the authorities.

Concerts and Festivals

Anti-regime singers and rock bands often performed in concerts organized by Otpor in cooperation with B92 radio. In Otpor's early days, concerts were crucial in attracting youngsters to join the movement. One iconic concert was held in Belgrade on November 22, 1999, "as a follow up to [the police] beating of students in [Otpor's] first march on November 11" and in commemoration of the 1996–97 student protests.[74] The concert was entitled "We Have a Situation" (*Imamo situaciju*). Attended by around 2,000 people, it was one of Otpor's foremost public platforms to declare the movement's goals. Political activism was accompanied by domestic rock bands such as Eyesburn, Love Hunters, Atheist Rap, Kanda Kodža i Nebojša, and Darkwood Dub. During the concert, Jovanović announced that this gathering would mark the last protest of students because the regime would be gone soon, and student demonstrations would no longer be necessary.[75] In the following month, Dragoljub Đuričić—a prominent drummer and musician who had performed in protest concerts since 1996—played in a concert organized in Kragujevac.[76] In Novi Sad, activists organized the concert "Fist in the Head" (*Šakom u glavu*) in October 1999 in order to attract new members because at the time the Otpor branch there was in its infancy. Aleksandar Savanović, Otpor activist and reporter for the tabloid *Blic*, observed that around 1,500 people attended the concert and that Otpor membership increased afterward.[77]

In 2000, organized concerts promoted the campaigns "He's Finished" and "It's Time." From July through October 2000, Otpor collaborated with B92, ANEM—a coalition of independent media—and various NGOs to organize a rock concert tour through at least twenty-five towns.[78] According to Popović, fifteen big concert events were organized for the "It's Time" campaign alone.[79] The concerts attracted approximately 150,000 participants. A disk jockey from B92 even remarked that the tour was the biggest "in the history of Serbian rock music."[80]

The EXIT music festival, which has since become an icon of youth movements in the Balkans, was first held in Novi Sad in the summer of 2000 as a part of Otpor's "Exit" election campaign. The festival was initiated by Dušan Kovačević, Bojan Bošković, and Ivan Milivojev, then students from the Philosophy Faculty of Novi Sad University and Otpor activists. It lasted for 100 days and was attended by approximately 20,000 spectators. The EXIT festival's slogan, "exit from ten years of madness," invoked resistance against the Milošević regime. Rock bands such as Darkwood Dub, Orthodox Celts, Eyesburn, Van Gogh, Atheist Rap, and Deca loših muzičara all performed at the festival. In addition, films with anti-regime subjects were shown and a variety of art performances, as well as discussion panels were organized. A few days before the election date (September 24, 2000), the festival concluded with the message "He's Finished" projected onto a screen on the stage.[81] An organizer notes that the EXIT music festival in 2000 was viewed at the time as the best event in Yugoslavia in at least a decade. With its backdrop of political turbulence, the festival marked a young generation's "fight for democracy and normal life [and] the rise from darkness to let the future begin."[82]

Together with the rock concerts, "caravans of celebrities" traveled to dozens of towns in Serbia to promote the campaign "It's Time."[83] In Aleksandrovac, for instance, Dejan Cukić (a pop-rock singer) and Sanja Ignjatović (a TV reporter) appeared together as guests for the concert event organized in August 2000.[84] And in Užice, Otpor activists invited Vlade Divac (a Serbian NBA basketball player) and Srđan Dragojević (a movie director) to meet with locals and to encourage them to go out and vote.[85]

Parties and Feasts

Otpor successfully turned forms of social gathering (i.e., parties and feasts) into platforms for recruiting new members and gaining publicity among locals. Throughout the campaigns "He's Finished" and "It's Time," there was at least one massive party organized in each area where an Otpor branch was active.[86] For instance, in Aleksandrovac, Otpor activists together with staff from the Center for Free Elections and Democracy (Centar za slobodne izbore i demokratiju—CeSID) organized a party in a local café to persuade the young to cast ballots in September 2000.[87] In the northern town of Zrenjanin, Lacmanović, who was also a bartender in a café where Otpor parties were usually held, estimates that his branch threw at least one party every week. He points out that "it was how [Otpor] got new members, and how [Otpor] built up good relationships among us and between us and the locals."[88]

At times, parties were organized across multiple Otpor branches to strengthen solidarity and publicize the election campaign. An exemplar was the "Mini-Festival: Nonstop Festival before the Election," which was a joint effort between Otpor Novi Sad and Valjevo, the Novi Sad radio station—FM 201, and the activist art group Led Art.[89] According to Goran Dašković, this was a massive "techno party" that went on for a week that attracted approximately 6,000 partyers. The party provided the fun and became a site for young people to socialize. Moreover, it was a channel for directly reaching and encouraging youngsters to vote.[90]

Feasts, characterized by food sharing, were incorporated into street actions that aimed to bridge the gap between Otpor activists and local town residents, or between activists and local police. An Otpor action entitled "Pick the Police Day" was a prime example. The action, which was synchronized across various towns, involved "fraternizing marches" and an "invasion" of police stations by hundreds of female activists, including mothers with children. They brought cakes, cookies, and flowers to the police.[91] In big cities (e.g., Belgrade), the police blocked the crowd from entering police stations, but in some smaller areas, such as Kragujevac and Aleksandrovac, police welcomed activists and even invited them inside the police stations to share the food. The reason for this could be that in smaller towns police were also the neighbors of Otpor members and supporters. Hence, to demonstrate "good manners" and maintain their relationship, they accepted the gifts.[92]

At times, Otpor activists organized "feasts" to give away free food to locals as a public relations gimmick. In Belgrade, for example, activists distributed two hundred kilograms of bread to passersby at a market in the Braće Jerković residential area. This was both humanitarian and a protest action. The donation put the spotlight on the regime-inflicted impoverishment experienced by many who could not even afford loaves of bread.[93] In a similar vein, Otpor activists in Aleksandrovac organized an action called "Just a Little Bit More" in September 2000. Aleksandrovac is located in the geographic region of "Župa" the main product of which is grapes. During the action, activists gave away grapes to passersby while spreading the message "Resistance because I am hungry."[94] In another action by the Aleksandrovac branch, when activists received a big piece of cake as a gift from Otpor supporters, they shared it with children in the city center.[95]

The sharing of food demonstrated the spirit of young activists to the Serbian public, portraying Otpor's altruistic image in contrast to the regime's warmongering image. The spirit of giving gifts and enjoying the fun of life underpins carnivalesque humor. Otpor merged this spirit with the will to resist the ruthless regime. By doing this, the movement gave rise to its "life-celebratory" approach to nonviolent resistance. In the words of Popović: "I think [that] we have succeeded [to bring down Milošević] because we simply loved life more than death. Generally those guys were the preachers of the death. Their hatred, their propaganda . . . their language smelled like death. And we won because we loved life more, and you can't beat life."[96]

Strategizing the Effects of Excorporation

Otpor's excorporation practices fully matured as integral components of the movement's advanced nonviolent strategy. Activists from branches across Serbia systematically created satirical street performances out of the regime's propaganda. There were no outright condemnations of the regime in these actions. Rather, they used the content of the regime's propaganda and twisted it to absurdity. Through this kind of operation, their actions subtly invalidated the claims underlying the regime's propaganda. Popular examples include "Dinar for a Change," the variety of "Reconstruction . . ." actions, and the "Nice Day for Terrorism" action.

Many satirical skits also dealt with the media's manipulation of information. Rather than blatantly criticizing the regime-controlled media, activists in cities such as Novi Sad, Zrenjanin, and Aleksandrovac carried out skits drawing on metaphors that represented the crisis of media control, with skits such as the "Media Eclipse," "The Fine Certificate," and "Brain Washing."

The tactical sophistication of satirical street events was most evident in the "Load and Unload 2000" action in which activists managed to turn the authorities into the "clowns." The earlier police raid on Otpor's office in Belgrade provided the plot for this action. While the core idea of the second raid remained the same (confiscation of activist publicity materials), there was a difference in the staged event because the new boxes confiscated by the police were empty.

Ideas for these satirical actions emerged from the content of the regime's propaganda, which the satire embraced in order to deconstruct it. Otpor's messages conveyed in the satirical actions made use of the rhetorical material provided by the regime. The actions were "populism-oriented" in this sense. However, they were concurrently anti-regime and populist in nature because the actions twisted the original rhetoric, replacing regime components with the movement's own messages.

As with satirical street theater, Otpor's parodic protest actions worked to subvert the regime on the basis of excorporation. They dealt with various sets of rhetoric and symbols common in society so as to undermine the symbolic foundation of the regime's authority. The actions were fundamentally parodic because they mimicked and parodied the regime's rhetoric. But in the process of mimicry, these actions severed the form from the content of that rhetoric. While the form was maintained through the act of imitation, the original content was usually replaced with Otpor's anti-regime message. In this way, the rhetoric that was initially foundational to the regime's authority was reappropriated by the movement to undermine it.

A conspicuous example of parody in an Otpor action was its "May Day" celebration. Leading activists deliberately organized the Otpor event in parallel with the Socialist Party event. Kragujevac was chosen as the site of the event for its symbolic associations with the regime's leftist ideology. Activists imitated the whole ritual of the Socialist Party's May Day event, including inviting workers to attend. However, they announced that the "real workers" were reclaiming the meaning of May Day from the "corrupt criminals" of the regime. In a similar fashion, at Otpor's First Congress they mimicked the Socialist Party's congress: activists had Otpor's allies congregate, leading figures delivered speeches in the "Leninist revolutionary" style, and participants generated a militaristic atmosphere via their haircuts and black leather jackets. However, Otpor's congress was held as a declaration of the movement's enlargement. This was a message to intimidate Milošević, but the act of intimidation was accomplished through the staging of a ritual originally belonging to the regime.

A number of Otpor's parodic protest actions were carried out to reclaim historical narratives from the Milošević regime. Examples include the "Relay Race" organized in Valjevo, the anniversary of Tito's birthday in Užice, and the reenactment of Tito's train trip organized as a farewell for Ivan Marović. These kinds of events and their associated historical narratives had been monopolized by the regime in an effort to establish its legitimacy as the heir to Tito's communism. Otpor activists reinterpreted and reconstructed the events so as to dismiss Milošević's claim. Similarly, subversion through parody also appeared in episodes where historical figures were "registered" as Otpor members. Activists "recruited" a number of heroic Serb personalities by draping their monuments with an Otpor flag or T-shirt. Counterfeit signatures of these famous figures were printed on Otpor's application forms to demonstrate that even Serb historical icons, once incorporated in the regime's nationalist rhetoric, had changed sides to support Otpor. History no longer played into the hands of the regime.

The satirical street performances and parodic protest actions staged in Otpor's campaigns worked to excorporate power. These actions brought about change in popular discourses. While relying on the very same rhetorical and symbolic sources that once empowered the ruling elites, satirical and parodic street actions rendered the original meanings of these sources absurd. Truth claims underlying the rhetoric or the sacredness of these symbols lost the firm ground on which the authority of the regime had rested. In some situations, satirical and parodic humor revealed cracks in the regime's rhetoric, allowing people to clearly see invalid claims to authority. Other humorous actions not only pointed out cracks in the regime's authority, but created those cracks. They provoked the regime to lose its temper and show its true face.

In the face of regime repression, the excorporation process of using humorous actions can accelerate a regime's decline in legitimacy. Non-violence scholars have explained how a nonviolent movement could gain political momentum by exposing a regime's oppression. For instance, inspired by the Japanese martial art of jujutsu (or jiu-jitsu), which uses the physical strength of one's opponent against that opponent, some activists have developed a concept of "political jiu-jitsu," which explores methods and consequences of using an opponent's repressive policies in weakening that opponent's own support networks. A repressive response to protesters who maintain resilience in their nonviolent discipline can shift loyalties among three primary groups: nonpartisan parties at the local and global level, the government's usual supporters and its apparatus, and the general grievance group.[97]

The dynamics of the "backfire" concept deals with publicizing repression to enhance the effect of "political jiu-jitsu."[98] For this process to be effective, two conditions are needed: the formulation of a collective perception that the repression is unjust and an outrage, and the communication of incidents of repression to the masses. Televised media, and lately the internet, are crucial for inciting an emotional response to such repression. As the numbers in the media audience become larger, attempts by a government to cover up its repression become harder. The impact of "political jiu-jitsu" can become much greater.[99]

Underlying these two concepts is the diminished legitimacy of rulers who have responded to unarmed challengers with the use of force. Political legitimacy is a prerequisite for a government to remain in power. Legitimacy can be established based on popular acceptance of a certain ruling group via elections, or established through other claims to legitimacy having little to no democratic process. In any case, legitimacy underpins the power to rule. It must be produced and sustained in ways that the populace will accept if they are to be governed by an elite group. In a conflict situation, a government's legitimacy may be undermined when authorities attack unarmed people because there is a fundamental understanding that the use of violence must be justified. For a government to be seen as legitimately acting against its own citizens, justification would usually entail criminalizing a person or a group as a threat to state security. However, when nonviolent activists demonstrate to the public that regime violence is unjustified, the use of force against unarmed citizens may result in declining legitimacy for those who use it or authorize it. If the perceived legitimacy of a group of elites allows them to govern the masses, then diminishing their legitimacy threatens the continuation of their governance.[100]

The dynamics of legitimacy politics hold true in the case of Otpor. In an effort to undermine Otpor's advanced campaigns, the regime's security forces routinely detained, interrogated, and, in a few cases, tortured activists for pasting posters and stickers, leading public gatherings, and distributing leaflets. The police readily claimed that Otpor activists were being manipulated by and were cooperating with the United States and its NATO allies, and were therefore traitors. From that perspective, repression could be perceived as legitimate by the Serbian public. However, when it came to activists' satirical street actions, such rationalizations became absurd. Because Otpor's actions were jocular and innocent, people saw them as politically nonthreatening. Hence, repression appeared to be an excessive response.[101]

Fundamentally, humorous protest actions create a situation where the justification for repression appears nonsensical. "Political jiu-jitsu" and "Backfire" theories suggest that several methods of nonviolent action can communicate the repressive image of a regime, thereby exposing the regime's illegitimacy. What humor does is different from other methods of nonviolent action in that it forces the opponent's repression to encounter its own absurdity. Humor reveals the unwise fabrication of justification needed for the repression of activists. Humorous street actions even invite onlookers to laugh at how ludicrous the justifications are. If the "excorporation" process works to generally subvert the truth claims of the opponent's propaganda, it also operates to disturb the coherence of a grand narrative justifying the regime's repressive actions. And incoherent justifications undermine the legitimacy of the regime.

Carnivalesque Imagination and Nonviolent Revolution

Otpor's carnivalesque events encouraged young activists to imagine a scenario of social change. The events were organized in different sites off the street. Rock concerts were held in town halls and public parks. Activists went to police stations, inviting officers for a dance, or sharing food with them. Parties were organized in cafés and pubs. Theatrical plays were performed on the river bank. What these carnivalesque events had in common was the offer of a platform on which to imagine alternative realities. Such a platform was particularly important for young Serbians who still found themselves trapped in Milošević's dictatorial rule on the eve of the year 2000. The title of the concert caravan "EXIT" reflected the aspiration of young people who made up the majority of Otpor's members. Many activists point out that these concerts and parties provided a metaphor of a world without the Milošević regime, a world they were attempting to materialize. In that imagined world, having fun and hanging out with friends was possible. There was no fear of being drafted to fight in wars. In that world, they hoped for a "normal" life in which there was no international isolation preventing them from attending concerts in other countries or from traveling abroad. It was a world where they could raise their children, provide them with food, housing, and a good education.[102]

The imagined world of "EXIT" does not imply political nihilism, because those wishing for it engaged heavily in Otpor's campaigns for democratic change. Despite their harsh repression, these activists risked their lives to make this other world possible. Carnivalesque events provided an imaginative space for the activists who were in the progress of struggling for social change. They offered a site for envisioning how this change could allow them to live life with fun and delight. Such a space could inspire activists who, in turn, spread their hopes and optimism—as elicited from carnivalesque events—to society more widely.[103]

As another form of carnivalesque event, Otpor's feasts, to some extent, created a platform for activists' interaction with the police, shifting the perceptions of their opponents. In some towns such as Kragujevac and Aleksandrovac, activists visited the authorities at police stations, offering them food and gifts. From a tactical viewpoint, this might have contributed to humanizing and thus disarming the police officers. But the impact of this carnivalesque humor on the regime's apparatus can perhaps be seen more appropriately at the level of a change in perspective. As Goran Dašković points out, "for a long time the Milošević regime had divided people in Serbia into those against it and those serving it." Through shared food and laughter and other participatory entertainment, carnivalesque events introduced a worldview in which divisions along a pro- versus anti- Milošević fault line were illusory. Those serving the regime were also neighbors and friends of those opposing it.[104]

Expressed differently, sharing food as an activity at carnivals potentially allowed the inclusion of those who would otherwise be defined as the "enemy." The feasts' inclusive nature opened a space for interaction among conflicting parties. Such a space constitutes within it the possibility for further dialogue and a chance for building constructive relationships, even among members of opposing factions. The dialogical interaction provided during the feasts enabled adversaries to overcome their predefined perceptions of each other.[105]

Carnivalesque humor's contribution toward overcoming cognitive blocks provides a crucial opportunity for reflection on the idea that there is a need to construct a parallel polity underlying a nonviolent revolution. Nonviolence practitioners and theorists proposed the idea of constructing alternative or parallel institutions when nonviolent resistance campaigns have been launched long enough and gained critical support from the populace. In some situations, alternative institutions can be established as a counterpart of the ongoing noncooperation programs that can put additional pressure on the regime being opposed. The idea of a parallel polity can be translated into forms of alternative economic, cultural, and political institutions.[106] A new system of tax collection, for instance, can be introduced as a path toward economic independence from the regime. Nonviolent action scholars such as Gene Sharp and Howard Clark consider the establishment of a parallel polity as a way of empowering the oppressed, paving the way for complete independence.[107] In a similar vein, Gandhi founded a constructive program that covered different processes of civil independence subsequent to the removal of the British colonization from

India. His idea was to foster sustainable development in India by encouraging a self-sufficient and community-based economy, the abolishment of untouchability, the introduction of basic education in villages, and the improvement of women's status in India, to name a few.[108]

The notion of the carnivalesque—the imagining of other possibilities—can be recognized as an initial step toward a parallel polity. Underlying Gandhi's constructive program initiative was the suggestion that a process of thinking of the alternatives is needed for nonviolent resistance to be able to overturn domination. The notion of an alternative polity recognizes that a dominant regime's influence can penetrate and dominate almost every sphere of life. Therefore, nonviolent activists need to be able to imagine a society that can transcend the current institutions confronting them.[109] Current nonviolence literature illustrates some of the concrete forms that alternative institutions may take in order to establish a parallel polity. However, there is little scholarly work on the process that helps people to reach this stage. Envisioning alternatives requires a shift in perspective, and without this, a cognitive block remains. The images of a counter-reality that can emerge in a carnival atmosphere can help those trapped in an oppressive situation to transcend this mental block by reminding them of the possibilities of a change from the status quo. That is, those subordinate to the structures of the current regime can set themselves free—gender prejudice can be lifted, civil liberty can be granted, and justice can be brought within reach. The carnivalesque brings into existence an outlook where social realities are subject to possibilities of change. For those engaging in a nonviolent struggle, this outlook comes with the hope of transforming their society from one of oppression to that of a caring polity, where citizens are treated equally. It is this hope that can translate into activists' persistent endeavors in pursuit of a nonviolent revolution.

Conclusion

The proliferation of Otpor's satirical street theater, parodic protest actions, and carnivalesque events reflected the significant position humor occupied the organization's campaigns. Satirical street theater had been developing since the 1996–97 protests, but Otpor lifted it to a new level of sophistication. Activists generally directed their satire at the regime's absurd propaganda and the ruling elites. Their parodic protest actions were invented to take back ownership of popular symbols on behalf of the public, symbols that had been monopolized by the regime. Theoretically, these impacts bring into frame the relationship between a movement's effective nonviolent strategy and organization, and the maximization of excorporation process. Not only did Otpor's humorous actions counter the regime's rhetoric and symbolism promulgated throughout Serbia, but they also annulled the logic of repression. Otpor's carnivalesque events such as concerts, festivals, parties, and feasts encouraged protesters to imagine realities alternative to the current oppressive situation. Imagining other possibilities constitutes a practice necessary for emancipation from "paradigms" favorable to a dominant system. This practice can set the stage for the founding of parallel institutions, an idea central to nonviolent revolution.

6

Localizing Strategic Humor

How Milošević Was Mocked across Serbia

Otpor's branch-based organization enabled the proliferation of humorous protest actions across Serbia. Nevertheless, on-the-ground reality showed that humor was not the preferred choice in every town. The degree to which independent media, NGO members, and opposition politicians were active in different areas shaped activists' decisions toward the use of humor. In major cities, the proliferation of humorous protest actions was related to the active role played by opposition forces in resistance campaigns. However, in other cities, activists' tactical calculations led to avoiding the use of humor, despite the support rendered by opposition figures. Similarly, in towns with an absence of opposition forces, activists bypassed humorous protest actions, viewing them as counterproductive or even as dangerous. Nevertheless, there were regime stronghold towns where activists opted for humor despite the threat of repression. An attempt to identify situations both favorable and unfavorable for the tactical use of humor is drawn from these observations.

The Interplay between Local Opposition Forces and Activists' Tactical Decisions[1]

The presence or absence of opposition forces in towns and cities was a strong influence shaping activists' decisions to opt for or bypass humorous protest actions. Chapter 4 demonstrated Otpor's strategic pillars: nonviolence, campaigning and public relations, and marketing techniques. Based on these pillars, activists conceived of a wide range of protest tactics, including the humorous protest actions detailed in chapter 5. Otpor's organizational structure also permitted a degree of autonomy for activists in their tactical decision-making. As a result, activists employed different protest tactics based on local knowledge of their various communities. These localization effects—varying ways of conceptualizing protest actions and their tactics—resulted in differing preferences for how humor should or should not be deployed in protest actions. And the active role played by opposition parties, anti-regime media, and NGOs in different localities helped shape the conditions and motivations for this local decision-making by Otpor.

Otpor's Protest Tactics Other Than Humorous Protest Actions

Otpor activists relied on humorous street actions chiefly to draw media attention and increase the movement's publicity. At times, these actions were staged along with using tactics such as publicizing repression, mounting small acts of resistance, and "door-to-door" methods. However, in various situations, activists opted for using these particular tactics without any supporting humorous action. Their reasons for avoiding the use of humor are related to specific advantages deriving from the particular tactics.

Publicizing police repression through rallies and press conferences could generate public outrage against the regime. Between March 1999 and March 2000, 190 Otpor activists were detained by the police. However, when the Anti-Terrorism Act came into force in May 2000, at least 2,000 Otpor activists were detained, approximately 300 of whom were apprehended five or more times.[2] To reverse the consequences of repression, Otpor asked for assistance from independent lawyers, nongovernmental organization staff, and, in many stronghold towns of opposition parties, local politicians. These networks of dissidents formed "rapid action teams." As soon as activists were detained, other activists sent out information to NGOs and lawyers who would document the arrest and provide legal aid. In some areas, opposition politicians assisted in negotiating with the police and bailing out activists. Simultaneously, other Otpor activists mobilized sympathizers in the locality, including parents of the detained and their neighbors, and gathered in front of the police station.[3] In addition, they contacted journalists to report the detention or set up a press conference to condemn the regime's heavy-handed reaction against young activists. In this way, Otpor advanced its publicity based on the regime's repression.[4]

Small acts of resistance—which included spray painting graffiti, wearing T-shirts, and pasting posters and stickers—enhanced visibility for Otpor throughout Serbia without exposing activists to the risk of repression. Resisting the regime through executing these acts was simple: ordinary citizens could wear T-shirts or paste stickers without registering themselves as Otpor members. Nevertheless, the impact could be profound. The mass production of these protest paraphernalia ensured the appearance of Otpor in almost every corner of Serbian cities. Especially in the stronghold towns of Slobodan Milošević's Socialist Party, the presence of Otpor's symbolism—through stickers and posters—could pose a serious threat because the party had been confident of its monopoly of presence in these towns. In addition, many activists regarded tactics such as pasting posters and painting graffiti safer than taking to the street as a part of a recognized protest group. At times, they carried out these actions at night, thereby concealing their identity from the police.[5]

The "door-to-door" or village outreach method accelerated the popularity of Otpor in small towns and villages without Otpor's reliance on the media. In the preceding chapter, we discussed Otpor's establishment of branches through cooperation with local leaders. Due to their prevailing influence amongst locals, these leaders could shape public opinion and convince people to vote against Milošević. Apart from this influence, Otpor activists visited residents in remote areas to persuade them to cast their ballots for the opposition parties in elections. Usually, while handing out flyers and stickers, activists would discuss the residents' own issues in addition to Otpor campaign messaging, and in this way activists could explicitly link local problems to the iniquities of the existing regime.[6]

Local Opposition Forces: Independent
Media, Opposition Parties, and NGOs

To promote greater effectiveness in their protest repertoires, Otpor formed cooperative networks among key dissident groups: anti-regime media, NGOs, and opposition parties.[7] Their contributions in assisting

Otpor varied from implementation of one tactic to another. With regard to humorous tactics, the active role of anti-regime media in major cities became the factor most relevant to activists' preference for this tactic, since they sought substantial news coverage for their campaigns.

A prominent step taken by anti-regime media that benefitted Otpor was the establishment of the Association of Independent Electronic Media (ANEM) by the radio station B92 in June 1993, enabling collaboration between Otpor activists and local journalists. ANEM linked local radio and television stations, which were mainly liberated from the control of SPS after the 1996 municipal elections. In 1998, more than thirty local radio and television stations were supportive members of ANEM.[8] They attracted an audience of approximately 1.7 million Serbians in mid-2000, compared to the 1.5 million viewers of state-run Radio Television of Serbia.[9] Generally, local radio and television channels broadcast international news programs such as BBC and CNN, along with national TV productions (Vin, TV Mreža, and TV B92).[10] Since the regime had taken over the B92 office in Belgrade on May 17, 2000,[11] ANEM became the only independent media coalition, and operated outside Belgrade by transmitting their signal from Bosnia.[12]

According to Veran Matić of B92, "ANEM was the backbone of Otpor."[13] Leading activists from Otpor could not agree more. Ivan Marović emphasized that the widespread coverage by local media was crucial for Otpor's publicity in minor cities: "[T]here were not many national independent media . . . , [but] there were tons of local . . . newspapers and radio stations. That was the majority of coverage that Otpor got."[14] There might be small towns without access to independent media because the local radio and television stations or newspaper did not have enough funding to disseminate copies or stretch the signal to remote areas.[15] Nevertheless, in the localities without access to ANEM's networks, people still found ways to access alternative information by tuning to radio stations from neighboring towns.[16]

Otpor's other media allies included the daily *Glas javnosti*, *Danas*, and the tabloid *Blic*. Milja Jovanović notes that in 2000, out of 350 issues of the tabloid *Blic*, approximately 250 contained coverage of Otpor actions: "We might not be the main story, but we would always have photographs on the front page."[17] Despite the limited circulation (some 200,000 copies nationally), *Blic*'s hybrid characteristics—serving as a mouthpiece for the opposition and being part of the commercial press—meant it posed a threat to the regime. In early May 2000, the government printing house refused to publish copies of newspapers for *Blic*, claiming there were paper shortages. In July, *Danas* and *Glas javnosti* received the same treatment.[18]

The 1996 municipal elections and subsequent protests were turning points that significantly strengthened opposition parties and NGOs. Although the details of precisely what role these opposition groups had in encouraging Otpor activists to opt for humorous protest action remains unclear, the fact that these groups were present does help account for the construction of an "opposition infrastructure" and the anti-regime frame of mind. The scale of their support for Otpor may be reflected in the fact that forty-one cities and towns where the coalition Zajedno had won local elections subsequently became footholds for Otpor's organization. The opposition-dominated local governments provided Otpor activists with office facilities and vehicles for transporting promotional material. In some areas, opposition politicians exercised their influence to protect activists from police torture and bail them out in cases of detention.[19]

The 1996–97 protests were followed by an increase in the numbers of different nongovernmental organizations established in regional cities such as Novi Sad, Subotica, Niš, Podgorica, Vršac, Kikinda, Pančevo, Čačak, Kraljevo, Valjevo, Užice, Kragujevac, Leskovac, Bor, Novi Pazar, and Pirot.[20] The majority of emerging NGOs generally promoted human rights, democratization, and regime change.[21] After the NATO air strikes in 1999, existing NGOs established a coalition "Yugoslav Action." At the same time, civil parliaments were founded in many cities throughout Serbia (e.g., Čačak, Valjevo, Užice, Kraljevo, Leskovac).

The election campaigns ("It's Time" and "Exit") marked the nationwide collaboration that had been established among nongovernmental organizations, opposition parties, and Otpor. Along with spreading the message to "get out and vote" in towns and cities, on the day of election, nongovernmental organizations conducted exit polls and monitored ballot counting.[22] The latter was spearheaded by the Center for Free Elections and Democracy (CeSID) which collaborated with Otpor branches in most cities and towns.[23] It was the case that in many localities Otpor activists worked for CeSID, while the staff of CeSID assisted Otpor with logistical issues such as the transportation of material.[24] In major cities where the Trade Union Confederation (also known as "Independence" or Nezavisnost) had played an active role in anti-regime activism, cooperation between Otpor and the Union tended to be constructive. Otpor activists and workers often organized events together. A prime example was the May Day celebration held in Kragujevac.[25]

The Influence of Local Opposition Forces on Activists' Preference for Humorous Protest Actions

In sixteen of the cities and towns where Otpor's campaigns were launched, opposition forces were influential in determining activists' preference for humorous protest actions in a number of different ways. In some major cities, the active role played by the independent media, opposition politicians, and NGO group members encouraged the proliferation of humorous protest actions. However, in other cases, the prominence of opposition leaders influenced activists to downplay humorous protest actions. In a similar vein, regime stronghold cities saw little if any humorous protest action because it was perceived as too dangerous. Nevertheless, there were exceptions in regime-controlled towns with a history of civic protests. In these areas, activists opted for non-provocative street skits.

Areas Where the Opposition's Active Role
Enabled the Proliferation of Humorous Protest Actions

In Belgrade, Novi Sad, Zrenjanin, Kragujevac, Kraljevo, and Užice, the resilience of local media and NGOs and the control opposition parties exerted in municipal governments allowed humorous protest actions to proliferate. All of these cities were established as footholds of the Democratic Party (DS) and the Serbian Renewal Movement (SPO) in the wake of the 1996 municipal elections. In addition, local media and NGOs had been strongly involved in anti-regime activities. Between 1999 and 2000, at least five satirical street theater performances were staged in Belgrade and Novi Sad, and six street skits in Zrenjanin, Kragujevac, Kraljevo, and Užice, were reported in the newspapers.

The cooperation between Otpor activists and anti-regime journalists in these six cities determined the proliferation of humorous street actions. Since Otpor's inception, activists conceived the function of humorous protest actions to facilitate public relations. The actions were designed to draw media attention so as to popularize the movement, and the vibrant role of independent media in major cities were amenable to this objective.

The cooperation between Otpor activists in Belgrade and independent journalists was constructive. The capital city was the powerhouse of the liberal-oriented press, ranging from radio station and online news service B92, the national newspapers *Danas* and *Glas javnosti*, the tabloid *Blic*, the weekly news magazines *NIN* and *VREME*, the bi-weekly journal *Republika*, and the news agency BETA.[26] Otpor-supportive media that primarily covered the humorous protest actions included *Blic*, *Glas javnosti*, *Danas*, and B92 news online. Prior to planned street actions, journalists from these allied organizations usually received notice from Otpor's Belgrade press team. During these actions, they would visit the site, take photos, and sometimes interview activists. If there was police intervention, independent journalists were invited to attend Otpor's press conference. Their reports of the regime's repression of activists who only did "funny things on the street" usually generated public outrage against the regime.[27]

In smaller cities such as Novi Sad and Zrenjanin, it appeared that local journalists took on the role of being Otpor activists. This tendency helped improve news coverage of Otpor's protest actions. Aleksandar Pavlović, who was a correspondent for *Blic* in Novi Sad, arranged for articles concerning a number of Otpor's satirical street events there published in *Blic*.[28] As a consequence, local actions in Novi Sad appeared in the national media. Pavlović pointed out an additional benefit of being both a journalist and an Otpor activist: "As a journalist [of *Blic*], I had access to . . . information from the police. For example, when Boško Perošević [president of the SPS in Vojvodina] was killed in May 2000, the regime accused Otpor activists of killing him. I had inside information about this."[29] Pavlović shared this leaked information with the accused activists, who subsequently decided to cease their activism for a brief period so as to avoid an arbitrary arrest. Meanwhile, other leading activists and human rights lawyers helped discredit these fraudulent accusations.[30]

In Zrenjanin, Darko Šper, a local correspondent for B92 and the news agency BETA, worked alongside Otpor activists. He joined Otpor in 1999, taking charge of the public relations team. His role as a journalist was to facilitate the reporting of street actions in Zrenjanin, not only for the B92 website but also for publication in *Blic*.[31] Šper explains that "[Otpor] did a really good job in Zrenjanin because many actions were shown and reported on TV programs and radio stations. Our actions were unconventional. . . ." These actions, according to Šper, also received international coverage on Radio Free Europe, Deutsche Welle, and Voice of America.[32]

In Užice, Radio Luna, Radio Užice, and TV Alfa—all operated under ANEM—all covered Otpor's street actions, especially in the early days. In the words of Marko Simić, TV crews were invited to film Otpor's street skits, which were then broadcast on TV, "and on the following day there were more people joining [Otpor]."[33]

Local media in Kragujevac provided coverage not only to city residents, but also to other neighboring towns without access to their own civic media. Independent journalism in Kragujevac sprang up after the 1996 elections in which opposition parties took control of the city assembly.[34] Despite constant suppression by the regime, Kragujevac was "perhaps the town with the best media coverage in the whole of Serbia." Important press outlets included the television stations City TV, 34 M, and Dečija TV; the radio stations Radio Kragujevac Channels 1 and 2, Narodni Radio 34, Bis, and Radio 9; and a weekly newspaper, *Nezavisna svetlost*. A privately owned TV station, KANAL 9, offered an additional mouthpiece for dissidents in Kragujevac.[35]

Media reporting of Otpor's humorous protest actions and police interventions helped the Kragujevac team achieve further popularity. According to Zoran Matović, "half of Otpor actions in Kragujevac were humorous."[36] They conveyed a message that connected everyday economic hardship with the existence of the regime. The humorous edge provided by Otpor's street actions was attractive to the media and "that was why [Otpor's] message spread quickly."[37] In addition, Matović points out that cooperation with local press outlets was particularly crucial when activists were arrested during street skits.[38]

In Kraljevo, the radio and TV station Ibarske Novosti was the main provider of news coverage about Otpor's street skits. This local opposition mouthpiece had constantly criticized the regime. As a result, the authorities attempted to close down the station several times. For instance, in the spring of 2000, Ibarske Novosti's TV station license was revoked. Otpor activists led the inhabitants of Kraljevo in staging a protest in front of the TV station, and later the license was reinstated.[39] Vladimir Marović, Otpor coordinator for Kraljevo, explains that the resilience of Ibarske Novosti encouraged activists to stage humorous street events. Its journalists thought of these actions as both creative and subversive.[40]

Given their prominence, we need to consider the influence of two other anti-regime groups on Otpor's use of humor. In the cities and towns where humorous street actions flourished, the opposition parties had occupied the majority of seats in local governments since the 1996 election, and human rights organizations had strongly criticized the state's violation of civil rights. Compared to the role of the media, the contribution of these other members of the anti-regime front to the proliferation of humor seems at first only oblique. However, even if a preference for humorous tactics was less apparent amongst these groups, at the level of operational need the opposition parties' and NGOs' offers of office facilities, joint protest activities, and acts of symbolic solidarity (e.g., the wearing of Otpor T-shirts) generally set the stage for the operation of Otpor's local branches. By helping to provide broad community support, these other organizations set activists free to create a wide range of protest actions, including their signature comedic sketches. In addition, politicians' influence and the legal services provided by human rights organizations constituted a crucial mechanism that mitigated the impact of regime repression. In this way, then, the contributions of these groups can be understood as essential elements facilitating Otpor's objectives. Hence, the regime's repressive mechanisms became counterproductive and only served to further Otpor's claims of the regime's illegitimacy.

There can be no reasonable doubt about the influence of opposition parties in Belgrade, as the city had been the locus of protests against vote rigging since 1991.[41] In the 1996 municipal elections, the Democratic Party (DS) won a majority of city council seats, and the council then elected Zoran Đinđić to become the mayor of Belgrade. This defeat was evidence that not only had the opposition parties won control over the strategic geography of the capital city, but also over 22 percent of the population in Serbia. And this number also represented 40.2 percent of the workforce in Serbia.[42]

Although Otpor had established ties in Belgrade with opposition parties, activists tried to maintain their image of political nonpartisanship. In an effort to maintain this image, some leading Otpor activists refrained from openly endorsing opposition party candidates, but nevertheless did acknowledge that those parties were at least "instrumental" in advancing objectives that Otpor also shared.[43] The loose partnership between Otpor in Belgrade and the opposition parties translated into occasional joint rallies, such as the walk from Novi Sad to Belgrade in April 2000 that put public pressure on the opposition coalition to remain united. In May 2000, Đinđić, during a speech in Belgrade, urged members of the Belgrade Assembly and those in other opposition towns to "undertake risks" on behalf of Otpor's young activists in their localities.[44] In addition, Siniša Šikman points out that both the DS and the SPO provided support in the form of office facilities and materials storage.[45]

In Novi Sad, the DS and the Vojvodina Coalition (Koalicija Vojvodina or "KV") took control of local government in the 1996 municipal elections.[46] Observers noted that the rise of the Vojvodina Coalition in particular reflected general discontent among the Hungarian minority and urban voters toward the "rigid centralist system" of the Serbian state.[47] This apparently regional concern can be interpreted in light of historical ties between Novi Sad and the Austro-Hungarian Empire, and the widespread settlement of Hungarians in the city during this period. Novi Sad residents generally view themselves as belonging to a broader European civilization, and for many of them at the time, Milošević and his populist policies reeked of Balkan provincialism.[48]

The level at which Democratic Party politicians cooperated with Otpor in Novi Sad and neighboring municipalities was relatively substantial. Miodrag Jovović, former president of the DS's branch in the Vojvodinian

town of Vrbas north of Novi Sad and the current deputy provincial sec-
retary for the Government of Vojvodina, points out that the opposition
coalition always worked in partnership with Otpor in Novi Sad. For
instance, when police began their widespread crackdown in mid-2000,
they routinely confiscated Otpor's promotional materials shipped from
Belgrade. Jovović volunteered to solve this problem by smuggling the
materials in his car. In addition, when activists were detained in Vrbas,
where Jovović could exercise a degree of influence, he helped to negotiate with local authorities for their release. The negotiations, according to
Jovović, were mostly successful because "the police, except for the secret
police, which were the strong arm of the regime, understood that the DS
had some degree of influence and that regime was about to fall."[49] The
situation was similar in Novi Sad where the influence of local politicians
on the police was evident. For instance, on March 18, 2000, two deputy
mayors succeeded in negotiations with the chief of police, leading to the
release of two Otpor activists.[50]

In Kragujevac, because of a decade of economic recession and military
mobilization, there was growing resentment toward the regime. In the
early 1990s, workers—especially those from the Yugoslav automobile and
arms factory "Zastava"—were affected by the dismantling of Yugoslavia
and the wars.[51] Consequently, the unemployment rate in Kragujevac rose
by up to 50 percent.[52] Young men were drafted to the front line, and many
never made it home. This loss generated public outrage, driving thousands to stage antiwar demonstrations in Kragujevac in 1991.[53] The 1996
election that saw the SPS's defeat in Kragujevac proved that this sentiment
was widespread.[54]

With an opposition-dominated local government, Otpor in Kragujevac
received symbolic endorsement and at times concrete assistance from the
opposition parties. For instance, in June 2000 members of the opposition
coalition collectively wore Otpor T-shirts during the assembly session.[55]
In terms of concrete cooperation, Matović notes that the local government
offered office facilities to Otpor activists.[56] And occasionally, activists and
the DS politicians held their rallies together. For example, in May 2000,
in response to rising state repression, Otpor and the DS gathered at least
10,000 residents of Kragujevac and marched through the city.[57]

In Zrenjanin, Kraljevo, and Užice, the opposition's victories in the 1996 election set the scene for development of anti-regime movements.[58] For instance, in Zrenjanin, the Zajedno coalition, the Vojvodina Coalition, and the Party of Vojvodina won thirty-seven municipal seats, while the SPS obtained only thirty-one seats.[59] And in the western city of Užice, the opposition coalition won the SPS by seventy votes.[60] The SPS vote rigging in these cities sparked public outrage that led to civic protests.[61] It was found that many protesters were former SPS loyalists.[62]

The relationship between opposition politicians and Otpor activists in these three cities varied from close cooperation to entirely separate operations. In Zrenjanin and Kraljevo, opposition politicians provided vehicles for activists to transport promotional material from Belgrade. When activists were detained, they helped to negotiate their release. At times, opposition politicians invited Otpor activists to deliver speeches at their rallies.[63] However, the situation in Užice was quite different. Otpor retained its distance from local politicians, although, according to Simić, activists occasionally attended activities organized by the opposition, and vice versa.[64]

Otpor activists in Belgrade, Novi Sad, Kragujevac, Užice, Zrenjanin, and Kraljevo emphasized that NGOs took an active role in providing legal consultations to them and exposing regime repression to the public. While Otpor activists in these cities referred to "independent lawyers" as those providing legal assistance, it is clear that the Belgrade-based Humanitarian Law Center (HLC) played a leading role. With offices in major cities, including Novi Sad, the center documented and published cases of police repression that occurred between May and September 2000. Dragana Piletić pointed out that there were "seven to eight staff from the HLC providing legal assistance for Otpor activists" in cases of detention. The services rendered ranged from legal consultation to filing complaints against the state for offenses perpetrated on Otpor activists and other NGO members.[65] In court cases against the state, the HLC condemned the detention of Otpor activists as unlawful. The spotlight was put on the police's excessive use of force in response to activists' street actions, which were carried out "in a humorous way" and caused no harm to public order.[66]

Areas Where Activists Did Not Opt for Humorous
Protest Actions Despite the Opposition's Active Role

The active role played by local opposition forces at times led Otpor activists to adopt an alternative approach to humorous street actions. There are at least five cities where there were only between one and three humorous street actions carried out that received media coverage between 1999 and 2000. These numbers were low in these locations despite the degree of control opposition parties exerted in the municipal governments, and despite the active roles played by independent media and local NGOs. These cities were Subotica, Niš, Čačak, Valjevo, and Kruševac.

In these cities, activists tended to downplay humorous protest actions because of the consistent cooperation they achieved working with prominent anti-regime figures who had established respect among the locals. Combining humor with political activism could potentially compromise this respect, and thereby undermine the objectives of Otpor's publicity campaigns. Marović points out that "these [local leaders] were really prominent, and activists . . . never used humor [in these cities] because it would hurt them. That's why [Otpor headquarters] didn't force them to use humor."[67]

In Subotica, Niš, and Čačak, the opposition parties took over the local governments in 1996, setting the stage for Otpor's activism in these areas. In Subotica, the party known as the Alliance of Vojvodina Hungarians (Vajdasági Magyar Szövetség or "VMSZ") won the majority of votes in the 1996 municipal elections. In a similar vein, this election saw the opposition coalition replace the SPS in local government in Niš and Čačak. While the DS candidate for mayor Zoran Živković dominated the political scene in Niš,[68] Velimir Ilić, then from the SPO, was elected as mayor of Čačak.[69] Due to the outrage toward electoral fraud, the new mayors of Niš and Čačak dismantled the branches of the SPS in their cities.[70]

The role of Otpor activists in Niš overlapped with those of opposition-dominated local governments.[71] This contributed to the prioritization of conventional protest methods (e.g., rallies and petitions) over humor. The shift in protest repertoires between these two periods of leadership in the Niš branch of Otpor epitomized this. In 1999, Milan Stefanović, a student leader of Niš's 1996–97 protests, ran the Otpor office. There was a substantial amount of news coverage about humorous protest actions.[72] However, this trend changed when Aleksandar Višnjić, who held the membership of the Democratic Party, took over the Otpor office at the end of 1999. Rallies and political speeches became the more common protest events than street skits. And these events were usually organized as a part of DS electoral campaigns, rather than on behalf of the entire opposition coalition.[73]

In Kruševac and Valjevo, the opposition parties did not win the 1996 municipal elections, but Otpor's campaigns were nevertheless strengthened by local dissidents without political party affiliation. In Kruševac, it was Srđan Milivojević who played a central role creating an anti-regime atmosphere in his hometown. He had participated in the protests against the communist regime since 1987. In 1991, he took part in anti-regime protests, and in 1998, Milivojević was drawn to the idea of resisting the ruthless regime with nonviolent methods. He eagerly approached Otpor Belgrade seeking to establish an Otpor branch in Kruševac, wanting "the people of Serbia to realize that the authorities can be replaced and that they are supposed to serve the people, rather than the other way around."[74]

In Valjevo, dissent was expressed by both local influential personalities and ordinary citizens. The well-known painter Bogoljub Arsenijević "Maki" led the first anti-regime protest in Valjevo on June 17, 1992. On July 12, 1999, he vandalized Valjevo City Hall to demand the overthrow of Milošević.[75] During the latter incident, Milivojević, who was already active in Otpor, met Maki and Goran Dašković, and he convinced them to lead Otpor in Valjevo. In addition to Maki's rebellious acts, the residents of Valjevo themselves had long voiced their disagreement with the regime. For instance, in 1991, during the Serbo-Croatian war, draftees took to the streets in protest against the regime's military mobilization. In solidarity with citizens from other cities and towns where votes were rigged in 1996, people in Valjevo carried out daily rallies.[76] In this regard, even though the opposition parties were not in power in local government, the "atmosphere" of resistance had long been generated in Valjevo.

Both of the leading rebellious figures in Kruševac and Valjevo regarded humor as potentially counterproductive for their protest movements. For Milivojević, satire was a viable tool for protesting against the regime. However, he thought that seriousness, rather than humor, provided Otpor with greater credibility in the view of the general public.[77] Likewise, although Maki had, at times, combined ridicule in his artwork to subvert the regime,[78] Dašković preferred a politically "serious" approach to organizing Otpor's protest events in Valjevo. He commented further that if there were any humorous undertakings by his team, they were likely to serve as a "response to anger and fear," rather than a planned protest action.[79]

The local media and NGOs that were active in Subotica, Niš, Čačak, Valjevo, and Kruševac also did not contribute toward enabling the proliferation of humorous protest actions. The activists in these places did however receive substantial assistance from these opposition forces, ranging from office facilities and legal services to news reports of their repression. This wide range of support allowed activists to devise different tactics that they thought would potentially maximize their support base. In other words, the tremendous cooperation that activists received from local media and NGOs broadened activists' tactical options. This environment convinced them that humorous protest actions were not the most effective way to capitalize on their available resources.

Subotica serves as a useful example. Robertino Knjur surmised that "small acts of resistance" could be more effective than humor in increasing Otpor's publicity. This tactical preference was influenced by the extensive legal services the branch received from their Belgrade-based lawyers when harassed by local authorities. Knjur points out that in his area, pasting posters and graffiti at night usually attracted police intervention and detention of the activists involved. When that occurred, Otpor and their lawyers would respond by filing complaints and publicizing the illegal detention. For Knjur, reversing the consequences of police abuses was the most effective means of increasing Otpor's publicity in their locality. He provided two examples for comparison: When his crew staged a satirical performance in the downtown area, there were no arrests. Thus, the action provided no substantial advantage for Otpor's public relations. But in another incident where activists put up posters, seventeen of them were given jail sentences. This enraged the town residents, while turning the detainees into local heroes.[80]

In Niš, the function of humor as a public relations tactic was insignificant because of the close cooperation between local media and the opposition-dominated local government, which enabled news coverage of any type of anti-regime activities. After the DS came to power in 1996, citizens of Niš could access alternative information from at least seven local television stations and ten radio stations.[81] Freedom of expression in Niš clearly connected with this dominance of the DS in local government. For instance, when B92 in Belgrade was seized by the regime, the Mayor of Niš declared that a similar raid undertaken against the media in his city could spark a civil war.[82] The close ties between the two anti-regime forces in Niš allowed any kind of action by Otpor to be covered by the media without having to rely on the novelty of humorous tactics.[83]

Despite the absence of an Otpor branch in Čačak, local press and NGOs there had nevertheless long been representing the idea of *otpor* (resistance) in their own way. As of the year 2000, there were three television channels in Čačak, and ten radio stations. The strongest oppositional mouthpiece emerging from the civic protests in 1996 was Radio Ozon. At the time of the regime's ban on foreign media, it bravely aired news programs from the BBC, Radio Free Europe, Voice of America, and Deutsche Welle. Control by opposition parties in local government ensured an increase in freedom of the state-run RTV Čačak.[84] According to Dragan Savković, from the City Parliament of Čačak (Građanski parlament Čačak), civil society in Čačak was vital in facilitating Otpor's local campaigns. Key nongovernmental organizations included the Trade Union, representatives of the City Parliament of Serbia (Građanski parlament Srbije) and Civic Initiatives (Građanske inicijative).[85]

The "rapid action team" that effectively publicized activists' detention constituted the most substantial support Otpor received from the Čačak NGOs and the media. Željko Trifunović, Otpor's Čačak coordinator, pointed out that police often arrested activists during street actions and even those simply wearing Otpor T-shirts. To use this repression to Otpor's advantage, his team developed a standard media tactic: each arrest would be followed by a press conference. Local journalists who had already opposed the regime were more than willing to spread news of police abuses by reporting these occurrences. In addition, activists established collaborative relationships with local NGOs and political figures. The former helped launch lawsuits against abusive authorities, while the latter exercised their influence to protect detained activists from police assaults.[86]

In Čačak, well-established oppositional forces overrode the significance of Otpor. As a seasoned NGO member, Savković contends that Otpor presented a serious threat to the regime in towns without a strong network of dissidents. But the movement's contribution in Čačak only added to already existing anti-regime activities: "Otpor was strengthened unbelievably quickly throughout Serbia, but not in Čačak because the opposition in Čačak has always been strong. However, Otpor was important in many cities where the opposition was absent."[87]

Due to the presence of widespread anti-regime activities already in Čačak, the function of humor as a *stimulus* for public participation in resistance campaigns became unnecessary. Savković considers the humorous protest actions of Otpor as having a minor role in popularizing the message of resisting the regime there. This is fundamentally because this message had been promulgated by local opposition forces long before the founding of Otpor. Many citizens of Čačak had already prepared themselves to enter into a phase of full-scale civil disobedience. Therefore, instead of using humor, Savković prioritized other "serious" activities such as vote monitoring or workers' strikes because they could inflict substantial damage on the regime.[88]

In Valjevo and Kruševac, activists point out that "small acts of resistance" and public gatherings usually induced police interventions, and local radio stations preferred to report those rather than humorous protest actions. In Valjevo, the independent media outlet that cooperated most with Otpor was the radio station "Patak." In the words of Dašković, "[Otpor activists] informed this radio station of everything [they] did, and the message spread all over Serbia."[89] Although there was no independent media in Kruševac, Otpor activists relied on coverage by Radio Trstenik from the neighboring town of the same name, and Radio Kraljevo operated by Ibarske Novosti. Vladimir Žarković notes that these radio stations reported numerous actions by Otpor in Kruševac, "and that was a good way to recruit new members."[90] However, both coordinators emphasized that public gatherings and activists putting up posters normally attracted police repression. And the media were prone to report these kinds of incidents, rather than when activists staged humorous protest actions. This led to street demonstrations and small acts of resistance tending to enhance Otpor's popularity in Kruševac.[91]

In some remote areas, humorous protest actions could be culturally inappropriate because many thought of political campaigns as formal. Dašković explained that in villages surrounding Valjevo, "it wouldn't be effective to carry out humorous actions because people there saw themselves as serious." Accordingly, his crews improvised with different methods to enable Otpor's campaigns to resonate with the local populace. Dašković recognized how severely villagers had suffered from the economic recession, and that one-on-one conversation could demonstrate the linkage between their economic problems and Milošević as the source of them. Eventually, people came to understand that votes for the opposition coalition could improve their livelihoods.[92]

Based on this experience, Dašković developed the tactic of "village outreach" in a systematic way. For instance, he would prepare "a team of three boys who would then initiate a spontaneous conversation with villagers" in a village coffee shop or a beer bar. They might "ask villagers about their cows and farms . . . , [learning] what their problems were so they could connect those problems to regime [policies]." In this way, activists anticipated that people's anger about the causes of their problems was a useful resource, and Otpor could extend their message across apparent cultural and ideological differences by connecting with actual local concerns.[93]

Žarković also opted to spread Otpor's message in the rural areas of Kruševac through a similar village outreach program, which primarily involved pasting posters and stickers around villages. In addition, he would select Otpor representatives from similar communities who could explain to villagers that Otpor members were not traitors, as claimed by the regime. Nor were they affiliated with any particular political party. Otpor was simply a group of young people who wanted other "people to live a better life."[94] Žarković believes that because they relied on personal conversation as the key communication method, humorous protest actions were unnecessary.[95]

Areas Where Humorous Protest Actions Did Not Flourish
Due to the Near Absence of Opposition Forces

Humorous street actions did not flourish in cities where opposition forces were weak and there was little tradition of civic uprising. A common characteristic of these localities was the Socialist Party's dominance in local government. Although a few independent media and nongovernmental organizations may have existed in such locales, they struggled to survive the harassment of local government. This environment accounts for the fact that in many locations, Otpor was the only opposition force present. This "one-man-show" status in these localities shaped activists' tactical decisions in two important ways. First, due to the prevailing threats of the SPS, staging overt protest actions—be it through public assembly or humorous street skits—could put activists at risk. The cooperation between local government and the police force implied that activists in these areas potentially faced repression on a higher level than in other areas. Second, due to the weakness of opposition forces, the Otpor branch constituted the only significant emblem of anti-regime activism. Accordingly, even undertaking small acts of resistance, such as pasting posters and stickers, was perceived as a serious threat by local authorities. Thus, activists considered humorous street actions to be superfluous.[96]

The SPS remained relatively influential in at least 140 municipalities in Serbia after the 1996 municipal elections. These included Sremska Mitrovica (northwest of Belgrade and the administrative center of the Srem district in Vojvodina province), Smederevo (forty kilometers southeast of Belgrade), and Požarevac (east of Belgrade).[97] The influence of the SPS in these localities was large and beyond the reach of electoral politics. For instance, the steel industry had been the main source of income for the locals of Smederevo. The biggest factory was run by Dušan Matković, an SPS politician who in 1995 was appointed vice president of the party. His factory employed approximately 10,000 workers whose family members comprised approximately 40 percent of the 100,000 residents of Smederevo.[98]

Being the hometown of Milošević and his wife, Požarevac was controlled not just by the SPS, but specifically by his son, Marko Milošević.

Turning the town into his personal fiefdom, Marko Milošević owned the amusement park "Bambipark," cell phone shops, a café, an internet company, as well as the town's biggest dance club, "Madonna." One of his close business partners was the notorious bank robber and warlord Željko Ražnatović or "Arkan."[99] The locals were fearful of his ostensible omnipotence to the point that even during the NATO bombings, employees of the Madonna club did not dare to take days off.[100]

Anti-regime protests in these cities were a risky business. In Sremska Mitrovica, Nemanja Crnić, who would later become the coordinator of the Otpor branch there, explains that he attempted to lead a civic protest in his city in 1996–97 in spite of the landslide victory of the SPS. The aim "was to reduce the people's fear and to show [them] that there was somebody who dared to think differently." However, Crnić admits that "it was more difficult to build an opposition movement [in Sremska Mitrovica] than in Novi Sad or Belgrade" fundamentally because local authorities often threatened and abused dissidents.[101]

The situation was similar in Požarevac. Momčilo Veljković, a founder of the Otpor branch there, points out that the 1996 protest in Požarevac was organized by politicians from the SPO. At the outset, there were around thirty participants. Nonetheless, Vuk Drašković emphasized that "it was more significant to have thirty people protesting [in Požarevac] than in other cities because an anti-regime activity was very difficult here." During the protest in February 1997, Veljković was a street vendor selling liberal newspapers in Marko Marković's café. Consequently, he experienced a police beating, a period of detention at a police station, and defamation by the regime, which claimed he was mentally disabled.[102]

Due to constant repression by local authorities, Otpor activists who were also active in the opposition parties had a difficult time even establishing an office. Consider Smederevo as an example. In September 1999, Dušan Kocić spent almost six months just to convince somebody to rent an office to him for Otpor. Kocić explains that it was difficult for Otpor to gain support from locals due to his affiliation with the Civic Alliance of Serbia (GSS) party. And the repression increased once he eventually found office space for Otpor—Kocić was monitored by the police more closely than ever.[103]

Some independent local media did manage to establish a presence in Smederevo, Požarevac, and Sremska Mitrovica. In the first two cities, the emergence of ANEM in 1993 enabled the operation of local radio and television stations, and newspapers such as *Smederevac, Naš glas* (in Smederevo), Radio BOOM 93, TV Ritam, and *Korak* (in Požarevac).[104] In Sremska Mitrovica, because the local media (such as Radio M) was run by regime figures, opposition activities tended to be reported in the national tabloid *Blic*.[105]

Nevertheless, anti-regime journalists working in these three cities encountered various forms of repression, and their cooperation with Otpor only raised the level of police harassment. Local journalists were either close allies of Otpor or Otpor activists. However, unlike the situation in Novi Sad or Zrenjanin where the opposition parties dominated local politics and provided a level of protection, the overlapping role of journalists in these regime-dominated areas provided an additional pretext for local government to suppress media freedom. For instance, when *Blic* reported on the Otpor action "Goran Matić, Tell Us Who Killed Slavko Ćuruvija?"—which focused on *Dnevni telegraf*'s murdered journalist and was held in front of Sremska Mitrovica's state-run Radio M—the newspaper was sued by Matić, then the minister of information.[106] In Milošević's hometown, the repression of local media was similarly harsh. In July 2000, TV Ritam could not air its programs due to the regime revoking its license.[107] And during a rally in May 2000, Mile Veljković, *Danas*'s senior journalist and the editor-in-chief of Požarevac's Club Inn TV, was detained together with two Dutch journalists.[108]

Nongovernmental organizations in Smederevo and Požarevac struggled to survive, while they were almost nonexistent in Sremska Mitrovica. In Smederevo and Požarevac there were two registered NGOs, compared to five strong NGOs in Užice, for instance.[109] Despite the Trade Union Confederation's (also known as "Independence") cooperation with Otpor in various major cities, in Smederevo the state-supported Trade Union Federation dominated the scene of so-called "workers' activism."[110] In "Srem" district, the near absence of NGOs was notable. Duško Radosavljević, then vice president of the Executive Council of Vojvodina, notes that in eight municipalities of Srem district there were "barely ten nongovernmental organizations," with two NGOs in Sremska Mitrovica compared to between seventy and eighty NGOs in neighboring Novi Sad. He commented further that despite attempts by those with the requisite funds to establish new NGOs in these localities, the regime bureaucracy obstructed their establishment.[111]

Without substantial cooperation and support from opposition parties, independent media, and NGOs, humorous protest actions proved counterproductive because they exposed Otpor activists to the risk of harsh repression. Unlike activists in the opposition stronghold cities, those in Sremska Mitrovica and Smederevo received little protection when experiencing repression. They had limited access to independent lawyers or human rights activists, while local opposition politicians were short of influence over the police. In addition, ongoing media suppression prevented local journalists from publicizing acts of repression. Put differently, the formation of a "rapid action team" in these cities was virtually impossible. Otpor activists could make little use of police intervention in street actions to increase the movement's publicity. Thus, they considered overt protest actions, especially humorous street performance, as unfitting in this context.[112]

In a similar vein, harsh repression in Smederevo was a key reason that Kocić avoided provocative humorous protest actions and disagreed with attempts to make use of mass arrests for the movement's publicity. Kocić explains that his team did not stage many humorous protest actions because "the opposition was not in power," and therefore there was no protection from police abuses.[113] This attitude was shaped by his experience of the first street performance staged in Smederevo. When his crew experienced the police raid, they struggled to form a rapid action team to publicize their repression.[114] Kocić adds that the failure to put pressure on the police usually happened in cities where the SPS was in power. In this context, Kocić regarded provocative actions like "Dinar for a Change"—which invited passersby to hit an image of Milošević pasted on a barrel—as too risky. Activists were afraid that by beating the barrel, they might themselves have been beaten not only by the local police, but also by "some gangsters who worked for the SPS."[115]

The high level of repression and the near absence of opposition forces in Sremska Mitrovica and Smederevo influenced activists to substitute street skits with small acts of resistance. On the one hand, pasting posters and stickers and spraying graffiti allowed Otpor supporters to express their dissent anonymously. Consequently, they were likely to get away without experiencing any harsh repression. On the other, due to the near absence of opposition forces, Otpor was recognized as the leading engine of resistance in these localities. Without even taking to the street, their tactics posed a serious threat to the SPS authorities. For instance, by the end of the campaign "He's Finished" in Sremska Mitrovica, Crnić suggested that pasting stickers "He's Finished" on the SPS's posters for the election campaign frustrated local authorities the most. Although police repression remained, the consequences could have been worse had activists opted for street performance.

In addition, small acts of resistance enabled Otpor's presence in remote areas and facilitated effective village outreach. For example, Kocić points out that in Smederevo the widespread use of Otpor stickers and posters made it easier for activists to approach villagers. Throughout the election campaigns in 2000, he and his crew visited twenty-eight villages in Podunavlje district. When activists arrived, Otpor stickers and posters were there already. All they had to do was to talk with villagers, who most of the time eagerly asked activists about their campaigns. Villagers moreover "invited their neighbors to come listen to [Otpor activists]."[116]

The level of repression in Požarevac was comparatively higher than Sremska Mitrovica and Smederevo, but this situation proved conducive to Otpor's campaigns because it galvanized international acknowledgement of the movement. In March and May 2000, Otpor activists Zoran Milovanović, Radojko Luković, Nebojša Sokolović, and Momčilo Veljković were beaten and threatened by Milošević's son and his entourage. This provided an opportunity for Otpor to unveil the repressive face of the regime at the national and international level by launching the campaign "This Is the Face of Serbia." Veljković notes that these acts of beating, jailing, and accusing abused activists of committing criminal acts became headlines in international media such as the Radio Free Europe, BBC, Deutsche Welle, *Figaro*, and Aljazeera. The nationwide rallies that followed in response to the beatings in Požarevac were also reported worldwide.[117]

Despite these useful side-effects stemming from the regime's repression, Požarevac activists subsequently tried to avoid any protest actions that would potentially provoke further police abuses. For them, humorous performance carried an undesirable risk due to its provocative edge in explicitly ridiculing regime figures. By contrast, small acts of resistance were regarded as safer because they enabled ordinary people to express resentment against the regime without revealing their identity. Veljković explains that Otpor's material was distributed to people in the city. Soon after posters and stickers would be pasted on the walls and doors of Marko Milošević's cell phone shop, café, and night club. As the police kept removing these posters and stickers, Otpor activists responded by sticking Otpor stickers on advertisement posters for the Milošević-owned night club. Veljković recalls, "[w]hen the police took [Otpor] posters down, they saw that they also damaged posters of Marko's Madonna pub. The police were really angry."[118] He continues with another anecdote:

> There was one kid, twelve to thirteen years old, whose father was a police officer. Initially I didn't want to give him the material, but he kept asking me, so eventually I gave the material to him. He hung the flag with Otpor fist around the tail of his dog. His father was really angry. . . . At the time when we were really watched over by the police, there was a young girl approaching our office and asking for some stickers. One day, she went to a police officer and patted the butt of that police with Otpor sticker. So, he walked around with the sticker and people could see the police's butt with the Otpor sticker.[119]

Areas Where Humorous Protest Actions Flourished
Despite the Near Absence of Opposition Forces

Humorous protest actions could flourish in areas where the SPS remained in control of municipal government, but only where there was a tradition of civic protests. These areas included Leskovac (on the border of Kosovo and the administrative center of Jablanica district), and Aleksandrovac (a town with a population of approximately 30,000 located between Kruševac and Kraljevo). Despite SPS-dominated local governments and the apathy of local media and NGOs, Otpor activists in these two municipalities managed to carry out approximately five humorous street performances that received media coverage in 2000.

The 1996 election did not remove the SPS from Leskovac's and Aleksandrovac's local governments.[120] Vladimir Stojković from Otpor Leskovac attributed the coalition's electoral loss to the lack of collaboration among the DS, the SPO, and the GSS. In addition, he points out that the SPS's monopoly of the local police generated fear among citizens, hindering anti-regime activities.[121] The situation was similar in Aleksandrovac where the SPS remained strong after the 1996 election. It was estimated that 90 percent of the town population voted for the SPS.[122] According to Dalibor Glišović, the Otpor coordinator, opposition politicians from DS, SPO, and GSS ran their offices in the town, but "they were quite weak."[123]

The near absence of opposition parties in Leskovac and Aleksandrovac enabled Otpor's representation as the only opposition force. However, there was a downside: unlike opposition stronghold cities, activists had to do things on their own. Dušan Pešić compared the Leskovac branch with Niš. In Niš, activists were able to use DS offices and facilities, which was in power in local government. In contrast, he and his crew in Leskovac had to set up and run the Otpor office without any assistance. Moreover, when arrests occurred, there were no local politicians to bail them out or advocate on their behalf, unlike in opposition stronghold cities.[124]

Similarly, local opposition parties had a marginalized role in Otpor's campaigns in Aleksandrovac. There was no agreement for collaboration in matters such as material transportation or negotiation with the police on behalf of activists. The only exception was Otpor's relationship with DS because Otpor's office "was above theirs, [so activists] had friendly, neighborly communications and at times cooperated in protest marches, mass rallies, and road blockades."[125]

NGOs in Leskovac and Aleksandrovac did not set the scene for anti-regime activities, either. The situation for local NGOs in Leskovac appears to have been better than in Aleksandrovac. In 1996, the Swedish Helsinki Committee of Human Rights funded the establishment of the Committee for Human Rights in Leskovac, which disclosed information about the state's violation of civil rights through the local news magazine *Human Rights* (*Ljudska prava*).[126] Throughout Otpor campaigns, the committee provided legal aid for detained activists and pressed demands for authorities to release them. For instance, in June 2000, Stojković was charged with "urg[ing] the violent deposition of the highest organs of government" because he sprayed an Otpor clenched fist on the façade of the police station. He was detained for at least thirteen hours for interrogation. Two days later, other activists were arrested as they prepared to rally requesting Stojković's release. The Committee for Human Rights in Leskovac held a press conference, condemning the unlawful practices of local authorities. Together with the Belgrade-based Humanitarian Law Center and the Lawyers' Committee for Human Rights (Komitet pravnika za ljudska prava or "YUCOM"), the Committee for Human Rights in Leskovac helped defend Stojković against the regime's allegations.[127]

According to Glišović, no human rights organizations operated in Aleksandrovac before the regime's downfall. For this reason the Otpor team created a network of town residents that could respond to police repression. As soon as activists were arrested, a number of people would gather in front of the police station, persistently demanding their release. By this method, even though activists received no legal assistance from independent lawyers, they ensured that a certain amount of pressure was applied against abusive practices by the authorities.[128]

In both Leskovac and Aleksandrovac, local media was under the SPS's control. For instance, TV Leskovac operated at the time of the Otpor campaigns, but it avoided reporting any news of anti-regime activities mainly because it feared losing its broadcast license, which was granted at the discretion of the municipal government.[129] Pešić points out that this status of local media made it harder for Otpor's street actions to get media coverage.[130] In a similar vein, Otpor Aleksandrovac struggled to make activists' presence felt in the local media, which was completely controlled by the SPS local government. Glišović recalls that "back then there was no local media that assisted [activists]."[131]

Despite limited political freedom, citizens' protests during the Kosovo war constructed an atmosphere of resistance even before Otpor arrived in these two municipalities. The unpopularity of the SPS in Leskovac worsened after the escalation of the Kosovo war followed by the NATO bombing. It is estimated that between 40,000 and 60,000 young men from Leskovac were drafted to serve at the front line in Kosovo. It was the third mobilization and inhabitants of the city felt that they had had enough.[132] This resentment only increased when NATO launched attacks that destroyed the city of Leskovac.[133]

The historic protest led by Ivan Novković emerged out of the NATO military intervention, paving the way for the popularity of Otpor in Leskovac against the backdrop of the SPS-dominated local government. In early July 1999, during a NATO air strike, Novković—a technician of state-run TV Leskovac—interrupted the airing of a basketball match. He incited people to "rally against the local government loyal to Milošević." Although immediately arrested by the police, his speech inspired many thousands to take to the streets. This unarmed uprising in a southern stronghold town of the SPS received coverage from international press such as CNN.[134]

Similarly, the impacts of the Kosovo war and military mobilization prompted the locals in Aleksandrovac to take to the streets. For instance, from May 17, 1999 onward, at least 3,000 parents and neighbors of the reservists drafted to the front line in Kosovo staged one of the first anti-war demonstrations in the town. They requested the return of Yugoslav soldiers from Kosovo, holding a banner that read, "We want our boys back, not their coffins." The protest lasted for ten days.[135]

Despite the dearth of independent media, the local history of anti-regime activities influenced Otpor activists in Leskovac and Aleksandrovac to opt for humor as a method of communication. Their use of humorous protest worked in two significant ways. First, it conveyed criticism of the regime that would normally be dismissed by local media. Such actions became a mouthpiece for those who found themselves already in a rebellious state of mind against the regime.[136] Second, by staging humorous protest actions on the street, activists demonstrated their fearlessness and creativity amidst threats of repression generated in the local media and by police intimidation. Such demonstrations, in many ways, lifted popular morale. They reminded city residents that the street belonged to young activists, not to the regime apparatus.[137]

The Aleksandrovac activists would have agreed with the Leskovac crew. Activists deliberately held street skits once a week in the downtown precinct to make Otpor's presence felt by inhabitants. Glišović points out that funny street actions became the trademark of Otpor in Aleksandro-vac. Even nowadays "people still recognize Otpor members when we walk in the town." Moreover, activists considered humor as a tool for expos-ing the regime's vulnerability to the locals. In the words of Glišović, "the basic thing is that humor could deal with fear, exposing people to positive energy, and that we all could do something to change the circumstances. Making people laugh belittles the regime."[138]

However, because there was no network of opposition parties and NGOs to minimize the scale of regime repression, activists in these two areas avoided provocative humorous protest actions. For instance, the Leskovac activists were careful about the kind of humor they used in their actions. Their assessment was that provocative or "in-your-face" humor, characteristic of the Belgrade-initiated action "Dinar for a Change," could cause them serious trouble. It would unnecessarily invite mafia abuse.[139]

Concerns about repression led activists to create symbolic humorous protest actions, aiming to spread the message of popular resistance rather than targeting specific regime personalities. An example was a Leskovac action in which activists distributed the flower "defiance," or *prkos* in Serbian, to passersby downtown. Because the symbolism of the flower did not constitute a direct insult against regime figures, activists avoided provoking a repressive police response. When it came to actions that tar-geted regime figures, activists opted for a more subtle form of offense. An instance demonstrating this was activists giving out "Julka" brand choco-lates. The product's package contained the image of a cow with a flower on its head, which activists readily associated with Mirjana Marković and her party. Despite this symbolic insult, the police could not arrest activists just because they gave away bars of chocolate.

In a similar fashion, humorous protest actions choreographed by the Otpor crew in Aleksandrovac contained symbolic criticisms of the regime. The fact that there were a "large number of SPS supporters in the town" generated self-censorship among town dwellers, hindering them from participating in any anti-regime activities. As a result, "passersby were too afraid even to watch [Otpor activists'] performance."[140] In deal-ing with this situation, activists carried out a symbolic skit such as the action "Brain Washing" where they showed a mock RTS program in parallel to the gesture of pouring water on a plastic model of a human brain. The action did not contain explicit insults of regime figures, but it was thought provoking. Activists expected that this approach could engage passersby in the process of self-reflection even though they might avoid paying attention to their demonstration for a long time. Occasionally activists organized "feasts" as a part of the election campaign, aiming to build a constructive relationship with locals. This approach was intended to strengthen citizen networks that could in turn work to put pressure on local authorities who arrested activists.[141]

Situations Favorable and Unfavorable for Humorous Protest Actions

This chapter has thus far demonstrated ways in which Otpor activists' preference for humorous protest actions was influenced by existing opposition forces (i.e., the dominance of opposition parties in municipal government, and the active role played by local media as well as NGOs). The first pattern was characterized by a proliferation of independent media, which encouraged activists to stage humorous protest actions. The key reason for this lay in the fundamental function of humor, as conceived by activists, to be a *stimulus* for media attention. And media coverage helped the movement to increase its popularity. The cooperation between Otpor and the opposition parties as well as NGOs also helped minimize the scale of repression induced by the provocative anti-regime edge of some humorous actions.

The second pattern relates to the nonproliferation of humorous protest actions in areas where the opposition parties held strong positions in local government. An alternate pattern arose where Otpor's campaigns in these areas were led by local rebellious heroes whose respect among the locals was well-established. In either case, combining the playful image of humor with political campaigns was understood to be unhelpful, and to potentially undermine the established respect and influence of oppositional forces. Moreover, the tremendous cooperation between these opposition forces had enabled Otpor activists' diversification of protest tactics, such as publicizing repression and using door-to-door methods. As with humor, these tactics proved useful for the movement's public relations.

Accordingly, activists viewed humorous protest actions as unnecessary in this context.

The third pattern demonstrated a correlation between the near absence of local opposition forces and the nonproliferation of humorous protest actions. In areas where the regime's proxies dominated local government, media freedom tended to be limited, the establishment of local NGOs was aborted, and repression heightened. This background led to two consequences. On the one hand, activists struggled to carry out much in the way of street protest, including humorous street performance, because they would reveal activists' identities in places where the authorities would readily target and repress activists. On the other, because of the quiescence of opposition forces, Otpor represented the single front willing to defy the regime. Accordingly, "small acts of resistance" such as pasting posters and graffiti painting could pose a serious threat to the regime's presence in local government. Humorous protest actions were perceived as superfluous and attracting unnecessary police abuse.

The fourth pattern showed a proliferation of humor despite the near absence of local opposition forces. As with the third pattern, in areas where the ruling party took control of the local government, opposition parties, the independent media, and NGOs played a marginal role in Otpor's campaigns. Nevertheless, these were towns where popular outrage against the regime was prevalent. Humorous protest actions, therefore, constituted a crucial way activists could reflect this popular frustration. In addition, due to the municipal government's suppression of independent media, activists could not advance the movement's publicity by relying on the local press. They saw that staging humorous protest actions solved this problem. By doing something funny on the street, activists could gain recognition at least from passersby. However, the lack of support from opposition parties and NGOs differentiated the humorous protest actions in these areas from those of the first pattern. Without a "rapid action team" working to minimize the scale of repression, activists preferred non-provocative and more symbolic skits. Utilizing this kind of humor enabled Otpor to gain a foothold in regime-dominated communities and to also avoid harsh repression.

Based on these observations, situations deemed favorable and unfavorable for humorous protest action can be characterized as follows:

Situation 1: Humorous protest actions can be effective in a context where anti-regime media flourishes. Cooperative relationships between activists and local journalists enable regular media coverage of humorous protest actions.

Situation 2: "Offensive" humorous protest actions that potentially provoke police repression can be effective in a context where opposition-dominated local government and NGOs can exert a certain degree of influence over high-ranking police officers. This influence can mitigate the scale of repression. In addition, for provocative humor to have political impact, activists need these two opposition allies to publicize police intervention in the actions. In doing so, activists can harness public outrage against the regime.

Situation 3: Humorous protest actions without direct insults of persons in power can be effective in places where the level of repression is high, but civic uprisings are common. Such actions constitute a low-risk protest method for locals who have long voiced their disagreement with the government.

Situation 4: Humorous protest actions without direct insults of persons in power can be effective in a locality where the media is under the regime's control and repression is high, but civic uprisings are common. "Doing something funny on the street" potentially draws the attention of passersby. It enables the movement's presence in the locality even without media coverage of protest actions.

Situation 5: Humorous protest actions are not appropriate in a context where activists are prominent figures in the locality. The playful image of humor can undermine the credibility of these figures among locals. As a result, the movement's publicity is at risk.

Situation 6: Humorous protest actions can be counterproductive for activists operating in areas where there is limited history of civic rebellion, where the regime takes complete control of the local government, and where repression is unusually harsh. It is counterproductive because the actions reveal activists' identities, thereby placing activists at personal risk of repression. Such risk is unnecessary because in these areas the regime is confident in its monopoly. Small acts of resistance are effective in disturbing this confidence, while allowing protesters to avoid repression.

TABLE 1. The Influence of Local Opposition Forces on Activists' Tactical Decisions

Cities or towns	Opposition forces			Protest tactics			
	Opposition parties as local government	Independent media	NGOs	Satirical and parodic protest actions with news coverage (1999–2000)	Small acts of resistance	Publicising repression	Door-to-door method
1 Belgrade	Yes	Yes	Yes	5	Yes	Yes	N/A
2 Novi Sad	Yes	Yes	Yes	5	Yes	Yes	Yes
3 Zrenjanin	Yes	Yes	Yes	5	Yes	Yes	Yes
4 Kragujevac	Yes	Yes	Yes	6	Yes	Yes	Yes
5 Kraljevo	Yes	Yes	Yes	6	Yes	Yes	Yes
6 Užice	Yes	Yes	Yes	6	Yes	Yes	N/A
7 Subotica	Yes	Yes	Yes	2	Yes	Yes	N/A
8 Čačak	Yes	Yes	Yes	3	Yes	Yes	N/A
9 Valjevo	No	Yes	Yes	3	Yes	Yes	Yes
10 Kruševac	No	Yes	Yes	1	Yes	Yes	Yes
11 Niš	Yes	Yes	Yes	3	Yes	Yes	N/A
12 Požarevac	No	Limited	Limited	0	Yes	Yes	No
13 Smederevo	No	Limited	Limited	1	Yes	No	Yes
14 Sremska Mitrovica	No	Limited	Limited	1	Yes	No	No
15 Leskovac	No	No	Limited	5	Yes	Yes	No
16 Aleksandrovac	No	No	No	5	Yes	N/A	Yes

Source: Table compiled by the author.

Conclusion

The pleasure of studying humor lies in its celebration of life over death. In a time of seemingly ubiquitous violence, we may become trapped in pessimism, thinking "Oh, there is no alternative to this destruction." Or worse, "There is no tomorrow." Humor resists this very dark force by encouraging us to redefine the situation we encounter in a positive light. In response to "there is no alternative," humor suggests: "Hey, look again and laugh your head off. You may find a way out! If not, keep laughing."

This search for alternatives sowed the seeds of this book, which attempts to empower organized movements with ammunition in the form of ideas for creative nonviolent actions aimed at social change. The experiences of pro-democracy movements in Serbia in the 1990s not only provide us with a reservoir of creativity, but also sheds light on the power that humor contributes to nonviolent struggle. The 1996–97 protesters and Otpor activists have demonstrated ways in which everyday jokes offer a cultural backdrop for humorous protest actions. This combination between cultural elements and political activism enabled discursive subversion of Milošević regime's truth claims, and carved out an imaginative as well as an emotive space crucial for the realization of a nonviolent revolution.

Humor as a Technology of Discursive Resistance

Humor excorporates existing discourses underpinning domination. Excorporation is a process that can take place even when those subordinated to a dominant system have no means of direct escape. While submerged within the system, subordinates can appropriate for their own purposes the means and logic of the system that has (temporarily) consolidated power in the dominant elite. By doing this, subordinates can

disturb the dominant system even while it continues attempting to total-
ize its control. This process of resisting from within a space of domination
can be seen in the work of satire and parody.

When satirical and parodic forms of humor are combined in protest
repertoires, the process of excorporation described above is put to work
subverting the opposed regime's truth claims. Satirical street theater and
parodic protest actions are created from the propaganda of ruling elites,
but the essence of the propaganda is twisted or exaggerated to the point
of absurdity. The aim is not to invalidate outright the truth claims of a
regime's propaganda. Rather, these actions subvert domination by targeting the inconsistency and incoherence of the elites' truth claims, or their
defamatory insinuations about activists.

Because these actions mimic the tone of elite truth claims, they become
their reflection. Yet, this reflection distorts the shape and form of the original, painting it as something ridiculous. This process serves to resist discursive domination both at the level of "truth" production and "truth"
consumption. Through the act of deforming to absurdity the opponent's
truth claims, satirical and parodic actions hinder ruling elites' attempts to
manipulate public opinion, whereby they strive to establish their promulgated propaganda as the "only" truth, denouncing alternative explanations as "lies." Meanwhile, satirical and parodic protest disturbs popular
dogma, reflecting what we have been led to believe is "the truth" in a distorted way. This type of protest action often demonstrates how a popular
willingness to accept beliefs and established norms that maintain the status quo, without questioning the motives of the elites favoring it, actually
enables subordination of the populace.

Humorous protest action brings to the fore an inconvenient fact: that a
widespread lack of critical thinking among the populace helps sustain the
system of their own domination. Humor invites people to see themselves
as complicit in their own subordination and exploitation by the regime.
And it invites them to see that embarking on a course of resisting oppression first requires self-reflection and a willingness to challenge their own
strongly held beliefs. In this way, humor offers a technology of nonviolent resistance that helps deal with domination at the level of popular
discourse.

Humor and Its Transformative Power

Carnivalesque humor offers a counter-reality of metaphors, enabling pro-testers to overcome perceptual limits a stultifying regime can engender and to see the possibilities that social change can present. Carnivals con-tain a world of alternative realities. Characteristically, they are festive ritu-als in which participants are encouraged to invert the predominant social hierarchy. Lower orders of society are allowed to insult elites. The popu-lace is permitted to ridicule sacred institutions and violate norms. Unre-served laughter, usually prohibited in religious teachings, is sanctioned in the carnival atmosphere. These permissions, although only tempo-rary, have historically provided a platform for uprisings by subordinates. Through carnivals, they have had a taste of overturning hierarchy. This carnival-inspired "breathing space" that momentarily portrays an imagi-nary egalitarian world encourages those trapped by injustice to envision a more just real world.

When a wide range of carnivalesque activities are incorporated into protest campaigns, they depict emancipatory scenes against a backdrop of oppression. These are scenes where people can defy authorities with jokes, feel the triumph of cosmopolitanism over xenophobia, exchange political views without fear of state persecution, and imagine lives with-out the everyday struggle merely to afford basic commodities. In many ways, carnivalesque protests constitute an "exit" for those trapped under dictatorship. Rather than conveying a nihilistic undertone, this exit expe-rience motivates them to make the temporary carnivalesque experience a permanent one. And achieving this is possible only when regime change and some degree of social reform can take place. Put differently, the com-bination of carnivals and protest campaigns results in a political project in which protesters are exposed to the possibility of a life beyond their regime-imposed reality. At the same time, they are inspired to pursue this other reality.

The carnivalesque process of imagining other realities can be seen in light of the notion of constructing a parallel polity, an idea central to conceptions of nonviolent revolution. In the nonviolence literature, con-crete suggestions have been made for dissidents to construct parallel institutions as a breakaway from the old regime. However, the creation of alternative institutions requires that an oppressed populace has the capability to see and imagine alternatives. Explanations of how such a cognitive process might be cultivated has been missing from ongoing discussion regarding the construction of parallel polities as pathways to nonviolent revolution. The carnivalesque can fill that gap.

In carnivalesque protests, participants are encouraged to relate their experiences to a metaphor of emancipation from hierarchical order. This metaphor contests popular perceptions that the dominant system will last eternally. It enables protest participants' acknowledgement of the possibilities of change in power relations between them and ruling elites. Only when there is an acknowledgement that other realities are possible can one realize the importance of establishing a parallel polity as a concrete form of independence from an existing regime. In other words, the carnivalesque provides a window into the possibility of independence that is fundamentally necessary in order to realize any real project to actually establish independence.

Another effect of carnivalesque humor is its ability to channel the protest atmosphere away from sorrow and antagonism toward joy and inventive creativity. When carnivalesque activities are organized in street protests, they tend to generate a euphoria of, among other things, being together on the street, dancing, playing music, whistling, banging of pots and pans, and joining in costume parades. The positive emotions help mitigate protesters' rage against the institutions of their adversaries, which initially drove them to the street. The emotive shift can influence protesters to refrain from provoking the authorities with verbal insults and physical sabotage. This positive influence generally enables street protests to maintain their nonviolent approach. And in the case of a protest crackdown, remaining nonviolent makes it difficult for the government to justify its repressive actions.

The search for protest methods that dissipate protesters' anger is uncommon in current academic debates regarding the nature of nonviolent resistance. Usually, scholars suggest methods of nonviolent action that aim to highlight grievances, making use of anger to strengthen a movement's political solidarity. The carnivalesque protest, however, introduces a different phenomenon. Cheerfulness, laughter, and fun can mobilize people to join street demonstrations. Carnivalesque activities not only express protest against a regime, they also create an atmosphere of humor and goodwill that (many times) serves as a barrier against harsh police crackdowns. It is hard for the police to justify brutal treatment against citizens who are merely singing, dancing, and play-acting. Protesters tolerate police scrutiny not necessarily because of an ethical imperative, but because it is more desirable to enjoy the street entertainment. They put up with the piercing cold of winter, not necessarily because of a firm ideological commitment, but because the fun of dancing on the street with their friends renders the cold bearable. In a carnivalesque protest, participants tend to refrain from provoking the security forces. Activists bear little "love" for their oppressors, but carnivalesque actions enable protesters to relate to the police as people—people they can play games with and tease for a bit of laughter who eventually become acquaintances developed through the sharing of food and drink.

Utopia in the Making

By way of concluding this conclusion, one should be reminded that despite this book's devotion to theoretical arguments illuminating humor's power, theory is inseparable from practice. Activists incorporate humor in their protest strategies for several practical advantages such as fear reduction, entertainment value that is helpful in recruiting new members, prevention of burn-out among activists during prolonged campaigns, popularization of the movement to a wider public, and to help avoid harsh repression. When protest actions become too provocative for the regime, they may say that they were "only joking."[1] Humorous nonviolent action achieves more and operates deeper than theorizing about the functions of humor. Such action seeks to unravel complex webs of dominant power sustaining an unjust rule and its popular conformity. This stance proposes ways in which these webs of power can be cracked and weakened.

Nevertheless, one should be reminded that discursive resistance is normally an ongoing project. So is revolution. Serbian movements of the 1990s achieved certain objectives after Slobodan Milošević had been brought down in 2000. Serbian society as a whole, however, continued to face many challenges deriving from several remaining and dominant discourses such as nationalism and patriarchy (which were also obliquely addressed in some of the humorous actions mocking Milošević and his wife, for instance). Similar residual problems face numerous nonviolent movements around the world in the aftermath of removing an oppressive regime. Therefore, the discursive struggle goes on. Likewise, while this book posits that the transformative power of carnivalesque humor can help activists envision a road leading to "nonviolent revolution," this revolution should not be viewed as a single incident that transforms an entire society for the better once and for all. The carnivalesque connotes a constant renewal of realities, and cherishes the cycles of birth, death, and rebirth—and so the cycles continue. When the carnivalesque denotes the process of a nonviolent revolution, this cyclical generation and degeneration applies. A carnival of revolution is indefinite in the sense that one revolution might take place, followed by a discovery that the pursuit of further revolutions is needed.[2] This utopian world is always in the making.

Epilogue
Otpor's Legacy

The worst enemy of nonviolent creativity is not pessimism, but forgetting. October 5 marks the annual commemoration of the "Bulldozer Revolution," which resulted in ousting the "butcher of the Balkans"— Slobodan Milošević. In 2010, it was the 10th anniversary, and I expected to witness a grand celebration. Instead, there were only a quiet memorial ceremony and a few documentaries about the October 5 "revolution" broadcast on TV. To my surprise, these documentaries contained little reference to Otpor. My encounters with Serbian NGO workers during my field research similarly indicates this fading memory about Otpor's contribution to Serbian democratization. The tide of political instability subsequent to the year 2000 perhaps disappointed many Serbians who anticipated drastic changes and a better society.

One of the setbacks evident after the October 5 "revolution" was a return to conservatism. Despite his notorious reputation as a conservative nationalist, Vojislav Koštunica from the Democratic Party of Serbia (Demokratska stranka Srbije or "DSS") was nominated by the opposition coalition as its candidate in the 2000 presidential election, which he then won. The leader of the Democratic Party, Zoran Đinđić, whose political visions were starkly different from Koštunica's, initially agreed to take him on board for practical reasons—Koštunica was favored by both liberal and conservative voters. However, conflict between these two figures intensified and peaked when Đinđić cooperated with the International Criminal Tribunal for the Former Yugoslavia in cases against Milošević's entourage, who had taken part in crimes against humanity. In March

2003, he was assassinated. Many perceived the assassination as a symbolic loss of the "people's power," and associated it with vestiges of the Milošević regime. The nationalist response to Kosovo's declared independence in 2008, and the electoral victory of the center right Serbian Progressive Party (Srpska napredna stranka or "SNS") in 2012, to a large extent confirmed this belief.

For Serbian NGO workers I have met, the resurgence of conservative politicians showed that the October 5 "revolution" did not actually revolutionize Serbia. Some go so far as to define the change in 2000 as a "coup d'état in disguise," masterminded by the United States in an attempt to rearrange European geopolitics so as to strengthen its hegemony. This view aligns with accusations that Otpor was merely a puppet of the West, and reinforces arguments that dismiss Otpor's contributions to any Serbian political change. This mythology has also been used to explain the movement's dissolution in 2003, i.e., that Otpor's reason for existing vanished soon after the United States achieved its geopolitical goal.[1] Because Otpor as a movement had died and its members' motivations had always been heterogeneous, it could not defend itself. Barely a decade after 2000, Otpor had almost been forgotten in Serbia.

Nevertheless, the movement, particularly its creative and humorous approach to nonviolent struggle, is well remembered outside Serbia.[2] On the one hand, the role of Otpor as a global inspiration has been facilitated by the production of the Otpor film "Bringing Down A Dictator," which has been shown in training workshops across the globe.[3] Many activists in dictatorship countries such as Belarus, Iran, and Venezuela have downloaded the film from YouTube.[4] The inspiration bears its fruit in ideas for action. Otpor's playful and humorous style of protest is evident in many different places. For instance, activists from a Sudanese youth group, "We're Fed Up" (Girifina) that demands civil rights and the end of the abusive government (led by National Congress Party), replicated an Otpor humorous skit in an anti-corruption campaign. The activists produced a video clip based on the comic Otpor advertisement in which a woman demonstrates how to use a washing machine to remove the Milošević "stain" from a T-shirt. The Sudanese version simply replaced the washing machine with soap to wash away the current president.[5] In the 2011's anti-neoliberalism demonstrations that swept across the United States and Europe, episodes of carnivalesque protests that shared some characteristics with Otpor's humorous street actions were documented.[6]

Otpor veterans have also transferred their knowledge and skills in nonviolent strategies by leading training workshops. A small group of Otpor veterans founded the Center for Nonviolent Resistance (CNR) in 2002 and the Center for Applied Nonviolent Action and Strategies (CANVAS) in 2004.[7] CNR offered training workshops on nonviolent strategy to activists, particularly from Georgia and Ukraine. Its trainers used Otpor's humorous protest actions as examples of creative nonviolent methods, and these ideas influenced Georgian and Ukrainian activists. Otpor-style street skits were evident in demonstrations that contributed to toppling the authoritarian governments in Georgia in 2003 and Ukraine in 2004.[8] For its part, CANVAS provided training classes for over 1,000 activists in thirty-seven countries from its inception to early 2011.[9] Of those countries, activists in Syrian-occupied Lebanon, the Maldives, and recently Egypt carried out nonviolent campaigns that achieved democratic transition. Otpor's model of funny street actions was observed in those countries.[10]

In addition to their contributions to activism, the global legacy of Otpor's humorous approach to nonviolent protests lies in the carving out of theoretical space in nonviolence scholarship. Over the past decades, this body of knowledge has struggled to establish itself in the social sciences, and as it has achieved academic recognition, scholars have attempted to prove scientifically the strategic effectiveness of nonviolent action used in conflict situations. At the expense of this epistemological position, normative elements such as culture, emotion, and imaginative space have hardly been in the spotlight. However, if these elements constitute the sites of humor's operation as a vehicle of nonviolent struggle—as this book indicates—dismissing such elements may also result in overlooking several other nonviolent alternatives that share these sites of operation with humor. And failing to explore alternatives may hamper the growth of nonviolence scholarship, turning it into a mere study of static strategies to bring down powerful opponents. Accounts of humorous protests arising in Serbia in the 1990s effects a cultural and emotive turn in nonviolence scholarship. Expressed differently, humor serves not only as a "nonviolent weapon," but also as a channel of self-reflection that potentially brings about a theoretical dialogue among nonviolence researchers. This function potentially diversifies the field of nonviolence studies, rendering it imaginatively practical and theoretically profound.

Appendixes

Notes

Bibliography

Index

Appendix A
Research Methodology and Data Collection

The 1996–97 protests and Otpor serve as paradigmatic cases in this book. The paradigmatic case methodology illuminates a specific social event or actors in that event that potentially constitute a prototype or a theoretical model for a broad research subject that the case concerns. This methodology does not draw a generalization from the case in the sense that research findings can be applied across historical and geographical contexts. Instead, it allows elaborate research of a social event that shows a unique representation of a general subject of study. Because of its exemplary nature, the case is likely to form a conceptual foundation of its subject. The theoretical foundation may be contested and refined by subsequent research undertaken with the use of different cases.

The 1996–97 protests and the Otpor movement were selected as paradigmatic cases because they are exemplary in demonstrating humor's substantial contribution to successful nonviolent protests. On the domestic level, Milošević had survived waves of protests in the early 1990s, but it was through the carnivalesque protests in 1996–97 that his power started to crumble. Otpor's humorous street actions were developed from this period, but they became highly systematized over time. At the end of Otpor's campaigns, the national ridicule of Milošević created a crisis of legitimacy for him, setting the stage for his electoral defeat in September 2000. At the global level, Otpor's success has inspired a later generation of activists and the movement's humorous street actions have arguably set a global trend of protest repertoires. Generally, Otpor's humorous tactics became a blueprint for two groups of activists. The first group includes those without direct contact with Otpor activists. The second group consists of activists who received training workshops from Otpor veterans who discussed the effective use of humor.

The analysis of this book is based on insights and information obtained from two sources: semi-structured interviews and documentary research.

Semi-Structured Interviews

Between September and December 2010, forty-nine interviews were conducted. Interviewees have been classified into one of three groups. Members of the first group can be positioned within two sub-groups: leading student activists in the 1996–97 protests and founding members of Otpor active from 1998 to 2000. Some of the members of the first interview group were in both positions during these two periods of Serbian protest movements, while others were in either one or the other of the positions. The leading figures of the 1996–97 protests interviewed included the president of the Belgrade Students' Main Board—an ad hoc student group spearheading the student protests—and staff from security and program teams of student protests, as well as student leaders in other cities. Interviews were carried out with founding members of Otpor who were also veterans of student protests.

Interview questions for the first group revolved around the specific details of humorous protest actions they took part in or witnessed, their opinions about how these tactics came into being and the motivation and ideas behind the actions. Also important were questions identifying comparisons between characteristics of nonviolent actions in the 1996–97 protests and in Otpor's campaigns, and between humorous actions staged in the protests and in Otpor's campaigns. Other issues included activists' evaluations of the responses to humorous protest actions and their analysis of how nonviolence and humor are linked.

The second group of interviewees comprised rank-and-file participants in the 1996–97 protests, and regional activists of Otpor from sixteen regional cities and towns. The selection of rank-and-file protesters was less structured than that of Otpor activists. This is because the protests in 1996–97 were spearheaded by the opposition coalition and by student activists from Belgrade and university cities (Niš, Novi Sad, and Kragujevac). Organizers of the protests did not form a movement. They comprised an eclectic group of politicians and students, including artists and NGO members in Belgrade, who united over the course of four months of protests. With regard to the selection of regional Otpor activists, I traced the organizational structure of Otpor—which had its headquarters in Belgrade—to the branches in regional cities and towns. These regional branches were run by coordinators who supervised the planning of humorous protest actions in their areas. The insights of these local activists are crucial for understanding the influence of opposition forces on their decisions to stage humorous actions in areas under their supervision.

Interview questions for the second group were similar to those presented to the first group. Rank-and-file participants of the 1996–97 protests were additionally asked to provide their insights with regard to motivations for their participation in the protests, and evaluations of humorous actions staged in the protests. Otpor regional activists were asked to offer details of humorous street actions and the dynamics of Otpor's campaigns carried out in their cities and towns. These details also included their cooperation with opposition politicians, local journalists, and NGO members, responses to street actions, and the local history of rebellion against the authorities.

The third classified group was made up of nineteen interviewees, comprised of members from nongovernmental organizations in Serbia, scholars, artists, and political figures. They were involved in the 1996–97 protests or associated with Otpor's campaigns. Interview questions were designed to cross-check stories and information provided by interviewees in the first two groups. In addition, interviewees of this group were asked to provide stories of their involvement in the early 1990s protests, their insights into the atmosphere of the 1996–97 protests, and information about their cooperation with local activists of Otpor. With regards to humorous protest actions, the interviewees offered comparative evaluations between humorous protest actions in the 1996–97 protests and those of Otpor's campaigns. Lists of interviews with members of these three groups and dates of interviews and other communications follow.

The 1996–1997 Protests' Leading Student Activists
and Founding Members of Otpor

Čedomir Antić	Belgrade, Serbia, November 8, 2010
Ivan Marović	Belgrade, Serbia, November 1, 2010; December 12, 2010
Milan Milutinović	Belgrade, Serbia, October 6, 2010
Milan Stefanović	Niš, Serbia, October 7, 2010
Mile Ilić	Niš, Serbia, October 7, 2010
Milja Jovanović	Belgrade, Serbia, November 13, 2010
Nenad Belčević	Belgrade, Serbia, October 7, 2010
Nenad Konstantinović	Belgrade, Serbia, November 4, 2010
Pedrag Lečić	Belgrade, Serbia, September 23, 2010
Pero Jelić	Belgrade, Serbia, November 15, 2010

Siniša Šikman	Belgrade, Serbia, September 19, 2010; September 23, 2010; December 9, 2010; May 23, 2011 (e-mail message); and June 15, 2011 (e-mail message)
Srđa Popović	Belgrade, Serbia, September 9, 2010
Srđan Milivojević	Belgrade, Serbia, September 28, 2010
Stanko Lazendić	Novi Sad, Serbia, September 29, 2010 and December 6, 2010

The 1996–1997 Protests' Rank-and-File Participants and Regional Activists of Otpor

Boban Arsenijević	Niš, Serbia, October 8, 2010
Milica Popović	Belgrade, Serbia, November 21, 2010
Petar Milićević	Belgrade, Serbia, November 19, 2010
Vladimir Đumić	Belgrade, Serbia, November 15, 2010
Vojislav Milošević	Belgrade, Serbia, November 20, 2010
Aleksandar Pavlović	Novi Sad, Serbia, October 14, 2010
Aleksandar Savanović	Novi Sad, Serbia, October 14, 2010
Dalibor Glišović	Aleksandrovac, Serbia, November 16, 2010; May 29, 2011 (e-mail message); and December 31, 2011 (e-mail message)
Darko Šper	Novi Sad (Otpor Zrenjanin), Serbia, October 15, 2010
Dušan Kočić	Smederevo, Serbia, December 7, 2010
Dušan Pešić	Leskovac, Serbia, November 26, 2010
Goran Dašković	Valjevo, Serbia, December 2, 2010
Marko Simić	Užice, Serbia, November 12, 2010
Miloš Gagić	Novi Sad, Serbia, September 29, 2010
Miloš Milenković	Belgrade, Serbia, October 3, 2010
Momčilo Veljković	Požarevac, Serbia, November 19, 2010
Nemanja Crnić	Sremska Mitrovica, Serbia, October 15, 2010
Petar Lacmanović	Zrenjanin, Serbia, November 2, 2010; May 6, 2011 (e-mail message); and December 27, 2011 (e-mail message)
Robertino Knjur	Kanjiža (Otpor Subotica), Serbia, October 16, 2010
Vladimir Marović	Belgrade (Otpor Kraljevo), Serbia, December 3, 2010; December 13, 2011 (e-mail message); and December 27, 2011 (e-mail message)

Vladimir Stojković	Leskovac, Serbia, November 26, 2010
Vladimir Žarković	Kruševac, Serbia, November 16, 2010
Zoran Matović	Kragujevac, Serbia, November 9, 2010
Željko Trifunović	Valjevo (Otpor Čačak), Serbia, November 9, 2010

Members of Nongovernmental Organizations
in Serbia, Scholars, Artists, and Political Figures

Antonije Pušić (Rambo Amadeus)	Belgrade, Serbia, September 16, 2010
Borka Pavićević	Center for Cultural Decontamination, Belgrade, Serbia, September 13, 2010
Đorđe Balzamović	Škart, Belgrade, Serbia, October 28, 2010
Dragan Savković	City Parliament of Čačak, Čačak, Serbia, November 17, 2010
Dragana Piletić	Humanitarian Law Center, Belgrade, Serbia, October 13, 2010
Dušan Juvanin	Democratic Party, Zrenjanin, Serbia, November 2, 2010
Milena Dragićević-Šešić	University of Arts, Belgrade, Serbia, September 8, 2010
Milodrag Jovović	Democratic Party, Novi Sad, October 15, 2010 and December 4, 2010
Suzana Jovanić	Fund for an Open Society of Serbia, Belgrade, Serbia, September 24, 2010
Velimir Stanojević	Serbian Renewal Movement (former), and New Serbia Party (current), Čačak, Serbia, November 17, 2010
Veran Matić	B92, Belgrade, Serbia, September 20, 2010

Documentary Research

Documents were collected to supplement information provided by interviewees. These documents were also useful for cross-checking factual details of Otpor's actions that were initially obtained from activists, assessing media coverage of Otpor's humorous protest actions, and gauging public perception towards Otpor's campaigns in general. The documents are categorized into four groups: (1) personal records of protest actions; (2) protest newsletters, pamphlets, and leaflets published by protesters in 1996–97 and Otpor activists; (3) newspapers, online news services, and reports of nongovernmental organizations; (4) picture books, films, and documentaries that record protest events in 1996–97 and Otpor's campaigns.

Appendix B

Chronology of Nonviolent Struggle in Serbia in the 1990s

December 1990	First multi-party election held in Serbia.
March 9, 1991	Vuk Drašković, the leader of the Serbian Renewal Party leads a mass demonstration that is harshly crushed by the regime.
March 10–14, 1991	Students occupy Terazije Square in Belgrade, demanding the release of those arrested during the crackdown.
June and July 1992	Students stage protests, demanding immediate elections and the removal of Milošević regime.
November 3, 1996	First round of the federal and municipal elections held.
November 17, 1996	Second round of municipal elections held.
November 19, 1996	Protest against vote rigging starts in Niš.
November 21, 1996	First protest march staged in Belgrade.
November 25, 1996	Belgrade University students form ad hoc committees for protest organization.
December 14, 1996	Approximately 200 students from Novi Sad set off on a twenty-hour march to Belgrade.
December 17, 1996	Niš students stage a march from Niš to Belgrade.
December 20, 1996	Thirty students from Kragujevac march to Belgrade.
December 24, 1996	Socialist Party supporters clash with protesters in Belgrade.
January 1–8, 1997	Students and Belgrade protesters carry out "Cordon against Cordon" action.
February 23, 1997	Opposition protests conclude and Zoran Đinđić is inaugurated as mayor of Belgrade.

March 27, 1997	Election for the chairperson and for representatives of the newly-founded "Student Parliament" held.
July 23, 1997	Slobodan Milošević appointed as president of Federal Republic of Yugoslavia.
September 21, 1997	Parliamentary and presidential elections held in Serbia. Zoran Đinđić's Democratic Party leads election boycott.
September 30, 1997	Zoran Đinđić ousted from position as mayor of Belgrade.
May 26, 1998	University Act enacted.
October 20, 1998	National Assembly enacts Public Information Act. Otpor also founded this month.
November 3, 1998	Otpor's clenched fist symbol is sprayed for the first time on a wall in Belgrade. Consequently, four activists arrested.
Mid-November, 1998	Srđa Popović, Branko Ilić, and Ivan Andrić interrupt the ceremony of the 61st anniversary of the Economics Faculty, Belgrade University.
November 17, 1998	"We Are Paving the Way" march takes place from Belgrade to Novi Sad.
March 24–June 9, 1999	NATO conducts air strikes against Yugoslavia. Otpor suspends its activism.
August 1999	Otpor and other student organizations release "Declaration for the Future of Serbia." Otpor resumes its activism.
November 22, 1999	The concert "We Have a Situation" organized.
January 13, 2000	Otpor organizes the Orthodox New Year party. Campaign "This Is the YEAR" launched.
February 17, 2000	Otpor holds first congress that transforms it from a student movement into People's Resistance Movement (Narodni pokret Otpor). Campaign "It's Spreading" launched.
April 14, 2000	Activists from Novi Sad march to Belgrade under the theme "This Is the Last March." Pressure focused on opposition coalition to remain united.
May 2, 2000	Marko Milošević beats up Otpor activists Radojko Luković, Nebojša Sokolović, and Momčilo Veljković.

	In response, Otpor launches campaign "This Is the Face of Serbia."
May 13, 2000	Boško Perošević, president of the Socialist Party in Vojvodina, assassinated. Otpor activists Stanko Lazendić and Miloš Gagić accused of committing murder.
June 29, 2000	Regime outlaws Otpor as a terrorist organization.
July 27, 2000	Otpor launches the campaign "He's Finished" ("*Gotov je*").
August 2000	Election campaign "It's Time" ("*Vreme je*") announced.
September 8, 2000	Otpor activists in Vladičin Han arrested and tortured by the local police.
September 24, 2000	Official election reports indicate that Slobodan Milošević has again won the presidency, but the results are widely recognized as falsified. Democratic Opposition of Serbia responds with nationwide strikes and demonstrations.
October 5, 2000	Strikes and mass demonstrations culminate in Milošević's acceptance of electoral loss. He steps down from power the following day.

Notes

Introduction

1. Quoted in Laurence M. Bogad, "Tactical Carnival: Social Movements, Demonstration, and Dialogical Performance," in *A Boal Companion*, eds. Jan Cohen-Cruz and Mady Schutzman (London: Routledge, 2006), 46.

2. Padraic Kenney, *A Carnival of Revolution* (Princeton, NJ: Princeton Univ. Press, 2002), 160–64.

3. See more in Janjira Sombatpoonsiri, "Playful Subversion: Red Sunday's Nonviolent Activism in Thailand's Post-2010 Crackdown," *Peace and Policy* (2015, forthcoming).

4. See, for example, John Dear, *The God of Peace: Toward a Theology of Nonviolence* (New York: Orbis, 1994); Krisha Mallick and Doris Hunter, *An Anthology of Nonviolence* (London: Greenwood, 2002).

5. See more in Joan V. Bondurant, *Conquest of Violence: The Gandhian Philosophy of Conflict* (Berkeley: Univ. of California Press, 1967); Arne Naess, *Gandhi and Group Conflict: An Exploration of Satyagraha Theoretical Background* (Oslo: Universitetsforlaget, 1974); and Joan V. Bondurant, "Satyagraha versus Duragraha: The Limits of Symbolic Violence," in *Gandhi, His Relevance for Our Times: A Volume of Contemporary Studies in Gandhian Themes Presented to Sri R. R. Diwakar on His Seventieth Birthday by the Workers of the Gandhi Smarak Nidhi*, eds. G. Ramachandran and T. K. Mahadevan, accessed September 12, 2009, http://www.mkgan dhi.org/g_relevance/chap05.html. See also Thomas Weber, *Conflict Resolution and Gandhian Ethics* (New Delhi: Gandhi Peace Foundation, 1991).

6. Gene Sharp, *The Politics of Nonviolent Action* (Boston: Porter Sargent, 1973), 705–11.

7. Etienne de La Boétie, *The Politics of Obedience: The Discourse of Voluntary Servitude*, trans. Harry Kurz (New York: Free Life, 1975), 70–72.

8. It should be noted that the nexus between oppressive and contemptuous dimensions of humor is widely discussed by scholars within humor research. See, for example, Richard Stephenson, "Conflict and Control Function of Humour," *American Journal of Sociology* 56, no. 6 (1951); Marvin R. Koller, *Humour and Society: Explorations in the Sociology of Humour* (Houston: Cap and Gown, 1988); and Jerry Palmer, *Taking Humor Seriously* (New York: Routledge, 1994).

9. See, for example, Max Gluckman, *Rituals of Rebellion in South-East Africa* (Manchester, UK: Univ. of Manchester Press, 1954); Anton C. Zijderveld, *Reality in a Looking-Glass: Rationality through an Analysis of Traditional Folly* (London: Routledge, 1982); Hans Speier, "Wit and Politics: An Essay on Laughter and Power," *The American Journal of Sociology* 103, no. 5 (1998): 1352–1401; and Alexander Rose, "When Politics Is a Laughing Matter," *Policy Review* (December 2001/January 2002): 59–71.

10. Gregor Benton, "The Origins of the Political Joke," in *Humour in Society: Resistance and Control*, eds. Chris Powell and George E. C. Paton (London: Macmillan, 1988), 54.

11. See, for example, Laurence M. Bogad, *Electoral Guerrilla Theatre: Radical Ridicule and Social Movements* (New York: Routledge, 2005); Benjamin Shepard, "The Use of Joyfulness as a Community Organizing Strategy," *Peace and Change* 30, no. 4 (2005): 436–37; Marjolein't Hart and Dennis Bos, eds., *Humour and Social Protest* (Cambridge: Press Syndicate of the Univ. of Cambridge, 2007); and Benjamin Shepard, *Queer Political Performance and Protest: Play, Pleasure and Social Movements* (New York: Routledge, 2010).

12. Jörgen Johansen, "Humor as a Political Force, or How to Open the Eyes of Ordinary People in Social Democratic Country," *Philosophy and Social Action* 17, no. 3–4 (1991): 7–23; Maiken Jul Sørensen, "Humor as a Serious Strategy of Nonviolent Resistance to Oppression," *Peace and Change* 33, no. 2 (2008): 167–90; and Khalid Kishtainy, "Humor and Resistance in the Arab World and Greater Middle East," in *Civilian Jihad: Nonviolent Struggle, Democratization and Governace in the Middle East*, ed. Maria J. Stephan (London: Palgrave Macmillan, 2009).

13. Sharp, *The Politics of Nonviolent Action*, 19–23. See also Doug Bond, "Nonviolent Action and the Diffusion of Power," in *Justice without Violence*, eds. Paul Wehr, Heidi Burgess, and Guy Burgess (London: Lynne Rienner, 1994), 59–80.

14. Sharp, *The Politics of Nonviolent Action*, 10–24, 67. Sharp notes: "Nonviolent action is a means of combat, as is war. It involves the matching of forces and the waging of 'battles,' requires wise strategy and tactics, and demands of its 'soldiers' courage, discipline, and sacrifice. This view of nonviolent action as a technique of active combat is diametrically opposed to the popular assumption that, at its strongest, nonviolent action relies on rational persuasion of the opponent, and that more commonly it consists simply of passive submission." See also Kurt Schock, "Nonviolent Action and Its Misconceptions: Insights for Social Scientists," *Political Sciences and Politics* 36, no. 4 (2003): 705–11.

15. Sharp, *The Politics of Nonviolent Action*, 733–41.

16. Ibid., 742–68. See also Clarence M. Case, *Non-Violent Coercion: A Study in Methods of Social Pressure* (New York: Century, 1923), 320–96; Erica Chenoweth and Maria J. Stephan, *Why Civil Resistance Works: The Strategic Logic of Nonviolent Conflict* (New York: Columbia Univ. Press, 2011), 46–55.

17. See criticisms in Paul Routledge, "Entanglements of Power: Geographies of Domination / Resistance," in *Entanglements of Power: Geographies of Domination / Resistance*, eds. Paul Routledge, Joanne P. Sharp, Chris Philo, and Ronan Paddison (London: Routledge,

2000), 1–42; Roland Bleiker, *Popular Dissent, Human Agency and Global Politics* (Cambridge: Cambridge Univ. Press, 2000); and Stellan Vinthagen, "Power as Subordination and Resistance as Disobedience: Nonviolent Movements and the Management of Power," *Asian Journal of Social Science* 34, no. 1 (2006): 1–21.

18. See, for example, Michel Foucault, *Madness and Civilization* (New York: Vintage/ Random House, 1973); Michel Foucault, *The Birth of the Clinic: An Archeology of Medical Perception*, trans. A. M. Sheridan (New York: Vintage/Random House, 1975); Michel Foucault, *Discipline and Punishment: The Birth of the Prison*, trans. Alan Sheridan (New York: Vintage/ Random House, 1979); John Gaventa, *Power and Powerlessness: Quiescence and Rebellion in an Appalachian Valley* (Oxford: Clarendon, 1979); and Theodor W. Adorno, *The Culture Industry* (New York: Routledge, 2001).

19. Michel Foucault, *Power/Knowledge—Selected Interviews and Other Writings 1972–1977*, ed. Colin Gordon (New York: Pantheon, 1980), 142.

20. Michel de Certeau, *The Practice of Everyday Life* (Berkeley: Univ. of California Press, 1984), 91–110, 165–89.

21. de Certeau, *The Practice of Everyday Life*, 91–110, 165–89.

22. Ibid., 29–42.

23. John Fiske, *Understanding Popular Culture* (London: Routledge, 1989), 1–21.

24. Bleiker, *Popular Dissent, Human Agency and Global Politics*, 210–11.

25. Fiske, *Understanding Popular Culture*, 81–102, 106–14; Bleiker, *Popular Dissent, Human Agency and Global Politics*, 201–2; and Vinthagen, "Power as Subordination and Resistance as Disobedience," 17–18.

26. For elaborate discussions on the subversive role of humor in different genres, see for example John Morreall, *Taking Laughter Seriously* (Albany: State Univ. of New York Press, 1983); Mahadev L. Apte, *Humor and Laughter: An Anthropological Approach* (London: Cornell Univ. Press, 1988); and Michael Mulkay, *On Humor: Its Nature and Its Place in Modern Society* (Cambridge: Polity, 1988).

27. Peter L. Berger, *Redeeming Laughter: The Comic Dimension of Human Experience* (New York: Walter de Gruyter, 1998), 158.

28. Berger, *Redeeming Laughter*, 158. See also Brian Connery and Kirk Combe, eds., *Theorizing Satire* (New York: St. Martin's, 1995); Dustin Griffin, *Satire: A Critical Introduction* (Lexington: Univ. Press of Kentucky, 1994).

29. Charles A. Knight, "Satire, Speech, and Genre," *Comparative Literature* 44, no. 1 (1992): 22–41.

30. Arthur Koestler, *The Act of Creation* (London: Pan, 1964), 73–75. See also Berger, *Redeeming Laughter*, 160.

31. Linda Hutcheon, *A Theory of Parody: The Teachings of Twentieth-Century Art Forms* (Champaign: Univ. of Illinois Press, 2000), xiv.

32. Mikhail Bakhtin, *The Dialogic Imagination: Four Essays*, trans. Vadim Liapunov and Kenneth Brostrom, ed. Michael Holquist (Austin: Univ. of Texas Press, 1981), 53–55;

G. D. Kiremidijan, "The Aesthetics of Parody," *Journal of Aesthetics and Art Criticism* 28, no. 2 (1969): 231–42; Terry Caesar, "Impervious to Criticism: Contemporary Parody and Trash," *SubStance* 20, no. 64 (1991): 69–79; and Hutcheon, *A Theory of Parody*, 30–49.

33. Carnivals have been historically central to many societies. In Europe, the origin of carnivals dates back to the Roman Saturnalia, which later on influenced the Feast of Fools (*fête des fous*) in France and the "feast of the ass," for instance. In Latin America, carnivals have been organized that combine Catholic religious processions with indigenous rituals. There is also a long tradition of carnivals in Hindu society (the Feast of Krishna or "Holi") and mainland Southeast Asia (Water festival or "Songkran"). In Africa, carnivals are merged with weddings, funerals, and the rites after male circumcision. See more in James C. Scott, *Domination and the Arts of Resistance* (New Haven, CT: Yale Univ. Press, 1990), 172–82; Mary Douglas, "Jokes," in *Implicit Meanings: Essays in Anthropology*, ed. Mary Douglas (London: Routledge, 1984), 90–114; and Apte, *Humor and Laughter*, 156–60.

34. David Kunzle, "World Upside Down: The Iconography of a European Broadsheet Type," in *The Reversible World: Symbolic Inversion in Art and Society*, ed. Barbara A. Babcock (Ithaca, NY: Cornell Univ. Press, 1978), 39–90; Mikhail Bakhtin, *Rabelais and His World*, trans. Helene Iswolsky (Bloomington: Indiana Univ. Press, 1984), 83; and Scott, *Domination and the Arts of Resistance*, 173.

35. Bakhtin, *Rabelais and His World*, 83–84.

36. Peter Burke, *Popular Culture in Early Modern Europe* (New York: Harper and Row, 1978), 123.

37. David Gilmore, *Aggression and Community: Paradoxes of Andalusian Culture* (New Haven, CT: Yale Univ. Press, 1987), 98, cited in Scott, *Domination and the Arts of Resistance*, 174–75.

38. Scott, *Domination and the Arts of Resistance*, 168. See also John Docker, *Postmodernism and Popular Culture: A Cultural History* (Cambridge: Cambridge Univ. Press, 1994), 189–97; Victor Turner, *The Anthropology of Performance* (New York: PAJ, 1988), 24.

39. Bakhtin, *Rabelais and His World*, 303–436.

40. Don Handelman, "The Ritual-Clown: Attributes and Affinities," *Anthropos* 76 (1981): 321–70; Jacques le Goff, "Laughter in the Middle Ages," in *A Cultural History of Humor: From Antiquity to the Present Day*, eds. Jan Bremmer and Herman Roodenburg (Cambridge: Polity, 1997), 40–53.

41. Bakhtin, *Rabelais and His World*, 286. See also Allan Irving and Tom Young, "Paradigm for Pluralism: Mikhail Bakhtin and Social Work Practice," *Social Work* 47, no. 1 (2002): 19–29.

1. Laughing at the Misery

1. Milena Dragićević-Šešić, "The Art in Protest," in *The Last Decade: Serbian Citizens in the Struggle for Democracy and an Open Society, 1991–2001*, ed. Velimir Ćurgus Kazimir (Belgrade: Media Center, 2001), 39. See a different interpretation of Yugoslav artist movements

in Radina Vučetić, *Koka-Kola socijalizam: Amerikanizacija Jugoslovenske popularne kulture šezdesetih godina* [Coca-Cola socialism: The Americanization of Yugoslav popular culture in the 1960s] (Belgrade: Službeni glasnik, 2012). Vučetić argues that artist movements in Tito's period presented both openness and limits of dissidence. While acknowledging this aspect, this chapter focuses on the role of anti-communist artists that would later inspire protesters' ideas of humorous actions.

2. See RoseLee Goldberg, *Performance Art: From Futurism to the Present* (New York: Thames and Hudson World of Art, 2001), 50–96; Peter Bürger, *Theory of the Avant-garde* (Minneapolis: Univ. of Minnesota Press, 1984). This chapter by no means attempts a comprehensive explanation of the avant-garde art movement. For the purpose of discussing the artist's role in introducing humor into protest campaigns, I refer to "avant-garde" as a type of artwork created to reflect on and criticize the established norms of society. Hence, such artwork tends to be reformative, thought provoking, and usually oppositional to classic and market-based art.

3. Irina Subotić and Ann Vasić, "'Zenit' and Zenitism," *Journal of Decorative and Propaganda Arts* 17 (1990): 15; Vidosava Golubović, "The Zenit Periodical (1921–1926)," accessed June 15, 2011, http://digital.nb.rs/zenit/ english.html.

4. Irina Subotić, "Avant-Garde Tendencies in Yugoslavia," *Art Journal* 49, no. 1 (1990): 22–23.

5. Ivan Pravdić, "Student Performances: Guidelines for Possible Analyses or Theatre of the Masses—Walking from Failureville to Never-Never Land," in *Šetnja u mestu: građanski protest u Srbiji* [Walking on the spot: civil protest in Serbia], ed. Darka Radosavljević (Belgrade: B92, 1997), 38.

6. Padraic Kenney, *A Carnival of Revolution* (Princeton, NJ: Princeton Univ. Press, 2002), 181.

7. Alexei Monroe and Slavoj Žižek, *Interrogation Machine: Laibach and NSK (Short Circuits)* (Cambridge, MA: MIT Press, 2005), 3–5.

8. NSK, "The NSK State," *NSK,* accessed June 15, 2011, http://www.passport.nsk.si /en/about_us.

9. Kenney, *A Carnival of Revolution,* 181–82. Tito led the partisan movement and conquered the Nazis occupying the Yugoslav states during the Second World War. The fall of the Nazis, in this sense, gave rise to the power of Tito's communist party. The poster mocked the totalitarian nature that the communist regime shared with Nazism, despite their historical hostility.

10. Dijana Milošević, "Theatre as a Way of Creating Sense: Performance and Peacebuilding in the Region of the Former Yugoslavia," in *Acting Together: Performance and Creative Transformation of Conflict,* eds. Cythia E. Cohen, Roberto G. Varea, and Polly O. Walker (Oakland, CA: New Village, 2011), 23–44.

11. Erika Munk, "Before the Fall, Yugoslav Theaters of Opposition," *Theater* 31 (2001): 15; and Dragićević-Šešić, "The Art in Protest," 42.

12. Matthew Collin, *This Is Serbia Calling* (London: Serpent's Tail, 2001), 89.

13. Aleksandra Jovićević, "Everybody Laughed: Civil and Student Protest in Serbia 1996–97, between Theater, Paratheature and Carnival," in *Šetnja u mestu: građanski protest u Srbiji* [Walking on the spot: civil protest in Serbia], ed. Darka Radosavljević (Belgrade: B92, 1997), 51–52.

14. Đorđe Balmazović, in discussion with the author, October 2010. See also Annika Salomonsson, "Art Action Group Speaks to the World: Humble Artists Create Touching Work on the Trials of Humanity," accessed June 15, 2011, http://www.culturebase.net/artist .php?677.

15. Pravdić, "Student Performances," 38.

16. A breeding ground for Milošević's nationalist rhetoric had been formed by the history-based novel by Dobrica Ćosić, *A Time of Death* [Vreme smrti], which narrates the sufferings of Serbs during the First World War. The novel fundamentally questions the construction of Yugoslavia instead of a "greater Serbia" as an outcome of allying with the West. It was published in four volumes in the 1970s. The novel's second volume, *The Battle of Kolubara*, was chosen by the Yugoslav Drama Theater for production as a play. See Mattijs van de Port, *Gypsies, Wars and Other Instances of the Wild* (Amsterdam: Amsterdam Univ. Press, 1998), 83–85; Jasna Dragović-Soso, *Saviours of the Nation: Serbia's Intellectual Opposition and the Revival of Nationalism* (London: Hurst, 2002), 89–90; and Tim Judah, *The Serbs: History, Myth and the Destruction of Yugoslavia* (New Haven, CT: Yale Univ. Press, 2009), 34–37.

17. Ivan Čolović, *The Politics of Identity in Serbia* (New York: New York Univ. Press, 2002), 18–19.

18. Eric D. Gordy, *The Culture of Power in Serbia: Nationalism and the Destruction of Alternatives* (University Park: Pennsylvania State Univ. Press, 1999), 127. See also Dalibor Mišina, *Shake, Rattle and Roll: Yugoslav Rock Music and the Poetics of Social Critique* (Surrey, UK: Ashgate, 2013).

19. Generally, turbo folk singers were supported enormously by the government. Their music was produced and sold by state-run music companies. Turbo folk's lyrics were mainly patriotic, emphasizing warrior culture and the historical misery of Serbs. See Gordy, *The Culture of Power in Serbia*, 128–41; Ivana Kronja, "Turbo Folk and Dance Music in 1990s Serbia: Media, Ideology, and the Production of Spectacle," *Anthropology of East Europe Review* 22, no. 1 (2004): 103–14; and Alexei Monroe, "Balkan Hardcore: Pop Culture and Paramilitarism," *Central European Review* (June 19, 2000), accessed June 15, 2011, http://www.ce-review.org/00/24/monroe24.html.

20. Brana Mijatović, "'Throwing Stones at the System': Rock Music in Serbia during the 1990s," *Music and Politics* 2, no. 2 (2008): 2, accessed May 12, 2010, www.music.ucsb.edu /projects/musicandpolitics /archive/2008 . . . /mijatovic.pdf.

21. Antonije Pušić, in discussion with the author, September 2010. Pušić's caricaturist nature is noticeable in his pseudonym, which appropriates the last name of a Hollywood

action-adventure hero (John Rambo) and the middle name of an iconic classical composer (Wolfgang Amadeus Mozart).

22. Gordy, *The Culture of Power in Serbia*, 119.

23. Petar Janjatović, "Their Time Is Past," in *The Last Decade: Serbian Citizens in the Struggle for Democracy and an Open Society, 1991–2001*, ed. Velimir Ćurgus Kazimir (Belgrade: Media Center, 2001), 53. Serbian lyrics were translated into English by Jelena Vukičević, my research assistant.

24. The words *Karamba, karambita* originate from the popular comic book *Zagor*, from the 1970s. Originally published in Italian, this comic book was translated into Serbian and widely distributed throughout Yugoslavia during the 1970s. Zagor was a protector of the weak and the oppressed and possessed superhuman strength, as well as excellent wilderness survival skills. He was often accompanied by his friend, Chico, whose frequent use of the words *Karamba, karambita* (meaning "goodness gracious") inspired the title for Rambo's song. See Mijatović, "Throwing Stones at the System," 9–11; Gordy, *The Culture of Power in Serbia*, 119. Serbian lyrics are translated into English by Jelena Vukičević, my research assistant.

25. Mijatović, "Throwing Stones at the System," 6; Janjatović, "Their Time Is Past," 54; and Collin, *This Is Serbia Calling*, 63.

26. Gordy, *The Culture of Power in Serbia*, 116.

27. Janjatović, "Their Time Is Past," 54.

28. Pero Jelić, in discussion with the author, November 2010. Pušić further explains that his action was meant "to demonstrate to students that they should have "clean" politics alongside the re-painted and clean toilet."

29. Brana Mijatović, "(Com)Passionately Political: Music of Đorđe Balašević," *Anthropology of East Europe Review* 22, no. 1 (2004): 93.

30. Janjatović, "Their Time Is Past," 54.

31. Mijatović, "(Com)Passionately Political," 95.

32. Ibid., 97. See also Janjatović, "Their Time Is Past," 54.

33. Mijatović, "(Com)Passionately Political," 99–100. Serbian lyrics are translated into English by Jelena Vukičević, my research assistant.

34. When Balašević mentions "Resistance" in his lyrics, he is referring to "Otpor" as a movement, as well as the popular forces of resistance against the Milošević regime.

35. Mijatović, "(Com)Passionately Political," 93.

36. This concert was actually broadcast by the state-run TV channel, RTS2.

37. Nebojša Grujičić, "Koncert Đorđa Balaševića" [Đorđe Balašević's concert], *VREME*, December 7, 2000, accessed October 20, 2010, http://www.vreme.com/arhiva_html/518/20 .html.

38. Monroe and Žižek, *Interrogation Machine*, 130; Laibach, *Nova Akropola*, Cherry Red Records, 1985, compact disc.

39. Kenney, *A Carnival of Revolution*, 181–82.

40. Laibach, *NATO*, Mute Records, 1994, compact disc.

41. Simon Bell, "Laibach: Post-Ideological Trickster," *EXEUNT Magazine*, May 23, 2012, accessed November 19, 2012, http://exeuntmagazine.com/features/laibach-ludic-paradigm-of-the-post-ideological-age/2/. It should be noted that Laibach experienced regime oppression from time to time because of its use of symbolic incorporation. For instance, in 1982 the Yugoslav authorities investigated and banned Laibach for "apparent use of military expedients in a show," and again in 1983 for "inappropriate" use of symbols.

42. Paul Hockenos, "Serbia's New New Wave," *In These Times*, March 5, 2001, accessed October 20, 2010, http://www.inthesetimes.com/issue/25/07/hockenos2507.html; Marc W. Steinberg, "When Politics Goes Pop: On the Intersections of Popular and Political Culture and the Case of Serbian Student Protests," *Social Movement Studies* 3, no. 1 (2004): 3–29.

43. Milana Vujkov, "Black Humor in Serbian Films of the Early Eighties and Its Cultural Consequences: The Cinema of Slobodan Šijan and Dušan Kovačević" (master's thesis, Univ. of London, 2005), 25–33; Dina Iordanova, "Conceptualizing the Balkans in Film," *Slavic Review* 55, no. 4 (1996): 882.

44. Van de Port, *Gypsies, Wars and Other Instances of the Wild*, 101; Andrew Horton, "Laughter Dark and Joyous in Recent Films from the Former Yugoslavia," *Film Quarterly* 56, no. 1 (2002): 23–28.

45. See more in Pavle Levi, *Disintegration in Frames: Aesthetics and Ideology in the Yugoslav and Post-Yugoslav Cinema* (Redwood City, CA: Stanford Univ. Press, 2007), 11–56; Nebojša Jovanović, "*Futur Antérieur* of Yugoslav Cinema, or, Why Emir Kusturica's Legacy Is Worth Fighting For," in *Retracing Images: Visual Culture after Yugoslavia*, eds. Daniel Šuber and Slobodan Karamanić (Boston: Brill Academic, 2012).

46. Vujkov, "Black Humor in Serbian Films of the Early Eighties and Its Cultural Consequences," 15.

47. *Doomsday Is Near / It Rains in My Village* [Biće skoro propast sveta], directed by Aleksandar Petrović (Yugoslavia and France: Avala Film, Les Productions Artistes Associés, 1969), film.

48. Horton, "Laughter Dark and Joyous in Recent Films from the Former Yugoslavia," 23.

49. *Who's Singin' over There* [Ko to tamo peva], directed by Slobodan Šijan and Dušan Kovačević (Serbia: Centar Film, 1980), film.

50. *Balkan Spy* [Balkanski špijun], directed by Dušan Kovačević and Božidar Nikolić (Yugoslavia: Union Film, 1984), film.

51. Carol S. Lilly, "Film Reviews," *American Historical Review* 104, no. 4 (1999): 1429; Čolović, *The Politics of Identity in Serbia*, 39–47.

52. See also Gordana P. Crnković, *Post-Yugoslav Literature and Film: Fires, Foundations, Flourishes* (London: Bloomsbury Academic, 2012).

53. Local comedy shows, especially the Bosnian *Top lista nadrealista*, were popular throughout the former Yugoslavia. The analysis in this section does not explore the impact

of this TV show on Serbian humorous protests, focusing instead on *Monty Python* because of Otpor activists' reference to *Monty Python* as their main source of inspiration.

54. Marcia Landy, *Monty Python's Flying Circus: TV Milestones Series* (Detroit, MI: Wayne State Univ. Press, 2005), 3.

55. For these skits, see *The Complete Monty Python's Flying Circus*, directed by Ian Mac-Naughton and Terry Hughes (London: British Broadcasting Corporation (BBC) and Python (Monty) Pictures, 1982), DVD.

56. Vujkov, "Black Humor in Serbian Films of the Early Eighties and Its Cultural Consequences," 11.

57. Dalibor Glišović, in discussion with the author, November 2010; Miloš Gagić, in discussion with the author, September 2010; Petar Milićević, in discussion with the author, November 2010, Belgrade, Serbia; Vojislav Milošević, in discussion with the author, November 2010.

58. See, for example, Collin, *This Is Serbia Calling*, 105; Taras Kuzio, "Civil Society, Youth and Societal Mobilization in Democratic Revolutions," *Communist and Post-Communist Studies* 39 (2006): 375; Maiken Jul Sørensen, "Humor as Nonviolent Resistance to Oppression" *Peace and Change* 33, no. 2 (2008): 167–90; Stephen Zunes, "The Leftist Attack on Nonviolent Action for Democratic Change," *Centre for Applied Non-Violent Action and Strategies* (CANVAS), 2008, accessed April 15, 2010, www.canvasopedia.org/legacy/files /various/Leftist_Attack_on_NVA.doc; and Wayne Grytting, "Gandhi Meets Monty Python: The Comedic Turn in Nonviolent Tactics," *Waging Nonviolence* (October 28, 2011), accessed November 3, 2011, http://wagingnonviolence.org/2011/10/gandhi-meets-monty -python-the-comedic-turn-in-nonviolenttactics/?utmsource=feedburner&utmmedium= feed&utmcampaign=Feed%3A+Waging Nonviolence+%28Waging+Nonviolence%29.

59. Lada Stevanović, "Ridiculed Death and the Dead: Black Humor, Epitaphs and Epigrams of the Ancient Greeks," Glasnik Etnografskog Instituta SANU 55, no. 1 (2007): 202.

60. Duško Doder, *The Yugoslavs* (London: George Allen and Unwin), 24–25, cited in Van de Port, *Gypsies, Wars and Other Instances of the Wild*, 112; Judah, *The Serbs*, 11.

61. Vladimir Kolesarić, Mirjana Krizmanić, and Antun Rohaček, "Humor in Yugoslavia," in *National Styles of Humor*, ed. Avner Ziv (New York: Greenwood, 1988), 206.

62. See Judah, *The Serbs*, 279–94.

63. Robert Thomas, *Serbia under Milošević / Politics in the 1990s* (London: Hurst, 1999), 161–65; Judah, *The Serbs*, 371, 108–9.

64. Thomas, *Serbia under Milošević / Politics in the 1990s*, 161–65.

65. Gordy, *The Culture of Power in Serbia*, 170, 187–88.

66. Thomas, *Serbia under Milošević / Politics in the 1990s*, 166.

67. Judah, *The Serbs*, 339–40; Lenard J. Cohen, *Serpent in the Bosom: The Rise and Fall of Slobodan Milošević* (Boulder, CO: Westview, 2002), 394–95; and Sabrina P. Ramet, *Balkan Babel: The Disintegration of Yugoslavia from the Death of Tito to the Fall of Milošević* (Boulder, CO: Westview, 2002), 342–45.

68. Collin, *This Is Serbia Calling*, 87; Velimir Ćurgus Kazimir, "From Islands to the Mainland," in *The Last Decade: Serbian Citizens in the Struggle for Democracy and an Open Society, 1991–2001*, ed. Velimir Ćurgus Kazimir (Belgrade: Media Center, 2001), 14.

69. Collin, *This Is Serbia Calling*, 87; Kazimir, "From Islands to the Mainland," 14.

70. An example of an antagonistic joke appears in a Serbian folk song that mocks Montenegrins as being traitors, ungrateful for the Serbian "liberation" of them from the Austro-Hungarian Empire. See Milovan Đilas, *Land without Justice* (New York: Mariner, 1958), cited in Judah, *The Serbs*, 105.

71. Srđan Vučetić, "Identity Is a Joking Matter: Intergroup Humor in Bosnia," *Space of Identity* 4, no. 1 (2004): 14, accessed April 2, 2010, pi.library.yorku.ca/ojs/index.php/soi/article/view/8011/7168.

72. Boris Mitić, "Aphorism," accessed July 9, 2011, http://www.dribblingpictures.com/flash_eng/drbbpct.html; Dan Bilefsky, "Dark One-Liners Shine a Light on the Mood of Serbs," *New York Times*, December 2, 2007, accessed May 8, 2011, http://www.nytimes.com/2007/12/02/world/europe/02serbia.html.

73. Mitić, "Aphorism." These and most of the following aphorisms are selected from the documentary film *Goodbye, How Are You?* [Doviđenja, kako ste?], directed by Boris Mitić (Serbia: Dribbling Pictures, 2009); Mitić has collected aphorisms from different places in Serbia between the years 1969 and 2009.

74. Gordy, *The Culture of Power in Serbia*, 190.

75. Mitić, "Aphorism."

76. Ibid.

77. Collin, *This Is Serbia Calling*, 106.

78. Mitić, "Aphorism."

79. Milica Popović, in discussion with the author, November 2010.

80. Hubert L. Dreyfus, Stuart E. Dreyfus, and Tom Athanasiou, *Mind over Machine: The Power of Human Intuition and Expertise in the Era of the Computer* (Oxford: Basil Blackwell, 1986).

81. Sigmund Freud, *Jokes and Their Relation to the Unconscious*, trans. Angela Richard and James Strachey (New York: Norton, 1963), 140; Arthur Koestler, *The Act of Creation* (London: Pan, 1964), 42.

82. Mary Douglas, "Jokes," in *Implicit Meanings: Essays in Anthropology*, ed. Mary Douglas (London: Routledge, 1984), 98.

83. Pernille Ammitzbøll and Lorenzo Vidino, "After the Danish Cartoon Controversy," *Middle East Quarterly* 14, no. 1 (2007): 3–11.

84. Dreyfus, Dreyfus, and Athanasiou, *Mind over Machine*, 5.

85. See, for example, Ulrich Marzolph, "Reconsidering the Iranian Sources of a Romanian Political Joke," *Western Folklore* 47, no. 3 (1988): 212–16.

86. This line of argument is influenced by the concept of *habitus* coined by Pierre Bourdieu.

87. Although he does not discuss comic experience specifically, the notion of *habitus*—embodied history—can be applied to understand the intuitive practice of culture. See more in Pierre Bourdieu, *Outline of a Theory of Practice* (Cambridge: Cambridge Univ. Press, 1977), 54–65. In social movement theories, the influence of culture at the level of perception is conceptualized as "cognitive praxis," "idea/ideology-based practice." See more in Ron Eyerman and Andrew Jamison, *Social Movements: A Cognitive Approach* (Cambridge: Polity, 1991), 45–65.

88. Aleksandar Pavlović, in discussion with the author, October 2010; Goran Dašković, in discussion with the author, December 2010; Marko Simić, in discussion with the author, November 2010; Srđa Popović, in discussion with the author, November 2010; Vladimir Stojković, in discussion with the author, November 2010.

89. Milica Popović, in discussion with the author, November 2010; Milja Jovanović, in discussion with the author, November 2010; Nenad Belčević, in discussion with the author, October 2010; Petar Lacmanović, in discussion with the author, November 2010; Zoran Matović, in discussion with the author, November 2010.

2. Coming to the Fore

1. *Tito among the Serbs for the Second Time* [Tito po drugi put medju Srbima], directed by Zemilir Zilnik (Belgrade: B92, 1993), DVD.

2. Theodor W. Adorno, *The Authoritarian Personality* (New York: W. W. Norton, 1993).

3. See also Eric D. Gordy, *The Culture of Power in Serbia: Nationalism and the Destruction of Alternatives* (University Park: Pennsylvania State Univ. Press, 1999); Matthew Collin, *This Is Serbia Calling* (London: Serpent's Tail, 2001); Sabrina P. Ramet, *Balkan Babel: The Disintegration of Yugoslavia from the Death of Tito to the Fall of Milošević* (Boulder, CO: Westview, 2002); Lenard J. Cohen, *Serpent in the Bosom: The Rise and Fall of Slobodan Milosevic* (Boulder, CO: Westview, 2002); and Ivan Čolović, *The Politics of Identity in Serbia* (New York: New York Univ. Press, 2002).

4. Prior to the 1990s, popular protests had been a common political scene in Serbia. Among others, popular protests that were dubbed the "Anti-Bureaucratic Revolution" in 1988 to 1989 brought Slobodan Milošević and his Socialist Party of Serbia to power. The protests were staged by Serbs in the (former) autonomous provinces of Kosovo and Vojvodina, demanding the resignations of non-Serb heads of local governments. See also Robert Thomas, *Serbia under Milošević / Politics in the 1990s* (London: Hurst, 1999), 32–43; Cohen, *Serpent in the Bosom*, 74–79; and Nebojša Vladisavljević, *Serbia's Anti-Bureaucratic Revolution: Milošević, the Fall of Communism and Nationalist Mobilization* (New York: Palgrave Macmillan, 2008).

5. Mirjana Prosić-Dvornić, "Enough! Student Protest '92: The Youth of Belgrade in Quest of 'Another Serbia,'" *Anthropology of East Europe Review* 11, nos. 1–2 (1993), accessed September 21, 2010, http://condor.depaul.edu/rrotenbe/aeer/aeer11_1/prosic-dvornic.html. The 1991 protest was symbolically associated with the Czech Velvet Revolution, and thereby

was labeled the "Velvet" Revolution. There was an expectation at the time that a democratic transition could take place in Serbia as it had in Czechoslovakia in 1989.

6. Veran Matić, in discussion with the author, September 2010. See also Velimir Ćurgus Kazimir, "From Islands to the Mainland," in *The Last Decade: Serbian Citizens in the Struggle for Democracy and an Open Society, 1991–2001*, ed. Velimir Ćurgus Kazimir (Belgrade: Media Center, 2001), 12; Collin, *This Is Serbia Calling*, 26. The B92 station attempted a prank before this public skit. In early 1992, DJs at B92 imposed a "self-ban" on the station, a prank that aimed to respond to the prospect of the regime ban. The announcement of the ban generated a chaotic and "frantic" reaction from fans. Matić explained that some enraged fans took to the street, smashing windows, while others called in to the station and burst into tears. Eventually, the staff of B92 decided to put an end to the prank as the reaction from longtime listeners became too overwhelming. The regime did not intervene in the operation of B92, at least for a while.

7. Veran Matić, in discussion with the author, September 2010. See also Milena Dragićević-Šešić, "The Street as Political Space: Walking as Protest, Graffiti, and the Student Carnivalization of Belgrade," *New Theatre Quarterly* 17 (2001): 75; Prosić-Dvornić, "Enough! Student Protest '92."

8. Dragićević-Šešić, "The Street as Political Space," 56.

9. Dubravka Knežević, "Marked with Red Ink," in *Radical Street Performance: An International Anthology*, ed. Jan Cohen-Cruz (London: Routledge, 1998), 57.

10. Bojana Šušak, "An Alternative to War," in *The Road to War in Serbia: Trauma and Catharsis*, ed. Nebojša Popov (Budapest: Central European Univ. Press, 2000), 494–95; Dragićević-Šešić, "The Street as Political Space," 75.

11. Knežević, "Marked with Red Ink," 55.

12. Prosić-Dvornić, "Enough! Student Protest '92."

13. Collin, *This Is Serbia Calling*, 61.

14. Prosić-Dvornić, "Enough! Student Protest '92"; Nebojša Popov, "The University in an Ideological Shell," in *The Road to War in Serbia: Trauma and Catharsis*, ed. Nebojša Popov (Budapest: Central European Univ. Press, 1996), 323. See also Bora Kuzmanović, *Studentski protest '92: socijalno-psihološka studija jednog društvenog događaja* [The student protest '92: a social-psychological study of a social event] (Belgrade: Institut za psihologiju Filozofskog fakulteta, knjižara Plato, 1993).

15. Knežević, "Marked with Red Ink," 55–56.

16. Prosić-Dvornić, "Enough! Student Protest '92"; Ivan Pravdić, "Student Performances: Guidelines for Possible Analyses or Theatre of the Masses—Walking from Failureville to Never-Never Land," in *Šetnja u mestu: građanski protest u Srbiji* [Walking on the spot: civil protest in Serbia], ed. Darka Radosavljević (Belgrade: B92, 1997), 39; Popadić, "Student Protests," 135; Knežević, "Marked with Red Ink"; Collin, *This Is Serbia Calling*, 51; and Dragićević-Šešić, "The Street as Political Space," 75.

17. Prosić-Dvornić, "Enough! Student Protest '92"; Pravdić, "Student Performances," 39; and Popadić, "Student Protests," 146.

18. Knežević, "Marked with Red Ink," 56.

19. Prosić-Dvornić, "Enough! Student Protest '92"; Knežević, "Marked with Red Ink," 56. For the political use of the epic composed by Vuk Karadžić, see Tim Judah, *The Serbs: History, Myth and the Destruction of Yugoslavia* (New Haven, CT: Yale Univ. Press, 2009), 34–37; Mattijs van de Port, *Gypsies, Wars and Other Instances of the Wild* (Amsterdam: Amsterdam Univ. Press, 1998), 124; and Čolović, *The Politics of Identity in Serbia*, 5–12.

20. "Sloba" is Milošević's nickname.

21. Prosić-Dvornić, "Enough! Student Protest '92."

22. Scott, *Domination and the Arts of Resistance.*

23. See an analysis in the case of the Polish Solidarity Movement in Colin Barker, "Fear, Laughter, and Collective Power: The Making of Solidarity at the Lenin Shipyard in Gdansk, Poland, August 1980," in *Passionate Politics: Emotions and Social Movements*, eds. Jeff Goodwin, James M. Jasper, and Francesca Polleta (Chicago: Univ. of Chicago Press, 2001), 175–94.

24. Regarding this line of argument, see also William A. Callahan, "Laughter, Critical Theory and Korea," in *Habermas and the Korean Debate*, ed. Sang-Jin Han (Seoul: Seoul National Univ. Press, 1998), 446–71.

25. Peter L. Berger, *Redeeming Laughter: The Comic Dimension of Human Experience* (New York: Walter de Gruyter, 1998), 1–13.

26. Johannes Climacus, *Concluding Unscientific Postscript*, trans. David Swenson (Princeton, NJ: Princeton Univ. Press, 1941).

3. Coming of Age

1. The administrative system in Serbia is divided into federal, regional, and municipal levels. The municipal level of administration is a form of local self-government. There are two types of local government: the city (*grad*) and municipality (*opština*).

2. The Left Coalition won by 64 seats out of 108 seats (59.3 percent) while Zajedno received 22 seats or 20.4 percent of the votes. See Sreten Vujović, "Protest as an Urban Phenomenon," in *Protest in Belgrade: Winter of Discontent*, ed. Mladen Lazić (Budapest: Central European Univ. Press, 1999), 206.

3. Čedomir Antić, in discussion with the author, November 2010. See also Laslo Sekelj, "Parties and Elections: The Federal Republic of Yugoslavia—Change without Transformation," *Europe-Asia Studies* 52, no. 1 (2000): 61.

4. Vujović, "Protest as an Urban Phenomenon," 198.

5. Dragan Ilić, "Hronika Protesta 'Zajedno'" [Chronicle of the Zajedno protest], in *Šetnja u mestu: građanski protest u Srbiji* [Walking on the spot: civil protest in Serbia], ed. Darka Radosavljević (Belgrade: B92, 1997), 114; Balkan Peace Team, "The Protests in Belgrade and

throughout Yugoslavia," December 7, 1996, Peace Brigades International Archive, London, accessed November 10, 2010, http://www.peacebrigades.org/archive/bpt/bpt96-14.html.

6. Ilić, "Hronika Protesta 'Zajedno'" [Chronicle of the Zajedno protest], 14.

7. Robert Thomas, *Serbia under Milošević / Politics in the 1990s* (London: Hurst, 1999), 288.

8. Lenard J. Cohen, *Serpent in the Bosom: The Rise and Fall of Slobodan Milošević* (Boulder, CO: Westview, 2002), 254.

9. Ilić, "Hronika Protesta 'Zajedno'" [Chronicle of the Zajedno protest], 120.

10. Balkan Peace Team, "The Protests in Belgrade and throughout Yugoslavia."

11. Thomas, *Serbia under Milošević / Politics in the 1990s*, 303.

12. Milan Milutinović, in discussion with the author, October 2010. See also Balkan Peace Team, "The Protests in Belgrade and throughout Yugoslavia."

13. Thomas, *Serbia under Milošević / Politics in the 1990s*, 304; Ilić, "Hronika Protesta 'Zajedno'" [Chronicle of the Zajedno protest], 116.

14. Ilić, "Hronika Protesta 'Zajedno'" [Chronicle of the Zajedno protest], 117; Thomas, *Serbia under Milošević / Politics in the 1990s*, 308.

15. Thomas, *Serbia under Milošević / Politics in the 1990s*, 307.

16. The Balkan Peace Team, "The Protests in Belgrade and throughout Yugoslavia," December 7, 1996 (Peace Brigades International Archive, London); Ilić, "Hronika Protesta 'Zajedno'" [Chronicle of the Zajedno protest], 117.

17. Cohen, *Serpent in the Bosom*, 252.

18. Ilić, "Hronika Protesta 'Zajedno'" [Chronicle of the Zajedno protest], 120. Regarding the chronology of the 1996–97 protests, see also appendix B.

19. Prior to the 1996–97 protests, there were just a few student organizations, namely the League of Students, the Student Union, and the Student Federation. The former was controlled by the Socialist Party and had long taken over "student activism" of major universities. See Cohen, *Serpent in the Bosom*, 252, 263; Zoran B. Nikolić, "Students Divided: Belgrade—Struggle against Genes," *AIM*, September 8, 1997, accessed February 12, 2011, http://www.aim press.ch/dyn /trae/archive/data/199709/70912-029-trae-beo.html.

20. Čedomir Antić, in discussion with the author, November 2010; Ivan Marović, in discussion with the author, November 2010; Milena Dragićević-Šešić, in discussion with the author, September 2010; Pero Jelić, in discussion with the author, November 2010. See also Velimir Ćurgus Kazimir, "The Photograph as Protection," in *Šetnja u mestu: građanski protest u Srbiji* [Walking on the spot: civil protest in Serbia], ed. Darka Radosavljević (Belgrade: B92, 1997), 11–28; Maša Vukanović, "SP '96/'97. BG. YU. FAC. TOTUM. Files: faktografija studentskog Protesta 1996/97" [Facts about the Student Protest 1996/97], in *O studentima i drugim demonima: etnografija studentskog protesta 1996/97* [The students and other demons: ethnography of the student protest 1996/97), eds. Jadranja Milanović and Vuk Šećerović (Belgrade: TODRA, 1997), 10–12.

21. Čedomir Antić, in discussion with the author, November 2010; Milan Milutinović, in discussion with the author, October 2010.

22. Vukanović, "SP '96/'97. BG. YU. FAC. TOTUM. Files," 13–23.

23. Čedomir Antić, in discussion with the author, November 2010.

24. Milena Dragićević-Šešić, in discussion with the author, September 2010; Pero Jelić, in discussion with the author, November 2010.

25. Vukanović, "SP '96/'97. BG. YU. FAC. TOTUM. Files," 14.

26. Pero Jelić, in discussion with the author, November 2010.

27. Milan Stefanović, in discussion with the author, October 2010; Mile Ilić, in discussion with the author, October 2010.

28. Milan Stefanović, in discussion with the author, October 2010; Mile Ilić, in discussion with the author, October 2010. See also Zoran Kosanović and Uroš Komlenović, "The Rebelled Nis: A Week without Mile," *VREME*, December, 14 1996, accessed September 12, 2010, http://www.scc.rutgers.edu/serbian_digest/.

29. Milan Stefanović, in discussion with the author, October 2010.

30. Boban Arsenijević, in discussion with the author, October 2010. However, Arsenijević admitted that during the meeting sessions, there were debates about whether or not students should "radicalize" their actions if the number of participants declined.

31. Stanko Lazendić, in discussion with the author, September 2010 and December 2010; Miloš Gagić, in discussion with the author, September 2010.

32. Aleksandar Savanović, in discussion with the author, October 2010.

33. See "These Feet Are Not So Small. They Hold Great Wisdom for Us All" [Ove noge nisu male, mnogima su pamet dale], produced by Aleksandar Davić, Tolnai Szabolcs, and Nenad Milošević (Belgrade: Studio B, 1997), news footage; *Boom!*, December 2, 1996, accessed October 20, 2010, http://www.yurope.com/mirrors/protest96/pmf/boom/boom 12_16/boom16.html; and *Boom!*, December 23, 1996, accessed October 20, 2010, http://www.yurope.com/ mirrors/protest96/pmf/boom/boom1223/boom23.html.

34. Dušan Juvanin, in discussion with the author, November 2010. This deliberate generation of a sense of uncertainty among the Serbian populace was noticeable in the SPS's slogan launched in the 1990 election: "With us, there is no uncertainty" (*s nama nema neizvesnosti*). See Eric D. Gordy, *The Culture of Power in Serbia: Nationalism and the Destruction of Alternatives* (University Park: Pennsylvania State Univ. Press, 1999), 33.

35. Dušan Juvanin, in discussion with the author, November 2010. Another reason for the opposition parties' deliberate use of nonviolence may be related to Zoran Đinđić. The Democratic Party leader had extensive knowledge of civil disobedience and other forms of nonviolent resistance. He had also witnessed these methods at work during the 1968 nonviolent uprising of students in the former Yugoslavia. See Mirjana Prosić-Dvornić, "The Topsy Turvy Days Were There Again: Student and Civil Protest in Belgrade and Serbia, 1996/1997," *Anthropology of East Europe Review* 16, no. 1 (1998), accessed September 21, 2010, http://www.scholarworks.iu.edu /journals/index.php/aeer/article /view Article/691.

36. Matthew Collin, *This Is Serbia Calling* (London: Serpent's Tail, 2001), 50.

37. Ivan Vejvoda, "Civil Society versus Slobodan Milošević: Serbia 1991–2000," in *Civil Resistance and Power Politics: The Experience of Non-Violent Action from Gandhi to the Present,* eds. Adam Roberts and Timothy Garton Ash (Oxford: Oxford Univ. Press, 2009), 299.

38. *Boom!,* December 2, 1996, [no author; no article title; passage begins "Students are no children . . ."], accessed October 20, 2010, http://www.yurope.com/mirrors/protest96/pmf/boom/boom12_02/boom02.html.

39. Milan Milutinović, in discussion with the author, October 2010; Pero Jelić, in discussion with the author, November 2010; Petar Milićević, in discussion with the author, November 2010; Vladimir Đumić, in discussion with the author, November 2010; Vojislav Milošević, in discussion with the author, November 2010. See also *Students' Index against Vote Hijackers* [Indeksima protivu otmičara], directed by Miodrag Jakšić and Aleksandra Simić (Belgrade: Studio B, 2006), DVD.

40. Čedomir Antić, in discussion with the author, November 2010.

41. Pero Jelić, in discussion with the author, November 2010.

42. See also Milena Dragićević-Šešić, "The Street as Political Space: Walking as Protest, Graffiti, and the Student Carnivalization of Belgrade." *New Theatre Quarterly* 17 (2001): 75.

43. Prošić-Dvornić, "The Topsy Turvy Days Were There Again."

44. Thomas, *Serbia under Milošević / Politics in the 1990s,* 287; Collin, *This Is Serbia Calling,* 111.

45. Vujović, "Protest as an Urban Phenomenon," 20; Ilić, "Hronika Protesta 'Zajedno'" [Chronicle of the Zajedno protest], 114.

46. Petar Milićević, in discussion with the author, November 2010; Vojislav Milošević, in discussion with the author, November 2010. See also Prošić-Dvornić, "The Topsy Turvy Days Were There Again," *Boom!,* November 28, 1996, accessed October 20, 2010, http://www.yurope.com/mirrors/protest96/pmf/boom/boom11_28/boom28.html.

47. Lazar Džamić, "Of Midgets and Giants," in *Šetnja u mestu: građanski protest u Srbiji* [Walking on the spot: civil protest in Serbia], ed. Darka Radosavljević (Belgrade: B92, 1997), 78–79.

48. Džamić, "Of Midgets and Giants," 89.

49. Dejan Sretenović, "Noise," in *Šetnja u mestu: građanski protest u Srbiji* [Walking on the spot: civil protest in Serbia], ed. Darka Radosavljević (Belgrade: B92, 1997), 86–94; *Poludeli ljudi* [Belgrade follies], directed by Goran Marković (Belgrade: B92, 1997), documentary film.

50. Džamić, "Of Midgets and Giants," 82; Prošić-Dvornić, "The Topsy Turvy Days Were There Again"; and Collin, *This Is Serbia Calling,* 108.

51. Dragićević-Šešić, "The Street as Political Space," 78.

52. Vladimir Đumić, in discussion with the author, November 2010.

53. Suzana Jovanić, in discussion with the author, September 2010. Making noise to drown out the state's propaganda had also been undertaken in earlier nonviolent protests in Chile, Nepal, and Poland. See Paul Routledge, "Backstreets, Barricades, and Blackouts: Urban Terrains of Resistance in Nepal," *Environment and Planning: Society and Space* 12

(1994): 568–69; Stef Jansen, "Victims, Underdogs and Rebels: Discursive Practices of Resistances in Serbian Protest," *Critique of Anthropology* 20 (2000): 415; and *A Force More Powerful: A Century of Nonviolent Conflict*, episode two, directed by Jack DuVall and Peter Ackerman (Columbus, OH: Santa Monica Pictures LLC and A Force More Powerful Films, 1999–2000), multi-part documentary, DVD.

54. Stef Jansen, "The Streets of Beograd. Urban Space, and Protest Identities in Serbia," *Political Geography* 20 (2001), 51; Vesna Bjekić, "Investigation: '96 Protest under Magnifying Glass of Sociologists: "Time has Come to Replace Sloba," *AIM*, January 2, 1997, accessed April 24, 2011, http://www.aimpress.ch/dyn/trae/archive/data/199701/70102-006-trae-beo.html.

55. Collin, *This Is Serbia Calling*, 99–100, 106; Dragićević-Šešić, "The Street as Political Space," 77.

56. Siniša Šikman, in discussion with the author, September 2010. See also The Balkan Peace Team, "The Protests in Belgrade and throughout Yugoslavia."

57. *Belgrade Follies* [Podeli ljudi], directed by Marković; Collin, *This Is Serbia Calling*, 106.

58. Ilić, "Hronika Protesta 'Zajedno'" [Chronicle of the Zajedno protest], 118; Aleksandra Jovićević, "Everybody Laughed: Civil and Student Protest in Serbia 1996–97, between Theater, Paratheature and Carnival," in *Šetnja u mestu: građanski protest u Srbiji* [Walking on the spot: civil protest in Serbia], ed. Darka Radosavljević (Belgrade: B92, 1997), 58.

59. Thomas, *Serbia under Milošević / Politics in the 1990s*, 308–9.

60. Vujović, "Protest as an Urban Phenomenon," 201.

61. Jovićević, "Everybody Laughed," 55.

62. Dragićević-Šešić, "The Street as Political Space," 78.

63. Vujović, "Protest as an Urban Phenomenon," 203–4.

64. Ivan Marović, in discussion with the author, November 2010. See also *Students' Index against Vote Hijackers* [Indeksima protivu otmičara], directed by Jakšić and Simić, DVD.

65. Prošić-Dvornić, "The Topsy Turvy Days Were There Again."

66. Jansen, "Victims, Underdogs and Rebels," 49. See also Vujović, "Protest as an Urban Phenomenon," 203.

67. Marina Blagojević, "The Walks in a Gender Perspective," in *Protest in Belgrade: Winter of Discontent*, ed. Mladen Lazić (Budapest: Central European Univ. Press, 1999), 121.

68. Milan Milutinović, in discussion with the author, October 2010. See also Jansen, "Victims, Underdogs and Rebels," 398. The way police officers were voted on was also quite hilarious. The police identification numbers became the vote number of each officer. In order to vote, students and other protest participants would look at the police officer's "belts" and write down the numbers on paper.

69. Ivan Blagojević, "Moratorijum (19.1.97 - 27.1.97)" [Moratorium]. In *O studentima i drugim demonima: etnografi ja studentskog protesta 1996/97* [The students and other demons: ethnography of the student protest 1996/97], edited by Jadranja Milanović and Vuk Šećerović (Belgrade: TODRA, 1997), 97; Ilić, "Hronika Protesta 'Zajedno'" [Chronicle of the Zajedno protest], 130.

70. Milena Dragićević-Šešić, "The Iconography and Slogans of Civil Society and Civil Protest 96/97," in *Civil Society in the Countries in Transition*, ed. Nadia Skenderović (Subotica, Serbia: Agency of Local Democracy Center, Subotica and Open Univ. Subotica, 1999), 531.

71. Gordy, *The Culture of Power in Serbia*, 50.

72. Dragićević-Šešić, "The Iconography and Slogans of Civil Society and Civil Protest 96/97," 531–32.

73. Dragićević-Šešić, "The Iconography and Slogans of Civil Society and Civil Protest 96/97," 536; Collin, *This Is Serbia Calling*, 106.

74. Students of Belgrade University and of University of Arts, *Beograd je svet: studentski protest '96* [Belgrade is the world: student protest '96] (Belgrade: Ušće-Print [Fast Print], 1996), n.p.

75. Dragićević-Šešić, "The Iconography and Slogans of Civil Society and Civil Protest 96/97," 535–36.

76. Students of Belgrade University and of University of Arts, *Beograd je svet* [Belgrade is the world], n.p.

77. Ibid.

78. Dragićević-Šešić, "The Iconography and Slogans of Civil Society and Civil Protest 96/97," 536. The latter slogan also referred to the caution given by "Tito," who always patronizingly called students his "children." "Mira" is the nickname of Mirjana Marković. During the protests, she was frequently insulted as a "hen." In Serbia, referring to a woman as a hen is offensive, since this implies the woman is unintelligent.

79. Ivan Čolović, "Reading a Handful of Serbian Palms," in *Šetnja u mestu: građanski protest u Srbiji* [Walking on the spot: civil protest in Serbia], ed. Darka Radosavljević (Belgrade: B92, 1997), 62–74.

80. Students of Belgrade University and of University of Arts, *Beograd je svet* [Belgrade is the world], n.p.

81. Ibid.

82. Čolović, "Reading a Handful of Serbian Palms," 65.

83. Collin, *This Is Serbia Calling*, 118; Vujović, "Protest as an Urban Phenomenon," 202.

84. Slaviša Lekić, *Svi u napad iz BGD protesta '96* [All in the attack from Belgrade's protest '96], vol. 1 (Belgrade: BiS Press, 1997), 80.

85. Students of Belgrade University and of University of Arts, *Beograd je svet* [Belgrade is the world], n.p., italics added.

86. Vojislav Milošević, in discussion with the author, November 2010.

87. Lekić, *Svi u napad iz BGD protesta '96* [All in the attack from Belgrade's protest '96] , vol. 1, 48; Dragićević-Šešić, "The Iconography and Slogans of Civil Society and Civil Protest 96/97," 536; and Collin, *This Is Serbia Calling*, 110.

88. Čolović, "Reading a Handful of Serbian Palms," 62.

89. Students of Belgrade University and of University of Arts, *Beograd je svet* [Belgrade is the world], n.p., italics added.

90. Collin, *This Is Serbia Calling*, 106.

91. Čolović, "Reading a Handful of Serbian Palms," 71; Dragićević-Šešić, "The Iconography and Slogans of Civil Society and Civil Protest 96/97," 536. There were two contexts for interpreting this satire. During World War II the Nazis occupied Serbia and other Yugoslav states, and carried out killings of civilians. Serbs or Yugoslavs cooperating with the Nazi government in this period were often referred to as "traitors." This label had been employed to justify the state prosecution of dissidents. Another context which gave rise to the hypocrisy of the Milošević regime was its adoption of the Deutschmark as an official currency alongside the dinar. This policy was implemented in 1993 to curb hyper-inflation.

92. Dragićević-Šešić, "The Iconography and Slogans of Civil Society and Civil Protest 96/97," 536.

93. Čolović, "Reading a Handful of Serbian Palms," 67.

94. Tim Judah, *The Serbs: History, Myth and the Destruction of Yugoslavia* (New Haven, CT: Yale Univ. Press, 2009), 162. See more in Nebojša Vladisavljević, *Serbia's Anti-Bureaucratic Revolution: Milošević, the Fall of Communism and Nationalist Mobilization* (New York: Palgrave Macmillan, 2008), 109–43.

95. Dragićević-Šešić, "The Iconography and Slogans of Civil Society and Civil Protest 96/97," 532.

96. Collin, *This Is Serbia Calling*, 106.

97. Ibid., italics added.

98. Vladimir Đumić, in discussion with the author, November 2010, Belgrade, Serbia. See also Students of Belgrade University and of University of Arts, *Beograd je svet* [Belgrade is the world], n.p.

99. Čolović, "Reading a Handful of Serbian Palms," 66.

100. Dragićević-Šešić, "The Street as Political Space," 78–79; Thomas, *Serbia under Milošević / Politics in the 1990s*, 308; and Collin, *This Is Serbia Calling*, 206. It should be noted that a few days later, the same action was launched in the center of Belgrade, but with a smaller number of participants. As a result, traffic-jammers were assaulted by the police. See Branka Kaljević, "Police Torture in Belgrade: Brutal Beating Up of Citizens," *AIM*, December 31, 1996, accessed April 24, 2011, http://www.aimpress.ch/dyn/trae/archive/data/199612/61231-002-trae-beo.html.

101. Pero Jelić, in discussion with the author, November 2010. See also Vujović, "Protest as an Urban Phenomenon," 204; Dragićević-Šešić, "The Street as Political Space," 78.

102. *Boom!*, December 23, 1996, accessed October 20, 2010, http://www.yurope.com/mirrors/protest96/pmf/boom/boom12_23/boom23.html.

103. Jansen, "The Streets of Beograd: Urban Space, and Protest Identities in Serbia," 44.

104. Vujović, "Protest as an Urban Phenomenon," 201; Pravdić, "Student Performances," 41; and Dragićević-Šešić, "The Street as Political Space," 76.

105. Vujović, "Protest as an Urban Phenomenon," 202; Pravdić, "Student Performances," 41; and Dragićević-Šešić, "The Street as Political Space," 76.

106. Roksanda Ninčić, "Down by Law," *VREME*, December 14, 1996, accessed September 20, 2010, http://www.scc.rutgers.edu/serbian_digest/; Pravdić, "Student Performances," 41; and Dragićević-Šešić, "The Street as Political Space," 77.

107. Srđa Popović, in discussion with the author, September 2010. See also Branka Kaljević, "'96 Students' Protest: We Know What We Want," *AIM*, December 3, 1996, accessed April 24, 2011, http://www.aimpress.ch/dyn/trae/archive/data/199612/61205-004-trae-beo .html; and Ninčić, "Down by Law."

108. The context of the statement can be traced back to the rise of the Communist Party and its cooperation with the Allies during the Second World War, in which it outpaced the royalists or *četnik* in killing German occupiers. See Judah, *The Serbs*, 114–34.

109. Ivan Marović, in discussion with the author, November 2010; Pero Jelić, in discussion with the author, November 2010. See also Dragićević-Šešić, "The Street as Political Space," 79; and Jansen, "Victims, Underdogs and Rebels," 379.

110. Pero Jelić, in discussion with the author, November 2010. See also Dragićević-Šešić, "The Street as Political Space," 78.

111. *Boom!*, February 8, 1997, accessed October 20, 2010, http://www.yurope.com/mir rors/protest96/pmf/boom/boom02_08/boom08.html.

112. Nenad Konstantinović, in discussion with the author, November 2010; Siniša Šikman, in discussion with the author, September 2010. See also Milan Milošević, "The Civic Movement: Civic Resistance, Month One," *VREME*, December, 21 1996, accessed September 12, 1996, http://www.scc.rutgers.edu/serbian_digest/; Pravdić, "Student Performances," 41; and Prošić-Dvornić, "The Topsy Turvy Days Were There Again."

113. Jovićević, "Everybody Laughed," 52; Jansen, "The Streets of Beograd. Urban Space, and Protest Identities in Serbia," 43.

114. Pedrag Lečić, in discussion with the author, September 2010. See also *Boom!*, February 24, 1997, accessed October 20, 2010, http://www.yurope.com/mirrors/protest96 /pmf/boom/boom02_24/boom24.html.

115. Milan Milutinović, in discussion with the author, October 2010.

116. Pero Jelić, in discussion with the author, November 2010. See also Dragićević-Šešić, "The Street as Political Space," 79; Milošević, "The Civic Movement."

117. Milan Milutinović, in discussion with the author, October 2010; Siniša Šikman, in discussion with the author, September 2010. See also Maša Radonić, "Chronology of the Student Protest 96/97," in *Šetnja u mestu: građanski protest u Srbiji* [Walking on the spot: civil protest in Serbia], ed. Darka Radosavljević (Belgrade: B92, 1997), 131–32; and Dragićević-Šešić, "The Street as Political Space," 80.

118. Ivan Marović, in discussion with the author, November 2010.

119. See, for example, James M. Jasper, "The Emotions of Protest: Affective and Reactive Emotions in and around Social Movements," *Sociological Forum* 13, no. 3 (1998): 397–424.

120. Helena Flam, "Anger in Repressive Regime: A Footnote to Domination and the Arts of Resistance by James Scott," *European Journal of Social Theory* 7, no. 2 (2004): 183–84.

121. Leroy H. Pelton, *The Psychology of Nonviolence* (New York: Pergamon, 1974), 186.

122. Robert Burrowes, *The Strategy of Nonviolent Defense: A Gandhian Approach* (Albany: State Univ. of New York Press, 1996), 221.

123. Pelton, *The Psychology of Nonviolence*, 143, 199–204.

124. Richard B. Gregg, *The Power of Non-Violence* (London: George Routledge and Sons, 1935), 53.

125. Gene Sharp, *Social Power and Political Freedom* (Boston: Porter Sargent, 1980), 4; Gene Sharp, "What Are the Options for Action for Believers in Principled Nonviolence?," *Ahimsa Nonviolence* 1, no. 3 (2005): 197–203.

126. See, for example, Burrowes, *The Strategy of Nonviolent Defense*, 235–38; Gene Sharp, *Waging Nonviolent Struggle: 20th Century Practice and 21st Century Potential* (Boston: Porter Sargent, 2005), 390–94; and Erica Chenoweth and Maria J. Stephen, *Why Civil Resistance Works: The Strategic Logic of Nonviolent Conflict* (New York: Columbia Univ. Press), 57–58.

127. Borka Pavićević, in discussion with the author, September 2010; Petar Milićević, in discussion with the author, November 2010; Suzana Jovanić, in discussion with the author, September 2010; Vladimir Đumić, in discussion with the author, November 2010.

128. Dragićević-Šešić, "The Street as Political Space," 85, italics added.

129. Prošić-Dvornić, "Enough! Student Protest '92."

4. Fighting Milošević with Otpor's Clenched Fist

1. Robert Thomas, *Serbia under Milošević / Politics in the 1990s* (London: Hurst, 1999), 335–38. Prior to this, Milošević's term as the Serbian president had already elapsed, having served the two terms that the Constitution allowed. Instead of clinging to the Serbian presidency, Milošević took steps to further secure his power by having himself "elected" as the Yugoslav president. As a part of the remaining Federal Republic of Yugoslavia (FRY), Montenegro, represented by the Democratic Party of Socialists of Montenegro (Demokratska partija socijalista Crne Gore or "DSP"), protested this move. Nevertheless, Milošević arranged for the federal assembly meeting to hold the election of the new Yugoslav president. Representatives from Serbia's Left Coalition (SPS, JUL, and ND), defectors from the Montenegrin DSP and Vojislav Šešelj's SRS voted for Milošević. Representatives from the opposition coalition were absent from the meeting because of the opposition campaign to ban the whole federal assembly since its inception in November 1996.

2. Ibid., 342.

3. Lenard J. Cohen, *Serpent in the Bosom: The Rise and Fall of Slobodan Milošević* (Boulder, CO: Westview, 2002), 261.

4. Thomas, *Serbia under Milošević / Politics in the 1990s*, 320–24.

5. The division along the lines of their election stance, with pro- and anti-boycott groups, could also be discerned in student organizations founded after the 1996–97 protests.

On the one hand, numerous student leaders, such as Čedomir Jovanović and Čedomir Antić, who founded the Student Political Club, were active as members of the DS. Accordingly, this wing of student leaders supported Đinđić's decision to boycott the elections. On the other hand, students who spearheaded the Student Parliament (e.g., Slobodan Homen and Nenad Konstantinović) thought that the election was the only legal way to oust Milošević. Therefore, their "Stop the Tyranny" campaign aimed to mobilize votes throughout Serbia, including Kosovo, in support of the opposition coalition to defeat Milošević in the election.

6. The conflict between the DS and the SPO spread to local politics. For instance, on August 15, 1997, during the DS-led rally in Kraljevo, there was a clash between supporters of the two parties.

7. Thomas, *Serbia under Milošević / Politics in the 1990s*, 350–52. The assembly meeting was held without the presence of the DS and GSS representatives. Later, the SPO justified the ousting of Đinđić on the ground that he "abused his office by using his position as mayor of Belgrade in order to promote the campaign to boycott the election."

8. Cohen, *Serpent in the Bosom*, 262.

9. BETA (online news service), August 3, 1997, quoted in Thomas, *Serbia under Milošević / Politics in the 1990s*, 351.

10. Laslo Sekelj, "Parties and Elections: The Federal Republic of Yugoslavia. Change without Transformation," *Europe-Asia Studies* 52, no. 1 (2000): 70.

11. Human Rights Watch, "Deepening Authoritarianism in Serbia and the Purges of the Universities," *Human Rights Watch* 11, no. 2 (January 1999), accessed December 12, 2010, http://www.hrw.org/legacy/reports/1999/serbia/, 15.

12. Human Rights Watch, "Deepening Authoritarianism in Serbia and the Purges of the Universities," 17.

13. Sabrina P. Ramet, *Balkan Babel: The Disintegration of Yugoslavia from the Death of Tito to the Fall of Milošević* (Boulder, CO: Westview, 2002), 341.

14. Ibid., 341. In addition, the law prohibited any private radio and television station from "broadcast[ing] to an audience of more than 25 percent of the 10.5 million population."

15. Cohen, *Serpent in the Bosom*, 399.

16. Ramet, *Balkan Babel*, 353.

17. Milica Bjelovuk, "Rađanje Otpora u Srbiji" [The birth of Otpor in Serbia], *Glas javnosti*, January 11, 2001, accessed October 20, 2010, http://arhiva.glas-javnosti.co.yu/arhiva /2001.

18. Ramet, *Balkan Babel*, 346. See also Howard Clark, "The Limits of Prudence: Civil Resistance in Kosovo, 1990–98," in *Civil Resistance and Power Politics: The Experiences of Non-Violent Action from Gandhi to the Present*, eds. Adam Roberts and Timothy Garton Ash (Oxford: Oxford University Press, 2009), 277–95; Tim Judah, *The Serbs: History, Myth and the Destruction of Yugoslavia* (New Haven and London: Yale University Press, 2009), 320.

19. Judah, *The Serbs*, 322.

20. Human Rights Watch, "The Crisis in Kosovo" (February 2000), accessed April 2, 2010, http://www.hrw.org/legacy/reports/2000/nato/Natbm200-01.html. See also the Independent International Commission on Kosovo, *The Kosovo Report: Conflict, International Response, Lessons Learned* (Oxford: Oxford University Press, 2000).

21. Ivan Čolović, *The Politics of Identity in Serbia* (New York: New York University Press, 2002), 24–25.

22. Ramet, *Balkan Babel*, 310.

23. Judah, *The Serbs*, 328.

24. Human Rights Watch, "Deepening Authoritarianism in Serbia and the Purges of the Universities," 7.

25. Velimir Ćurgus Kazimir, "From Islands to the Mainland," in *The Last Decade: Serbian Citizens in the Struggle for Democracy and an Open Society, 1991–2001*, ed. Velimir Ćurgus Kazimir (Belgrade: Media Center, 2001), 28.

26. Human Rights Watch, "Deepening Authoritarianism in Serbia and the Purges of the Universities," 7.

27. Ramet, *Balkan Babel*, 342; International Press Institute, "Slavko Ćuruvija," accessed on April 10, 2011, http://www.freemedia.at/our-activities/justice-denied/impunity/slavko-curuvija/.

28. Matthew Collin, *This Is Serbia Calling* (London: Serpent's Tail, 2001), 156.

29. It should be noted that the original motivation behind the design of the clenched fist emblem was romantic rather than heroic. According to one anecdote, Nenad Petrović Duda drew a black and white graphic image of the clenched fist for an "Otpor girl" that he fell for. See Milica Bjelovuk, "Pesnica stvorena iz ljubavi" [The fist created out of love], *Glas javnosti*, January 12, 2001, accessed October 20, 2010, http://arhiva.glasjavnosti.co.yu/arhiva/2001.

30. Ivan Marović, in discussion with the author, November 2010; Marko Simić, in discussion with the author, November 2010. See also Bjelovuk, "Rađanje Otpora u Srbiji" [The birth of Otpor in Serbia]; CANVAS, "Ten Years Smarter?: Chronology of Events—A Brief History of Otpor" (Belgrade: Center for Applied Non-Violent Action and Strategies (CANVAS), 2008).

31. CANVAS, "Ten Years Smarter?" Although no arrest was made on the spot, Popović was captured and tortured by police from a special unit on the following day. See Human Rights Watch, "Deepening Authoritarianism in Serbia and the Purges of the Universities," 27.

32. Stanko Lazendić, in discussion with the author, September 2010. See also Alexandar Pavlović, "Spisak akcija Novosadskog Otpor-a" [Personal records of Otpor's action in Novi Sad].

33. Nenad Konstantinović, in discussion with the author, November 2010. See also CANVAS, "Ten Years Smarter? Otpor—Concepts and Meanings" (Belgrade: Center for Applied Non-Violent Action and Strategies (CANVAS), 2008).

34. Joshua Paulson, "Removing the Dictator in Serbia—1996–2000," in *Waging Non-violent Struggle: 20th Century Practice and 21st Century Potential*, eds. Christopher A. Miller, Hardy Merriman, and Gene Sharp (Boston: Porter Sargent, 2005), 317; Danijela Nenadić and Nenad Belčević, "Serbia—Nonviolent Struggle for Democracy: The Role of Otpor," in *People Power: Unarmed Resistance and Global Solidarity*, ed. Howard Clark (London and New York: Pluto, 2009), 27; and Olena Nikolayenko, "The Learning Curve: Student Protests in Serbia, 1991–2000," paper presented at the the Eleventh Annual Graduate Workshop, Kokkalis Program on Southeastern and East-Central Europe, Harvard University, Cambridge, MA, February 12–13, 2009, 17–18. These three sources all claimed that the goals of Otpor were free and fair elections, the abolition of the university law, and the abolition of the media law. A problem, however, is that these sources do little to differentiate between the means and goals, and the different stages of the radicalization of Otpor's goals. Otpor's leading activists conceived free and fair elections as an instrument to remove Slobodan Milošević legally. The anti-regime campaigns were fundamentally a program to convince the Serbian populace to vote against Milošević. The abolition of the two draconian laws was the initial goal of Otpor, which became radicalized after the movement gained increasing support from the international community.

35. Ivan Marović, in discussion with the author, November 2010.

36. Collin, *This Is Serbia Calling*, 178–79; Roger Cohen, "Who Really Brought Down Milosevic," *New York Times Magazine*, November 26, 2000, accessed October 20, 2010, http://www.nytimes.com/2000/11/26/magazine/whoreallybroughtdownmilosevichtml?scp=3&sq= OTPOR&st=cse&pagewanted=4&pagewanted=print ().

37. Vladimir Ilić, "The Popular Movement Otpor—Between Europe and Re-Traditionalization," Helsinki files, no.5, n.d., Policy Documentation Center, Center for Policy Studies, Central European University, Budapest, accessed October 20, 2010, http://www.pdc.ceu.hu/archive/00005016/01/Files05.doc.

38. Stanko Lazendić, in discussion with the author, December 2010. See also Ilić, "The Popular Movement Otpor—Between Europe and Re-Traditionalization."

39. Dušan Kočić, in discussion with the author, December 2010; Vladimir Stojković, in discussion with the author, November 2010. See also Nenadić and Belčević, "Serbia—Nonviolent Struggle for Democracy," 29.

40. Goran Dašković, in discussion with the author, December 2010; Marko Simić, in discussion with the author, November 2010; Dušan Pešić, in discussion with the author, November 2010.

41. Ilić, "The Popular Movement Otpor—Between Europe and Re-Traditionalization."

42. Ibid.; Ivana Franović, "Serbia Eight Years After," in *People Power: Unarmed Resistance and Global Solidarity*, ed. Howard Clark (London and New York: Pluto Press, 2009), 38.

43. Ivan Marović, in discussion with the author, November 2010.

44. See, for instance, the Independent International Commission on Kosovo, *The Kosovo Report*, 86; Ivan Vejvoda, "Civil Society versus Slobodan Milošević: Serbia 1991–2000," in *Civil Resistance and Power Politics: The Experience of Non-Violent Action from Gandhi to the Present*, eds. Adam Roberts and Timothy Garton Ash (Oxford: Oxford Univ. Press, 2009), 310–11.

45. Paulson, "Removing the Dictator in Serbia—1996–2000," 321. It should be noted that Otpor received financial support from the United States only after the NATO intervention in 1999. Slobodan Homen notes that in 1998 he asked for "two hundred US dollars" in the meeting with the US mission in Belgrade in order to print "some posters with Milošević's face on them." The US official denied the request on the ground that they "couldn't fund such a campaign that was directly involved with politics." See Matthew Collin, *The Time of the Rebels: Youth Resistance Movements and 21st Century Revolutions* (London: Serpent's Tail, 2007), 25.

46. Nenad Konstantinović, in discussion with the author, November 2010.

47. Vejvoda, "Civil Society versus Slobodan Milošević," 310. Vejvoda details how the vote campaigns were stimulated by the Bratislava process, which began as early as July 1999. The meeting was held in Bratislava, Slovakia, under the auspices of a Slovak NGO and governmental circles and the EastWest Institute from New York, with the participation of Serbian democratic parties, NGO leaders, union, and independent journalists. This led to the formation of a broad coalition across nongovernmental sectors and opposition parties. The creation of the Democratic Opposition of Serbia was a product of this process.

48. On August 4, 2000, DOS finally nominated Vojislav Koštunica as the candidate for the presidential election to be held on September 20. See Milan Milošević, "Koštunica na prkosima" [Koštunica in Defiance], *VREME* (August 26, 2000), accessed September 20, 2010, http://www.vreme.com/arhiva_html/503/index.html.

49. Ivan Marović, in discussion with the author, November 2010; Nenad Konstantinović in discussion with author, November 2010; Siniša Šikman, in discussion with the author, September 2010; Srđa Popović, in discussion with the author, September 2010.

50. Srđan Milivojević, in discussion with the author, September 2010.

51. Robertino Knjur, in discussion with the author, October 2010.

52. Anne M. Lucas, "Strategic Nonviolence and Humor: Their Synergy and Its Limitations" (bachelor's thesis, Kent State University Honors College, 2010), 114.

53. Ivan Marović, in discussion with the author, November 2010.

54. A statement of villagers in the southern town of Vladičin Han reflected this psyche: "If Milošević goes, everything will fall apart. Somebody will bomb us, the Kosovo Albanians will take our land, all hell will break loose. So we voted for him." See Cohen, "Who Really Brought Down Milošević."

55. Nenad Konstantinović, in discussion with the author, November 2010.

56. Milja Jovanović, in discussion with the author, November 2010.

57. Ivan Marović, in discussion with the author, November 2010.

58. Milja Jovanović, in discussion with the author, November 2010. See also Paul Hockenos, "Serbia's New Wave," *In These Times* (March 5, 2001), accessed October 20, 2010, http://www.inthesetimes.com/ issue/25/07/hockenos2507.html.

59. Steve York, "How Did We Succeed: Superior Propaganda for Advertising Freedom" (excerpt from an interview with Steve York), Centre for Applied Non-Violent Action and Strategies (CANVAS) (website), November 30, 2000, accessed March 4, 2010, http://www.canvasopedia.org/legacy/content/serbian_case/Otpor_propaganda.html.

60. York, "How Did We Succeed."

61. Milja Jovanović, in discussion with the author, November 2010.

62. Peter Ackerman and Jack DuVall, "Sticker Shock," excerpt of "The New World of Power" in *A Force More Powerful: A Century of Nonviolent Conflict* (2001), accessed May 25, 2011, http://www.aforcemorepowerful.org/films/bdd/story/otpor/sticker-shock.php; CANVAS, *CANVAS Core Curriculum: A Guide to Effective Nonviolent Struggle* (Belgrade, Serbia: Center for Applied Non-Violent Action and Strategies (CANVAS), 2007), 126.

63. Nenad Konstantinović, in discussion with the author, November 2010.

64. Nenadić and Belčević, "Serbia—Nonviolent Struggle for Democracy," 29.

65. Regarding the legal document from the Serbian Ministry of Internal Affairs that outlawed Otpor as a terrorist organization, see Humanitarian Law Center, "Police Crackdown on Otpor, Report No. 31" (Belgrade: Humanitarian Law Center, 2001), 12.

66. Nemanja Crnić, in discussion with the author, October 2010.

67. There are different estimates of the numbers of Otpor activists. Konstantinović estimates that 100,000 activists worked for Otpor's campaigns by the end of 2000, while Olena Nikolayenko in her conference paper estimates that 70,000 were active at the time of the election in September 2000. However, Šikman argues that an estimate of 80,000 registered activists is only a perception. Vladimir Ilić similarly concluded that numbering activists at 60,000 was "an over-estimation." Joshua Paulson, Danijela Nenadić, and Nenad Belčević estimate that between May and September 2000, Otpor members may have ranged between 20,000 and 30,000. Ivan Vejvoda estimates that Otpor comprised 18,000 activists, the lowest such estimate. See Ilić, "The Popular Movement Otpor—Between Europe and Re-Traditionalization"; Paulson, "Removing the Dictator in Serbia—1996–2000," 322; Nenadić and Belčević, "Serbia—Nonviolent Struggle for Democracy," 29; Vejvoda, "Civil Society versus Slobodan Milošević," 308; and Nikolayenko, "The Learning Curve, 1991–2000," 4.

68. Miloš Gagić, in discussion with the author, September 2010; Stanko Lazendić, in discussion with the author, December 2010.

69. Dušan Kočić, in discussion with the author, December 2010; Siniša Šikman, in discussion with the author, September 2010; Zoran Matović, in discussion with the author, November 2010. While the principle of "doing actions in a nonviolent way" was encouraged among local activists, there were situations when things got out of hand. For instance, Dušan Kočić, an Otpor coordinator from Smederevo, admits that some young activists

under his supervision believed that retaliation against police repression was justified. In a similar vein, Zoran Matović notes that it was difficult to explain to young activists why they should refrain from a violent reaction to police abuse, and he came across cases of activists' vandalism.

70. Ivan Marović, in discussion with the author, November 2010; Srđa Popović, in discussion with the author, September 2010.

71. Siniša Šikman, in discussion with the author, September 2010; Srđa Popović, in discussion with the author, September 2010; Zoran Matović, in discussion with the author, November 2010. See also Paulson, "Removing the Dictator in Serbia—1996–2000," 321–23.

72. Srđa Popović, in discussion with the author, September 2010. See also Ilić, "The Popular Movement Otpor—Between Europe and Re-Traditionalization."

73. Ivan Marović, in discussion with the author, November 2010; Siniša Šikman, in discussion with the author, September 2010. This idea was developed from Tito's partisan movement during the Second World War. Marović notes that in liberating villages under the occupation of Nazi troops, the communist rebels established the "Popular Committee." Committee members went to villages that were still free from Nazi occupation and encouraged locals to select their own leaders to run a Nazi resistance unit. When Nazi soldiers reached these areas, they found that local self-defense forces were already organized.

74. Čedomir Antić, in discussion with the author, November 2010; Milan Milutinović, in discussion with the author, October 2010; Pero Jelić, in discussion with the author, November 2010.

75. Ivan Marović, in discussion with the author, November 2010.

76. Ibid.

77. Siniša Šikman, in discussion with the author, September 2010.

78. Čedomir Antić, in discussion with the author, November 2010; Milan Milutinović, in discussion with the author, October 2010; Milena Dragićević-Šešić, in discussion with the author, September 2010; Pero Jelić, in discussion with the author, November 2010; Suzana Jovanić, in discussion with the author, September 2010.

79. Srđa Popović, in discussion with the author, September 2010.

80. Dalibor Glišović, in discussion with the author, November 2010; Milja Jovanović, in discussion with the author, November 2010; Petar Lacmanović, in discussion with the author, November 2010; Stanko Lazendić, in discussion with the author, September 2010.

81. Čedomir Antić, in discussion with the author, October 2010. The majority of former student activists whom I interviewed often mentioned that they heard about the funny actions performed by students in Belgrade. However, some said that it was not possible to repeat these actions in their cities or towns because the scale of protest was much smaller than Belgrade. Moreover, they pointed out that the use of humor was more necessary in Belgrade than in their areas because of the heavy presence of riot police in the capital city. By staging humorous protests, demonstrators could portray themselves as nonthreatening to the police officers.

82. Siniša Šikman, in discussion with the author, September 2010.

83. This number is based on the estimate of activists running the branches in key regional cities such as Novi Sad, Kragujevac, Užice, Kraljevo, and Leskovac. It should be noted that in smaller towns there might not be as many humorous protest actions staged throughout Otpor's campaigns. The local dynamics of the use of humor will be examined in chapter 6.

84. Nikolayenko, "The Learning Curve," 4. Paulson suggested that "over 100" Otpor branches may have been established in May 2000. See Paulson, "Removing the Dictator in Serbia—1996–2000," 322.

5. Strategic Humor

1. In Serbian, *setva* means sowing and *smena* means change, dismissal, and purge. As these two words rhyme, activists twisted the title of the regime's policy to name their own action, mocking the regime's policy. This approach to planning street protests appeared frequently in later Otpor actions.

2. Milja Jovanović, in discussion with the author, November 2010.

3. Siniša Šikman, in discussion with the author, September 2010.

4. Siniša Šikman, in discussion with the author, September 2010.

5. Ivan Marović, in discussion with the author, November 2010; Srđa Popović, in discussion with the author, September 2010. However, at the end of October 1999, Branko Ilić and Vukašin Petrović were arrested on site at one action the day after Ilić had announced the rally for pensioners would occur. See Ivan Marović and Dejan Ranđić, "Resistance (Otpor!) Info: After the Action 'Dinar for His Resignation' Two Activists of Otpor Have Been Taken into Custody," accessed March 4, 2010, http://groups.yahoo.com/group/balkans/message/353?l=1; Milica Bjelovuk, "Jedan dinar u zamenu za slobodu" [One dinar in exchange of freedom], *Glas javnosti*, January 14, 2001, accessed October 20, 2010, http://arhiva.glasjavnosti.co.yu/arhiva/2001.

6. "Studenski pokret 'Otpor': dinar za smenu" [The student movement Otpor: dinar for a change], *Danas*, October 11, 1999.

7. Human Rights Watch, "The Crisis in Kosovo," *Human Rights Watch*, February 10, 2000, accessed April 2, 2010, http://www.hrw.org/legacy/reports/2000/nato/Natbm200-01.html.

8. Aleksandar Pavlović, in discussion with the author, October 2010; Miloš Gagić, in discussion with the author, September 2010; Stanko Lazendić, in discussion with the author, September 2010. See also Aleksandar Pavlović, "Spisak akcija Novosadskog Otpor-a" [Personal records of Otpor's action in Novi Sad]; Matthew Collin, *The Time of the Rebels: Youth Resistance Movements and 21st Century Revolutions* (London: Serpent's Tail, 2007), 22–23.

9. "Akcija studentskog pokreta 'Otpor' u Novom Sadu" [Actions of the student movement Otpor in Novi Sad], *Danas*, November 5, 1999.

10. Robertino Knjur, in discussion with the author, October 2010.

11. Zoran Matović, in discussion with the author, November 2010.

12. "Message in a Bottle by 'Otpor' to President Milošević," *Blic*, April 21, 2000, accessed October 20, 2010, http://www.blic.rs/stara_arhiva/naslovna/129782/Message-in -a-bottle-by-Otpor-to-President-Milosevic.

13. Vladimir Marović, in discussion with the author, December 2010.

14. Goran Dašković, in discussion with the author, December 2010.

15. Dušan Pešić, in discussion with the author, November 2010; Vladimir Stojković, in discussion with the author, November 2010.

16. Aleksandar Pavlović, in discussion with the author, October 2010; Aleksandar Savanović, in discussion with the author, October 2010; Stanko Lazendić, in discussion with the author, September 2010.

17. Dalibor Glišović, in discussion with the author, November 2010. See also Dalibor Glišović, "Otpor! Actions—Aleksandrovac (District of Župa)" (personal records).

18. *Danas*, March 13, 2000, cited in Vladimir Ilić, "The Popular Movement Otpor— Between Europe and Re-Traditionalization," Helsinki files, no. 5, n.d., Policy Documentation Center, Center for Policy Studies, Central European University, Budapest, accessed October 20, 2010, www.pdc.ceu.hu/archive/00005016/01/Files05.doc.

19. Petar Lacmanović, personal records of street actions by Otpor Zrenjanin. The translation of the "fine certificate" from Serbian to English was provided by Lacmanović.

20. Petar Lacmanović, in discussion with the author, November 2010; Petar Lacmanović, e-mail message to author, May 7, 2011.

21. Željko Trifunović, in discussion with the author, November 2010.

22. *Blic*, March 30, 2000, cited in Ilić, "The Popular Movement Otpor—Between Europe and Re-Traditionalization."

23. Marko Simić, in discussion with the author, November 2010.

24. Petar Lacmanović, in discussion with the author, November 2010.

25. CANVAS, "Ten Years Smarter? Otpor—Concepts and Meanings" (Belgrade: Center for Applied Non-Violent Action and Strategies (CANVAS), 2008); Otpor, "Popular Movement Otpor (Resistance)," in *The Last Decade: Serbian Citizens in the Struggle for Democracy and an Open Society*, eds. Velimir Ćurgus Kazimir (Belgrade: Media Center, 2001), 374.

26. CANVAS, "Ten Years Smarter?: Chronology of Events—A Brief History of Otpor" (Belgrade: CANVAS, 2008).

27. "Otpor: To nije smak sveta, samo režim pada" [Otpor: It's not the end of the world, only the regime falls], *B92*, August 18, 1999, accessed April 8, 2011, http://www.b92.net /info/vesti/index.php?yyyy=1999&mm=08&dd=16&nav_category=1&nav_id=1143.

28. CANVAS, "Ten Years Smarter? Otpor—Concepts and Meanings"; Collin, *The Time of the Rebels*, 22.

29. "Otpor: Rođendanom na rođendan" [Otpor: Birthday on a birthday], *B92*, August 19, 1999, accessed April 8, 2011, http://www.b92.net/info/vesti/index.php?yyyy=1999&mm =08&dd=19&nav_ category=1&nav_id=1396; *Bringing Down a Dictator*, directed by Steve York and Peter Ackerman (Washington, DC: York Zimmerman, 2001), DVD.

30. Marko Simić, in discussion with the author, November 2010.

31. Goran Dašković, in discussion with author, December 2010.

32. *Danas*, April 17, 2000, cited in Ilić, "The Popular Movement Otpor—Between Europe and Re-Traditionalization."

33. Zoran Matović, in discussion with the author, November 2010.

34. Srđa Popović, in discussion with the author, September 2010.

35. Dušan Pešić, in discussion with the author, November 2010; Vladimir Stojković, in discussion with the author, November 2010.

36. *Bringing Down a Dictator*, directed by York and Ackerman, DVD. See also Petra Marković, "L'humour, pas la Guerre" [Humor, not war], *Liberation*, July 4, 2000, accessed August 20, 2010, http://www.liberation.fr/monde/0101341 292-l-humor-pas-la-guerre.

37. Marko Simić, in discussion with the author, November 2010.

38. Vladimir Marović, in discussion with the author, December 2010. See also Humanitarian Law Center, "Police Crackdown on Otpor, Report No. 31" (Belgrade: Humanitarian Law Center), 52.

39. Robertino Knjur, in discussion with the author, October 2010.

40. Between July and August 2000, police officers searched more than 500 flats of Otpor activists, often without warrants. The upsurge in police raids corresponded to the growing popularity of the "He's Finished" and "It's Time" campaigns. See Humanitarian Law Center, "Police Crackdown on Otpor, Report No. 31," 16–17.

41. Milja Jovanović, in discussion with the author, November 2010; Siniša Šikman, in discussion with the author, September 2010; Srđan Milivojević, in discussion with the author, September 2010. See also Otpor, "Popular Movement Otpor (Resistance)," 380.

42. Ivan Marović, in discussion with the author, November 2010.

43. Momčilo Veljković, in discussion with the author, November 2010.

44. Željko Trifunović, in discussion with the author, November 2010.

45. Dušan Pešić, in discussion with the author, November 2010; Vladimir Stojković, in discussion with the author, November 2010.

46. Darko Šper, in discussion with the author, October 15, 2010, Novi Sad (Otpor Zrenjanin), Serbia; Petar Lacmanović, in discussion with the author, November 2010.

47. Stanko Lazendić, in discussion with the author, September 2010. See also "Kod Zmaj Jovinog spomenika akcija pokreta 'Otpor': misli, pruži Otpor" [Near the monument of Zmaj Jova was the action of the Otpor movement: think, resist], *Danas*, December 17, 1999.

48. Milja Jovanović, "Rage against the Regime: The Otpor Movement in Serbia," in *People Building Peace II: Successful Stories of Civil Society*, eds. Paul van Togeren, Malin Brenk,

Marte Hallena, and Juliette Verhoeven, accessed October 20, 2010, http://www.people buildingpeace.org/thestories/print.php?id=136&typ=theme.

49. Milja Jovanović, in discussion with the author, November 2010; Miloš Gagić, in discussion with the author, September 2010; Siniša Šikman, in discussion with the author, September 2010. For news coverage at the time, see "Otpor organizuje proslavu Srpske nove godine" [Otpor organizes the celebration of Serbian New Year], *Danas*, December 27, 1999; Milica Bjelovuk, "Otpor sa novim likom" [New image of Otpor], *Glas javnosti*, January 10, 2001, accessed October 20, 2010, http://arhiva.glas-javnosti.co.yu/arhiva/2001. See also *Bringing Down a Dictator*, directed by York and Ackerman, DVD; Collin, *The Time of the Rebels*, 28–29; and CANVAS, "Ten Years Smarter? Chronology of Events."

50. Milja Jovanović, in discussion with the author, November 2010. Jovanović explains that the idea of "asking people to go home because there was nothing to celebrate" emerged during a discussion of events being organized for the New Year celebration. An activist admitted that it was hard for him to think about all these fun activities because he felt that there was nothing to celebrate. The whole crew decided that this was a good theme for the New Year celebration: to celebrate because there is nothing to celebrate.

51. *Bringing Down a Dictator*, directed by York and Ackerman, DVD; Anne M. Lucas, "Strategic Nonviolence and Humor: Their Synergy and Its Limitations" (bachelor's thesis, Kent State University Honors College, 2010), 89.

52. Srđan Milivojević, in discussion with the author, September 2010. See also *Bringing Down a Dictator*, directed by York and Ackerman, DVD.

53. Ivan Marović, in discussion with the author, December 2010.

54. Zoran Matović, in discussion with the author, November 2010.

55. *Glas Javnosti*, May 3, 2000 and *Blic*, May 3, 2000—both cited in Ilić, "The Popular Movement Otpor—Between Europe and Re-Traditionalization."

56. Ivan Marović, in discussion with the author, December 2010.

57. Dalibor Glišović, in discussion with the author, November 2010; Zoran Matović, in discussion with the author, November 2010. See also Otpor, "Popular Movement Otpor (Resistance)," 377; CANVAS, "Ten Years Smarter? Otpor—Concepts and Meanings."

58. Ivan Marović, in discussion with the author, December 2010; Marko Simić, in discussion with the author, November 2010.

59. *Glas javnosti*, May 5, 2000, cited in Ilić, "The Popular Movement Otpor—Between Europe and Re-Traditionalization."

60. Ibid.

61. Marko Simić, in discussion with the author, November 2010.

62. Humanitarian Law Center, "Police Crackdown on Otpor, Report No. 31," 53. The HLC also reports that a handful of activists were detained and assaulted by plainclothes police during the action.

63. Vladimir Marović, in discussion with the author, December 2010. See also Otpor, "Popular Movement Otpor (Resistance)," 379.

64. Humanitarian Law Center, "Police Crackdown on Otpor, Report No. 31," 55–57.

65. Goran Dašković, in discussion with the author, December 2010.

66. "Aktivisti studentske organizacije Otpor najavljuju: oblačenje Zmaj Jove u 'Otporovu' majicu" [Activists from the students organization Otpor announce: dressing of Zmaj Jova in Otpor T-shirt], *Danas*, December 23, 1999.

67. Otpor, "Popular Movement Otpor (Resistance)," 380.

68. Zoran Matović, in discussion with the author, November 2010. Although the action was undertaken in Kraljevo, not Kragujevac, this anecdote came from Matović who was then the Otpor coordinator for the entire central region of Serbia.

69. Siniša Šikman, in discussion with the author, September 2010.

70. Ibid. See also Otpor, "Popular Movement Otpor (Resistance)," 375.

71. Vladimir Marović, in discussion with the author, December 2010. See also Humanitarian Law Center, "Police Crackdown on Otpor, Report No. 31," 52.

72. Humanitarian Law Center, "Police Crackdown on Otpor, Report No. 31," 51.

73. Steve York, "How Did We Succeed: Superior Propaganda for Advertising Freedom" (excerpted from an interview with Steve York), *Center for Applied Non-Violent Action and Strategies* (CANVAS), November 30, 2000, accessed March 4, 2010, http://www.canvasopedia.org/legacy/content/serbian_case/Otpor_propaganda.htm#01.

74. Srđa Popović, e-mail message to author, May 10, 2011. See also Nebojša Grujičić, "R'n'R i protesti: kamenje na sistem" [Rock 'n' roll and protests: rocks at the system], *VREME*, December 27, 1999, accessed April 17, 2011, http://www.vreme.com/arhivahtml/464/14.html.

75. Nebojša Grujičić, "R'n'R i protesti" [Rock 'n' roll and protests].

76. Otpor, "Popular Movement Otpor (Resistance)," 374.

77. Aleksandar Savanović, in discussion with the author, October 2010. See also Pavlović, "Spisak akcija Novosadskog Otpor-a" [personal records of Otpor's action in Novi Sad]; "Pretučeni aktivisti DS-a, privođeni aktivisti 'Otpora'" [DS activists beaten and Otpor activists detained], *B92*, October 13, 1999, accessed May 22, 2011, http://www.b92.net/info/vesti/index.php?yyyy=1999&mm=10&dd=13&nav_id=2454&nav_category=1&version=print.

78. Veran Matić, in discussion with the author, September 2010.

79. Srđa Popović, e-mail message to author, May 10, 2011.

80. Matthew Collin, *This Is Serbia Calling* (London: Serpent's Tail, 2001), 208.

81. EXIT Festival, "EXIT 00: History," *EXIT Festival (2000)* (website), accessed May 22, 2011, http://www.exitfest.org/exit-festival-mainmenu-310/exit-istorija-mainmenu-309/2560-exit-00; Charlotte Philby, "Exit Festival, Novi Sad, Serbia," *The Independent*, July 16, 2008, accessed May 22, 2011, http://www.independent.co.uk/arts-entertainment/music/reviews/exit-festival-novi-sad-serbia-868551.html; Collin, *The Time of the Rebels*, 50; and Lonnie R. Sherrod, "Youth Activism in Serbia," in *Youth Activism: An International*

Encyclopedia, eds. Lonnie R. Sherrod, Constance A. Flanagan, Ron Kassimir, and Amy K. Syvertsen (Westport, CT: Greenwood, 2005), 567.

82. EXIT Festival, "EXIT 00." The EXIT music festival continues to be held annually. Dušan Kočić, an Otpor activist from Smederevo, has remained a key organizer since the festival's inception to the present day.

83. CANVAS, "Ten Years Smarter? Otpor—Concepts and Meanings."

84. Glišović, "Otpor! Actions—Aleksandrovac (District of Župa)."

85. Otpor, "Popular Movement Otpor (Resistance)," 379.

86. Ibid.

87. Glišović, "Otpor! Actions—Aleksandrovac (District of Župa)."

88. Petar Lacmanović, in discussion with the author, November 2010.

89. Aleksandar Pavlović, in discussion with the author, October 2010. See also Otpor, "Popular Movement Otpor (Resistance)," 376.

90. Goran Dašković, in discussion with the author, December 2010.

91. Lucas, "Strategic Nonviolence and Humor," 131.

92. Glišović, "Otpor! Actions—Aleksandrovac (District of Župa)." See also Lucas, "Strategic Nonviolence and Humor," 131.

93. Otpor, "Popular Movement Otpor (Resistance)," 380.

94. "Otpor simbolično zatvorio župsku berbu 2000" [Otpor closed the vineyard in Župa symbolically in 2000], *B92*, September 18, 2000, accessed April 8, 2011, http://www.b92.net/info/vesti/index.php?yyyy=2000&mm=09&dd=18&nav_category=1&nav_id=11963.

95. Glišović, "Otpor! Actions—Aleksandrovac (District of Župa)."

96. *Bringing Down a Dictator*, directed by Steve York and Peter Ackerman, DVD.

97. Gene Sharp, *The Politics of Nonviolent Action* (Boston: Porter Sargent, 1973), 657–95.

98. Brian Martin, *Justice Ignited: The Dynamics of Backfire* (Lanham, MD: Rowman and Littlefield, 2007), 3.

99. Sharp, *The Politics of Nonviolent Action*, 184–99.

100. Hannah Arendt, *On Violence* (London: Harcourt, 1970), 52–54.

101. Goran Dašković, in discussion with the author, December 2010; Ivan Marović, in discussion with the author, December 2010; Petar Lacmanović, in discussion with the author, November 2010; Siniša Šikman, in discussion with the author, September 2010; Stanko Lazendić, in discussion with the author, September 2010; Srđa Popović, in discussion with the author, September 2010; Zoran Matović, in discussion with the author, November 2010. See also, Srđa Popović, "Serbia Arena for Nonviolent Conflict: An Analytical Overview of an Application of Gene Sharp's Theory of Nonviolent Action in Milošević's Serbia," paper presented at the conference "Whither the Bulldozer? Revolution, Transition, and Democracy in Serbia," Belgrade, Serbia, January 30–31, 2001; Joshua Paulson, "Removing the Dictator in Serbia—1996–2000," in *Waging Nonviolent Struggle: 20th Century Practice and 21st*

Century Potential, eds. Christopher A. Miller, Hardy Merriman, and Gene Sharp (Boston: Porter Sargent, 2005), 324.

102. Dušan Kočić, in discussion with the author, December 2010; Marko Simić, in discussion with the author, November 2010; Nenad Belčević, in discussion with the author, October 2010; Oskar Konja, in discussion with the author, October 2010; Petar Lacmanović, in discussion with the author, November 2010; Vladimir Stojković, in discussion with the author, November 2010. See also Roger Cohen, "Who Really Brought Down Milošević," *New York Times Magazine*, November 26, 2000, accessed October 20, 2010, http://www.nytimes .com/2000/11/26/magazine/who-really-broughtdownmilosevic.html?scp=3&sq=OTPOR &st=cse&pagewanted=4&pagewanted=print; Collin, *The Time of the Rebels*, 42.

103. Dalibor Glišović, in discussion with the author, November 2010.

104. Goran Dašković, in discussion with the author, December 2010.

105. See also Allan Irving and Tom Young, "Paradigm for Pluralism: Mikhail Bakhtin and Social Work Practice," *Social Work* 47, no. 1 (2002): 19–29.

106. Sharp, *The Politics of Nonviolent Action*, 398–400; Robert Burrowes, *The Strategy of Nonviolent Defense: A Gandhian Approach* (Albany: State Univ. of New York Press, 1996), 204–6. See also Ralph Summy, "Gandhi's Nonviolent Power Perspective," paper presented at the International Peace Research Association Conference, University of Sydney, Sydney, Australia, July 6–10, 2010.

107. Sharp, *The Politics of Nonviolent Action*, 398–400; Howard Clark, "The Limits of Prudence: Civil Resistance in Kosovo, 1990–98," in *Civil Resistance and Power Politics: The Experiences of Non-Violent Action from Gandhi to the Present*, eds. Adam Roberts and Timothy Garton Ash (Oxford: Oxford Univ. Press, 2009), 287.

108. Mohandas K. Gandhi, *Constructive Programme: Its Meaning and Place* (Ahmedabad, India: Navajivan Trust, 1945).

109. Stellan Vinthagen, "Power as Subordination and Resistance as Disobedience: Nonviolent Movements and the Management of Power," *Asian Journal of Social Science* 34, no. 1 (2006): 16.

6. Localizing Strategic Humor

1. The observations made and conclusions drawn in this chapter are based on three aggregated sources of evidence. The interviews conducted with twenty-two coordinators of Otpor branches in sixteen towns and cities comprise the primary source. These interviews underpin assessments regarding patterns of activists' decision-making on whether to use humor. The second category of sources comprises news reports about Otpor's protest actions for those sixteen cities and towns. These reports enable an evaluation of how prolific these humorous actions became in the assessed areas, and act as a cross-reference for activists' anecdotes of protest events in their localities. The third category of sources comprises the collection of interviews with local politicians, journalists, and NGO members, and

reports about Otpor produced by them. This category of evidence sheds light on the degree of cooperation between Otpor and local opposition forces from a third party's viewpoint.

2. Humanitarian Law Center, "Police Crackdown on Otpor, Report No. 31" (Belgrade: Humanitarian Law Center, 2001), 11–19.

3. For example, in the Vojvodinian towns of Inđija and Novi Sad a group of Otpor activists' mothers was specially organized to respond to the mass detention of young activists who were children of locals. These mothers, neighbors, and teachers were well aware of the regime's unfounded allegations and were enraged by the harsh repression. See Branka Kaljević, "Parents and Children: Family Resistance," *VREME*, June 3, 2000, accessed September 20, 2010, http://www.exyupress.com/vreme/vreme77.html.

4. Goran Dašković, in discussion with the author, December 2010; Ivan Marović, in discussion with the author, December 2010; Pedrag Lečić, in discussion with the author, September 2010; Siniša Šikman, in discussion with the author, September 2010; Željko Trifunović, in discussion with the author, November 2010. See also *Bringing Down a Dictator*, directed by Steve York and Peter Ackerman (Washington, DC: York Zimmerman, 2001), DVD; Lenard J. Cohen, *Serpent in the Bosom: The Rise and Fall of Slobodan Milošević* (Boulder, CO: Westview, 2002), 400; and Vladimir Ilić, "The Popular Movement Otpor—Between Europe and Re-Traditionalization," Helsinki files, no. 5, n.d., Policy Documentation Center, Center for Policy Studies, Central European University, Budapest, accessed February 1, 2010, www.pdc.ceu.hu/archive/00005016/01/Files05.doc.

5. Robertino Knjur, in discussion with the author, October 2010.

6. Goran Dašković, in discussion with the author, December 2010; Vladimir Marović, in discussion with the author, December 2010; Vladimir Žarković, in discussion with the author, November 2010.

7. Ilić, "The Popular Movement Otpor—Between Europe and Re-Traditionalization."

8. Veran Matić, in discussion with the author, September 2010. See also Matthew Collin, *This Is Serbia Calling* (London: Serpent's Tail, 2001), 139.

9. Spasa Bošnjak, "Fight the Power: The Role of the Serbian Independent Electronic Media in the Democratization of Serbia" (master's thesis, Simon Fraser University, 2005), 95.

10. Velimir Ćurgus Kazimir, "From Islands to the Mainland," in *The Last Decade: Serbian Citizens in the Struggle for Democracy and an Open Society, 1991–2001*, ed. Velimir Ćurgus Kazimir (Belgrade: Media Center, 2001), 20.

11. Steven Erlanger, "Serbian Government Seizes TV Station in a Drive to Crush the Opposition to Milošević," *New York Times*, May 18, 2000, accessed October 20, 2010, http://www.nytimes.com/2000/05/18/world/serbian-government-seizes-tv-station-drive-crush-opposition-milosevic.html?pagewanted=all&src=pm; Vana Suša, "Studio B Has Been Fined Twice," *Central European Review*, May 12–June 11, 2000, accessed April 8, 2011, http://www.ce-review.org/00/20/serbianews20.html.

12. Collin, *This Is Serbia Calling*, 202.

13. Veran Matić, in discussion with the author, September 2010.

14. Ivan Marović, in discussion with the author, December 2010.

15. Siniša Šikman, in discussion with the author, December 2010.

16. Ivan Marović, in discussion with the author, December 2010.

17. Milja Jovanović, in discussion with the author, November 2010.

18. "Dear Readers," *Blic*, May 17, 2000, accessed October 20, 2010, http://www.blic.rs /stara_arhiva/naslovna/130375/Dear-readers; Crna Gora Medija Klub and Pat FitzPatrick, "Paper Shortage Forces Closure of Dailies," *Central European Review*, July 1, 2000, accessed May 22, 2011, http://www.ce-review.org/00/27/serbianews 27.html.

19. Velimir Stanojević, in discussion with the author, November 2010. See also Florian Bieber, "The Serbian Opposition and Civil Society: Roots of the Delayed Transition in Serbia," *International Journal of Politics, Culture and Society* 17, no. 1 (2003): 80–81. However, the relationship between opposition politicians and Otpor activists could be at odds. In some areas, despite the dominance of the opposition parties in municipal governments, Otpor activists did not always receive substantial cooperation. See, for example, "We shall Not Allow Civil War," *Blic*, May 16, 2000, accessed October 20, 2010, http://www.blic.rs /stara_arhiva/naslovna/130318/We-shall-not-allow-civil-war; *Danas*, May 22, 2000, cited in Ilić, "The Popular Movement Otpor—Between Europe and Re-Traditionalization."

20. Between 1970 and 1980 only six alternative groups were founded in Serbia. However, the number rose to 519 in December 1997. By the end of 2000, it was estimated that the number of inhabitants per activist amounted to 124, and 90 percent of them worked on a volunteer basis. See Maja Dzelatović, "Pokrenimo Sadašnjost" [Challenges of the present days], 60, presented at The Third Forum of Yugoslav Non-Governmental Organizations, Center for Democracy Foundation and Center for the Development of Non-Profit Sector, Belgrade, May 2001, accessed November 10, 2010, http://www.greekhelsinki.gr/english/reports/yngos-31 -10-1999.html; Cohen, *Serpent in the Bosom*, 264; and Žarko Paunović, "Ten Years of NGOs in the FR of Yugoslavia," in *The Last Decade: Serbian Citizens in the Struggle for Democracy and an Open Society*, ed. Velimir Ćurgus Kazimir (Belgrade: Media Center, 2001), 58.

21. Branka Petrović, Žarko Paunović, Aco Divac, Tea Gorjanc, and Vesna Nenadić, *Directory of Nongovernmental Non-Profit Organizations in the Federal Republic of Yugoslavia* (Belgrade: Centar za razvoj neprofitnog sektora, 1998), cited in Cohen, *Serpent in the Bosom*, 264–45.

22. Paunović, "Ten Years of NGOs in the FR of Yugoslavia," 60–61; Ivan Vejvoda, "Civil Society versus Slobodan Milošević: Serbia 1991–2000," in *Civil Resistance and Power Politics: The Experience of Non-Violent Action from Gandhi to the Present*, eds. Adam Roberts and Timothy Garton Ash (Oxford: Oxford Univ. Press, 2009), 312.

23. Dzelatović, "Pokrenimo Sadašnjost" [Challenges of the present days], 60. See also Eleanor Pritchard, "Anti-Opposition Activities," *Central European Review*, September 4, 2000, accessed May 22, 2011, http://www.ce-review.org/00/32/serbianews32.html.

24. Ivan Marović, in discussion with the author, November 2010 and December 2010.

25. *Danas,* May 22, 2000, cited in Ilić, "The Popular Movement Otpor—Between Europe and Re-Traditionalization."

26. See Eric D. Gordy, *The Culture of Power in Serbia: Nationalism and the Destruction of Alternatives* (University Park: Pennsylvania State Univ. Press, 1999), 63–70; Vladan Radosavljević, *Pištaljke i jaja* [Whistles and eggs] (Belgrade: Medija Centar, 1997).

27. Ivan Marović, in discussion with the author, November 2010; Milja Jovanović, in discussion with the author, November 2010; Srđa Popović, in discussion with the author, September 2010.

28. Aleksandar Pavlović, in discussion with the author, October 2010.

29. Ibid.

30. Stanko Lazendić, in discussion with the author, September 2010.

31. See, for example, the coverage of Otpor actions in Zrenjanin in "Message in a Bottle by 'Otpor' to President Milošević," *Blic,* April 21, 2000, accessed October 20, 2010, http://www.blic.rs/stara_arhiva/naslovna/129782/Message-in-a-bottle-by-Otpor-to-President-Milosevic.

32. Darko Šper, in discussion with the author, October 2010.

33. Marko Simić, in discussion with the author, November 2010.

34. "U Kragujevcu se formira štab za odbranu lokalne TV" [The headquarters for the defense of the local TV is founded in Kragujevac], *B92,* March 21, 2000, accessed May 16, 2010, http://www.b92.net/info/vesti/index.php?yyyy=2000&mm=03&dd=21&nav_category=1&nav_id=5503.

35. Uroš Komlenović, Zorica Miladinović, and Zoran Radovanović, "What Audiences in Belgrade, Niš, Kragujevac, Pančevo, Čačak . . . See and Hear: Air over Serbia," *VREME,* July 31, 2000, accessed September 20, 2010, http://www.exyupress.com/vreme/vreme77.html. See also, Milan Milošević, "The Media Wars: 1987–1997," in *Burn This House: The Making and Unmaking of Yugoslavia,* eds. Jasminka Udovički and James Ridgeway (Durham, NC: Duke Univ. Press, 2000), 127; Cohen, *Serpent in the Bosom,* 400; and Kazimir, "From Islands to the Mainland," 21.

36. Zoran Matović, in discussion with the author, November 2010.

37. Ibid.

38. Ibid.

39. Ivan Marović, in discussion with the author, December 2010. See also "Ponovo proradila TV Kraljevo" [TV Kraljevo re-opened], *B92,* March 25, 2000, accessed May 16, 2010, http://www.b92.net/info/vesti/index.php?yyyy=2000&mm=03&dd=25&nav_category=1&nav_id=5610.

40. Vladimir Marović, in discussion with the author, December 2010.

41. It should be noted that Milošević's Socialist Party had hardly been popular among Belgraders. For instance, in the parliamentary election in 1992, the SPS received only 18.8 percent of the total votes in "Old Town" (*Stari Grad*), the central area of the city. See Laslo Sekelj, "Parties and Elections: The Federal Republic of Yugoslavia. Change without

Transformation," *Europe-Asia Studies* 52, no. 1 (2000): 63; Republika Srbija Republički zavod za statistiku, "Prevremeni izbori za narodne poslanike skupštine republike Srbije 1993," cited in Gordy, *The Culture of Power in Serbia*, 55.

42. Sreten Vujović, "Protest as an Urban Phenomenon," in *Protest in Belgrade: Winter of Discontent*, ed. Mladen Lazić (Budapest: Central European Univ. Press, 1999), 198.

43. *Danas*, May 22, 2000, cited in Ilić, "The Popular Movement Otpor—Between Europe and Re-Traditionalization"; Ivan Marović, "Opposition as Tool," *VREME*, May 26, 2000, accessed May 16, 2010, http://www.exyupress.com/vreme/vreme72.html.

44. "New Rally on May 27," *Blic*, May 20, 2000, accessed October 20, 2010, http://www.blic.rs/stara_arhiva/naslovna/130464/ New-rally-on-May-27.

45. Siniša Šikman, e-mail message to the author, June 15, 2011.

46. "Novi Sad without the Socialists," *AIM*, December 21, 1996, accessed November 12, 2010, http://www.aimpress.ch/dyn/trae/ archive/data/199612/61221-005-trae-beo.html.

47. Aleksandar Pavlović, in discussion with the author, October 2010; Stanko Lazendić, in discussion with the author, September 2010 and December 2010. See also Teofil Pančić, "Election in FRY: Socialists Going On," *AIM*, November 6, 1996, accessed March 20, 2011, http://www.aimpress.ch/dyn/trae/archive/data/199611/61106-005-trae-beo.html.

48. Mattijs van de Port, *Gypsies, Wars and Other Instances of the Wild* (Amsterdam: Amsterdam Univ. Press, 1998), 37–60.

49. Miodrag Jovović, in discussion with the author, October 2010 and December 2010.

50. *Danas*, March 18–19, 2000, cited in Ilić, "The Popular Movement Otpor—Between Europe and Re-Traditionalization."

51. Tim Judah, *The Serbs: History, Myth and the Destruction of Yugoslavia* (New Haven, CT: Yale Univ. Press, 2009), 271. It should be noted that Zastava's arms production wing benefited from supplying arms for the Yugoslav army in the Bosnian war. Its profit was in decline only when the war was about to terminate at the end of 1994.

52. Jasminka Udovički, "Neither War nor Peace," in *Burn This House: The Making and Unmaking of Yugoslavia*, eds. Jasminka Udovički and James Ridgeway (Durham, NC: Duke Univ. Press, 2000), 291.

53. Milošević, "The Media Wars," 110.

54. "Hronologija lokalnih izbora u Srbiji" [Chronology of the local elections in Serbia], *B92*, November 30, 2004, accessed May 16, 2010, http://www.b92.net/specijal/lokalni2004/enciklopedija.php?nav_id=151196.

55. "Stevanović ponovo izabran sa gradonačelnika Kragujevaca" [Stevanović elected as the mayor of Kragujevac], *B92*, June 30, 2000, accessed April 8, 2011, http://www.b92.net/info/vesti/index.php?yyyy=2000&mm=06&dd=30&nav_category=1&nav_id=8462.

56. Zoran Matović, in discussion with the author, November 2010.

57. Suša, "Studio B Has Been Fined Twice."

58. Teofil Pančić, "Reports from Cities in Serbia," *VREME*, November 24, 1996, accessed May 16, 2010, http://www.scc.rutgers.edu/serbian_digest/.

59. Pančić, "Reports from Cities in Serbia"; Dušan Kovačev, "Zrenjanin: trajno zaustav-ljanje perspektive" [Zrenjanin: permanent termination of a perspective], *Nova Srpska Politička Misao,* December 9, 2008, accessed June 14, 2011, http://www.nspm.rs/politicki -zivot/zrenjanin-trajno-zaustavlj anje-perspektive.html?alphabet=l.

60. Pančić, "Reports from Cities in Serbia."

61. Milan Milošević, "Shell Them with Eggs!," *VREME,* December 1, 1996, accessed May 16, 2010, http://www.scc.rutgers.edu/serbian_digest/; Bojana Lekić, "Rebellion of Pro-vincial Towns," *AIM,* January 16, 1997, accessed April 24, 2011, http://www.aimpress.ch /dyn/trae/archive /data/199701/70112-003-trae-beo.html.

62. Dušan Juvanin, in discussion with the author, November 2010.

63. Petar Lacmanović, e-mail message to the author, December 2011; Vladimir Marović, e-mail message to the author, December 27, 2011.

64. Marko Simić, in discussion with the author, November 2010.

65. Dragana Piletić, in discussion with the author, October 2010; Vladimir Marović, in discussion with the author, December 2010. See also Humanitarian Law Center, "Police Crackdown on Otpor, Report No. 31," 131.

66. Humanitarian Law Center, "Police Crackdown on Otpor, Report No. 31," 47.

67. Ivan Marović, in discussion with the author, November 2010.

68. In February 2000 he was also a vice president of the party. See Vana Suša, "The Democratic Party (DP) Held Its Sixth Party Convention," *Central European Review,* March 4, 2000, accessed May 22, 2011, http://www.ce-review.org/00/9/serbianews9.html.

69. Shortly after the acceptance of the election result in 1997, Velimir Ilić founded his own party, New Serbia (Nova Srbija or "NS"), which has remained influential in the local government of Čačak ever since.

70. "Rapušten opštinski odbor SPS?" [SPS Municipal Committee dissolved?], *Naša borba,* February 28, 1997, cited in Robert Thomas, *Serbia under Milošević / Politics in the 1990s* (London: Hurst, 1999), 327.

71. This assessment is based on interviews with other Otpor activists. For instance, Nemanja Crnić from Sremska Mitrovica explains that "Otpor in Niš was connected with DS, so there was no real Otpor movement there." Vladimir Stojković from Leskovac simi-larly points out that the Otpor branch in Niš no longer existed by July 2000, and key activ-ists were involved in local election campaigns for leaders of the opposition coalition there. Šikman concludes that the line between Otpor and DS in Niš was blurred due to Otpor's coordinator for Niš, Aleksandar Višnjić, and his close ties with the Democratic Party.

72. See for instance the coverage of the action "Dinar for a Change" in "Studenski pokret 'Otpor': dinar za smenu" [The student movement Otpor: a dinar for a change], *Danas,* October 11, 1999; and the action "It's Not the End of the World, Only the Regime Falls" in "Otpor: To nije smak sveta, samo režim pada" [It's not the end of the world, only the regime falls], *B92,* August 18, 1999, accessed April 8, 2011, http://www.b92.net/info /vesti/index.php?yyyy=1999&mm=08&dd=16&nav_category=1&nav_id=1143. Other actions

such as "The President's Birthday" (detailed in chapter 5) and "Culture, Here I Come" were carried out in 1999. See Otpor, "Popular Movement Otpor (Resistance): Chronology of Actions 1999–2000," in *The Last Decade: Serbian Citizens in the Struggle for Democracy and an Open Society*, ed. Velimir Ćurgus Kazimir (Belgrade: Media Center, 2001), 375.

73. Siniša Šikman, e-mail message to the author, May 23, 2011. See also "United towards the Victory over Regime," *Blic*, May 27, 2000, accessed October 20, 2010, http://www.blic.rs/stara_arhiva/naslovna/130711/United-towards-the-victory-over-regime; "Niški Otpor će zatražiti prijem kod Đukanovića" [Otpor from Niš will request the reception from Đukanović], *B92*, July 28, 2000, accessed May 23, 2011, http://www.b92.net/info/vesti/index.php?yyyy=2000&mm=07&dd=28&nav_category=1&nav_id=9588.

74. Srđan Milivojević, in discussion with the author, September 2010.

75. Goran Dašković, in discussion with the author, December 2010. Consequently, Maki was beaten by authorities and sentenced to three years imprisonment, but he managed to escape from the hospital in Belgrade in March 2000. See Dragan Todorović, "Ko je Bogoljub Arsenijević Maki" [Who is Bogoljub Arsenijević Maki], *VREME*, June 24, 1999, accessed May 23, 2011, http://www.vreme.com/arhiva_htm 1/446/12.html; "Maki zbog teškog zdravstvenog stanja nije mogao da daizjavu" [Because of severe illness, Maki could not make a statement], *B92*, August 19, 2000, accessed May 16, 2010, http://www.b92.net/info/vesti/index.php?yyyy=1999&mm=08&dd=19&nav_category=1&nav_id=1398; and Vana Suša, "A Serbian Protest Leader Has Made a Dramatic Reappearance," *Central European Review*, March 31, 2000, accessed May 23, 2011, http://www.cereview.org/00/13/serbianews13.html.

76. Thomas, *Serbia under Milošević / Politics in the 1990s*, 288; Milošević, "The Media Wars," 110.

77. Srđan Milivojević, in discussion with the author, September 2010.

78. Todorović, "Ko je Bogoljub Arsenijević Maki" [Who is Bogoljub Arsenijević Maki].

79. Goran Dašković, in discussion with the author, December 2010.

80. Robertino Knjur, in discussion with the author, October 2010. See also, Milica Bjelovuk, "Otpor i opozicija, kokoška il jaje" [Otpor and the opposition, chicken or the egg], *Glas javnosti*, January 22, 2001, accessed September 20, 2010, http://arhiva.glas-javnosti.co.yu/arhiva/2001.

81. Cohen, *Serpent in the Bosom*, 400.

82. "Rally of Serbian Opposition for Freeing Studio B," *Free Serbia News*, May 17, 2000, accessed September 20, 2010, http://www.xs4all.nl/~freeserb/specials/broadcasts/17052000/e-index.html.

83. Dušan Pešić, in discussion with the author, November 2010; Vladimir Stojković, in discussion with the author, November 2010.

84. Željko Trifunović, in discussion with the author, November 2010. See also Komlenović, Miladinović, and Radovanović, "What Audiences in Belgrade, Niš, Kragujevac, Pančevo, Čačak . . . See and Hear."

85. Dragan Savković, in discussion with the author, November 2010.

86. Željko Trifunović, in discussion with the author, November 2010.

87. Dragan Savković, in discussion with the author, November 2010.

88. Ibid.

89. Goran Dašković, in discussion with the author, December 2010.

90. Vladimir Žarković, in discussion with the author, November 2010.

91. Goran Dašković, in discussion with the author, December 2010.

92. Ibid.

93. Ibid.

94. Vladimir Žarković, in discussion with the author, November 2010.

95. Ibid.

96. Ivan Marović, in discussion with the author, December 2010. In the interview with *VREME* in mid-2000, Marović offered similar comments: "[Otpor activists] are now well-known even in those environments where the opposition is weak, for example in Srbobran, Šid, and even in Požarevac. Honestly, we have made more trouble for the regime there in the last month and a half than the opposition during the last ten years." See Nenad Lj Stefanović, "What Is Otpor? Fist in the Eye of Regime," *VREME*, May 13, 2000, accessed October 20, 2010, http://www.ex-yupress.com/vreme/vreme39.html#otpor.

97. See Alex Kireev, "Serbia: Legislative Election 1996," November 3, 1996, accessed May 22, 2011, http://www.electoralgeography.com/new/en/countries/s/serbia/serbia-leg islative- election-1996.html.

98. Thomas, *Serbia under Milošević / Politics in the 1990s*, 326.

99. Matthew Collin, *The Time of the Rebels: Youth Resistance Movements and 21st Century Revolutions* (London: Serpent's Tail, 2007), 36; "Who's Who: Milošević Family," *BBC*, March 14, 2006, accessed May 13, 2011, http://news.bbc.co.uk/2/hi/europe/747130.stm.

100. Momčilo Veljković, in discussion with the author, November 2010.

101. Nemanja Crnić, in discussion with the author, October 2010.

102. Momčilo Veljković, in discussion with the author, November 2010.

103. Dušan Kocić, in discussion with the author, December 2010.

104. Radosavljević, *Pištaljke i jaja* [Whistles and eggs], 11; Zdenka Milivojević, "The Media in Serbia from 1985 to 1994," in *Serbia between the Past and the Future*, eds. Dragomir Pantić and Dušan Janjić (Belgrade: Institute of Social Sciences and Forum for Ethnic Relations, 1997), 388; and Milošević, "The Media Wars," 115.

105. Nemanja Crnić, in discussion with the author, October 2010.

106. Ibid. See also "'Blic' Daily Is Helping 'Beta' Agency," *Blic*, April 21, 2000, accessed October 20, 2010, http://www.blic.rs/stara_arhiva/naslovna/129785/Blic-daily-is-helping -Beta-agency. In the action, activists displayed a black box downtown, demonstrating that "this is the kind of media available during the administration of Goran Matić."

107. Komlenović, Miladinović, and Radovanović, "What Audiences in Belgrade, Niš, Kragujevac, Pančevo, Čačak . . . See and Hear."

108. Humanitarian Law Center, "Izveštaj: strah vlasti od Otpora u Srbiji" [Investigation: state terror against Otpor in Serbia], 2000, accessed May 22, 2011, http://www.hlcrdc.org/Izvestaji/577.sr.html.

109. Dzelatović, "Pokrenimo Sadašnjost" [Challenges of the present days], 80–84.

110. For instance, in countering the May Day celebration organized by Otpor in collaboration with the Trade Union Confederation "Independence," the Trade Union Federation carried out another event in Smederevo's city center. The event's main focus was on the impact of "the sanctions imposed on Yugoslavia" by "the international power wielders." See Vana Suša, "Thousands of Serb Workers and Supporters Gathered in Central Belgrade on International Workers Day," *Central European Review*, May 6, 2000, accessed April 20, 2011, http://www.ce-review.org/00/18/serbianews18.html.

111. Dzelatović, "Pokrenimo Sadašnjost" [Challenges of the present days], 18.

112. Nemanja Crnić, in discussion with the author, October 2010.

113. Dušan Kocić, in discussion with the author, December 2010.

114. Ibid.

115. Dušan Kocić, in discussion with the author, December 2010. Although there was no report of torture or abduction in Smederevo, there were cases in which the police forced activists to swallow their leaflets when caught in the act of distributing them. See Humanitarian Law Center, "Police Crackdown on Otpor, Report No. 31," 99.

116. Dušan Kocić, in discussion with the author, December 2010.

117. See examples of international coverage of the incident in Požarevac and subsequent rallies in "L'opposition manifeste" [The opposition's protest], *Figaro*, May 5, 2000, accessed May 23, 2011, http://recherche.lefigaro.fr/recherche/access/lefigarofr.php?archi ve=BszTm8dCk78Jk8uwiNq9T8CoS9GECSHiDi%2FQyLLLih82IdPUTn%2B4s5tPGWuEz OXfG%2BhdVGNlEauZy6BaSOXVcw%3D; "Opposition Activists to Rally across Serbia," *BBC*, May 13, 2000, accessed May 23, 2011, http://news.bbc.co.uk/2/hi/europe/747130.stm. In addition, the news highlighted the resignation of Judge Boško Papović, who refused to convict the arrested Otpor activists of attempted murder. See "'Defense' of Požarevac on Victory Day," *Free Serbia News*, May 9, 2000, accessed September 20, 2010, http://www .xs4all.nl/~freeserb/specials/report/0905200 0/e-index.html.

118. Momčilo Veljković, in discussion with the author, November 2010.

119. Ibid.

120. Kireev, "Serbia: Legislative Election 1996."

121. Dušan Pešić, in discussion with the author, November 2010; Vladimir Stojković, in discussion with the author, November 2010. See also Dragan Ilić, "The Chronical of the Zajedno Protest," in *Šetnja u mestu: građanski protest u Srbiji* [Walking on the spot: civil protest in Serbia], ed. Darka Radosavljević (Belgrade: B92, 1997), 115; Thomas, *Serbia under Milošević / Politics in the 1990s*, 288.

122. Dalibor Glišović, in discussion with the author, November 2010. See also Kireev, "Serbia: Legislative Election 1996."

123. Dalibor Glišović, in discussion with the author, November 2010.

124. Dušan Pešić, in discussion with the author, November 2010.

125. Dalibor Glišović, e-mail message to the author, May 29, 2011 and December 31, 2011.

126. Center for Human Rights in Leskovac, "O Nama" [About us], accessed May 25, 2011, http:// www.humanrightsle.org/o%20 nama.htm.

127. Humanitarian Law Center, "Police Crackdown on Otpor, Report No. 31," 125–27; "Aktivisti Otpora određen istražni pritvor" [Otpor activists detained], *B92*, June 22, 2000, accessed April 8, 2011, http://www.b92.net/info/vesti/index. php?yyyy=2000&mm=06&dd =22&nav_category=1&nav_id=8157&version=print; and "Onemogućen protest u Leskovcu" [Protests hindered in Leskovac], *B92*, June 22, 2000, accessed April 8, 2011, http://www.b92 .net/info/vesti/index.php?yyyy=2000&mm=06&dd=24&nav_category=1&nav_id=8213.

128. Dalibor Glišović, e-mail message to the author, May 29, 2011

129. TV Leskovac, "O Nama" [About us], accessed April 8, 2011, http://www.tvl.rs /index.php?opt ion=com_content&view= article &id=5&Itemid=8.

130. Dušan Pešić, in discussion with the author, November 2010.

131. Dalibor Glišović, e-mail message to the author, May 29, 2011. See also Radosavljević, *Pištaljke i jaja* [Whistles and eggs], 11–16.

132. Dušan Pešić, in discussion with the author, November 2010. See also "Ivan Novković—Simbol Otpora" [Ivan Novković—the symbol of resistance], *B92*, October 2, 2010, accessed May 24, 2011, http://www.b92.net/info/vesti/index.php?yyyy=2010&mm =10&dd=02 &nav_category=12& nav_id=462459.

133. "Twelve Die as NATO Hits Passenger Train," *Southnews*, April 12, 1999, accessed May 24, 2011, http://southmovement.alphalink.com.au/southnews/990412-trainhit.html; "Grdelica: NATO Bombing Victims Remembered," *B92*, April 12, 2008, accessed May 24, 2011, http://www.b92.net/eng/news/societyarticle.php?yyyy=2008&mm= 04&dd= 12&nav _id=49352.

134. "Opposition Petition Drive Calls for Milošević's Resignation: General Strike," *CNN*, July 7, 1999, accessed May 24, 2011, http://articles.cnn.com/1999-07-07/world/9907_07 _yugo.opposition.01_1_party-leader-zoran-djindjic-police-ban-uzice/2?_s=PM:WORLD.

135. "Newsline—May 19, 1999: First Big Antiwar Protests in Serbia," *Radio Free Europe*, May 19, 1999, accessed May 24, 2011, http://www.rferl.org/content/article/1141909.html; "Yugoslavia: NATO Reports Anti-War Demonstrations in Serbia," *Radio Free Europe*, May 9, 1999, accessed May 24, 2011, http://www.rferl.org/content/article/1091345.html.

136. Dušan Pešić, in discussion with the author, November 2010; Vladimir Stojković, in discussion with the author, November 2010.

137. Vladimir Stojković, in discussion with the author, November 2010.

138. Dalibor Glišović, in discussion with the author, November 2010.

139. Dušan Pešić, in discussion with the author, November 2010.

140. Dalibor Glišović, in discussion with the author, November 2010.

141. Ibid. See also Dalibor Glišović, "Otpor! Actions—Aleksandrovac (District of Župa)" (personal records).

Conclusion

1. See for example, Harry H. Hiller, "Humor and Hostility: A Neglected Aspect of Social Movement Analysis," *Qualitative Sociology* 6, no. 3 (1983): 255–65; Marjolein't Hart, "Humour and Social Protest: An Introduction," in *Humour and Social Protest*, eds. Marjolein't Hart and Dennis Bos (Cambridge: Press Syndicate of the Univ. of Cambridge, 2007), 1–34. A number of academic works and journal articles emphasize Otpor's conceptions of humor's political advantages. See, for example, Srđa Popović, "Serbia Arena for Nonviolent Conflict: An Analytical Overview of an Application of Gene Sharp's Theory of Nonviolent Action in Milošević's Serbia," paper presented at the conference "Whither the Bulldozer? Revolution, Transition, and Democracy in Serbia," Belgrade, Serbia, January 30–31, 2001; Joshua Paulson, "Removing the Dictator in Serbia—1996–2000," in *Waging Nonviolent Struggle: 20th Century Practice and 21st Century Potential*, eds. Christopher A. Miller, Hardy Merriman, and Gene Sharp (Boston: Porter Sargent, 2005); Maiken Jul Sørensen, "Humor as a Serious Strategy of Nonviolent Resistance to Oppression," *Peace and Change* 33, no. 2 (2008): 167–90; and Danijela Nenadić and Nenad Belčević, "Serbia—Nonviolent Struggle for Democracy: The Role of Otpor," in *People Power: Unarmed Resistance and Global Solidarity*, ed. Howard Clark (London: Pluto, 2009), 26–34.

2. Hannah Arendt, *The Human Condition* (Chicago: Univ. of Chicago Press, 1998).

Epilogue

1. See, for example, Dragan Plavšić, "Manufactured Revolutions?," *International Socialism* 107 (June 27, 2005), accessed April 20, 2011, http://www.isj.org.uk/?id=122; Jonathan Mowat, "Coup d'Etat in Disguise: Washington's New World Order 'Democratization' Template," *Global Research on Globalisation* (February 9, 2005), accessed May 10, 2012, http://globalresearch.ca/articles/MOW502A.html; Mark MacKinnon, *The New Cold War: Revolutions, Rigged Elections and Pipeline Politics in the Former Soviet Union* (New York: Carroll and Graf, 2007); and Carl Gibson and Steve Horn, "Exposed: Globally Renowned Activist Collaborated with Intelligence Firm Stratfor," *Occupy*, February 12, 2013, accessed April 21, 2012, http://www.occupy.com/article/exposed-globally-renowned-activist-collaborated-intelligence-firm-stratfor#sthash.MFBhr5UX.dpuf.

2. See, for example, Wayne Grytting, "Gandhi Meets Monty Python: The Comedic Turn in Nonviolent Tactics," *Waging Nonviolence*, October 28, 2011, accessed November 3, 2011, http://wagingnonviolence.org/2011/10/gandhi-meets-monty-python-the-comedic-turn-in-nonviolenttactics/?utm_source=feedburner&utm_medium=feed&utm_campaign=Feed%3A+WagingNonviolence+%28Wagi ng+Nonviolence%29.

3. Ali Nardone, "Humor as a Tool of Protest in Belarus," *New Tactics*, December 15, 2010, http://www.newtactics.org/en/blog/ali-nardone/humor-tool-protest-belarus; Janine

di Giovanni, "Blueprint for a Revolution," *Financial Times Magazine,* March 18, 2011, accessed April 15, 2011, http://www.ft.com/cms/s/2/0ad005b4-5043-11e09ad100144feab49a.html#a xzz1HEy0vQHi; and Véronique Dudouet, "Nonviolent Resistance and Conflict Transformation in Power Asymmetries," in Berghof Foundation, *The Berghof Handbook: Transforming Ethnopolitical Conflict,* eds. Alex Austin, Martina Fischer, and Norbert Ropers (Wiesbaden, Germany: VS Verlag, 2004), 10.

4. Nardone, "Humor as a Tool of Protest in Belarus."

5. For Girifina's video clip, see http://www.youtube.com/watch?v= 2o6Rxc_JZKg.

6. Grytting, "Gandhi Meets Monty Python"; Claire Tancons. "Occupy Wall Street: Carnival against Capital? Carnivalesque as Protest Sensibility," *E-Flux Journal* 30 (December 2011), accessed May 10, 2012, http://www.e-flux.com/journal/occupy-wall-street-carnival -against-capital-carnivalesque-as-protest-sensibility/.

7. CNR ceased operations in 2004.

8. John Simpson, "Serb Activists Helped Inspire Ukraine Protests," *Institute for War and Peace Reporting,* February 21, 2005, accessed February 28, 2011, http://iwpr.net/global -voices/serb-activists-helped-inspire-ukraine-protests; Dušan Stojanović, "Serbs Offer Nonviolent Revolution Advice," *Charter 97,* November 11, 2004, accessed February 28, 2011, http://charter97.org/eng/news/2004/11/01/serb; Taras Kuzio, "Civil Society, Youth and Societal Mobilization in Democratic Revolutions," *Communist and Post-Communist Studies* 39 (2006): 375–78; and Matthew Collin, *The Time of the Rebel: Youth Resistance Movements and 21st Century Revolutions* (London: Serpent's Tail, 2007), 183–86.

9. Shadow [pseud.], "CANVAS, Otpor, Pora: Serbia's Brand Is Non-Violent Revolution," *Cafébabel,* March 31, 2011, accessed August 20, 2011, http://www.cafebabel.co.uk /article/37103/egypt-revolution-serbia-otpor-pora-canvas-youth.html.

10. Anna Louie Sussman, "Laugh, O Revolution: Humor in the Egyptian Uprising," *Atlantic,* February 26, 2011, accessed February 28, 2011, http://www.theatlantic.com/inter national/archive/2011/02/laugh-o-revolution-humor-in-the-egyptian-uprising/71530/; Yolande Knell, "Egypt Protest: 'Carnival Atmosphere' among Demonstrators," *BBC,* January 31, 2011, accessed February 28, 2011, http://www.bbc.co.uk/news/world-africa-1232 8506?print=true; and Tina Rosenberg, "Revolution U: What Egypt Learned from the Students Who Overthrew Milošević," *Foreign Policy,* February 16, 2011, accessed August 20, 2011, http://www.foreignpolicy.com/articles/2011/02/16/revolution_u?sms_ss=gmail&at _xt=4d61f7e3d19 8e602%2C0. See also William J. Dobson, *The Dictator's Learning Curve: Inside the Global Battle for Democracy* (New York: Doubleday, 2012), 224–50.

Bibliography

Books, Book Chapters, Scholarly Articles, and Films

Adorno, Theodor W. *The Authoritarian Personality*. New York: W. W. Norton, 1993.

———. *The Culture Industry*. New York: Routledge, 2001.

Ammitzbøll, Pernille, and Lorenzo Vidino. "After the Danish Cartoon Contro-versy." *Middle East Quarterly* 14, no. 1 (2007): 3–11.

Apte, Mahadev L. *Humor and Laughter: An Anthropological Approach*. London: Cor-nell Univ. Press, 1988.

Arendt, Hannah. *On Violence*. London and New York: Harcourt, 1970.

———. *The Human Condition*. Chicago: Univ. of Chicago Press, 1998.

Bakhtin, Mikhail. *Rabelias and His World*. Translated by Helene Iswolsky. Bloom-ington: Indiana Univ. Press, 1984.

———. *The Dialogic Imagination: Four Essays*. Edited by Michael Holquist. Trans-lated by Vadim Liapunov and Kenneth Brostrom. Austin: Univ. of Texas Press, 1981.

Ballantyne, Glenda. *Creativity and Critique: Subjectivity and Agency in Touraine and Riceour*. Leiden and Boston: Koninklijke Brill, 2007.

Barbalet, J. M. *Emotion, Social Theory, and Social Structure*. Cambridge: Cambridge Univ. Press, 2001.

Barker, Colin. "Fear, Laughter, and Collective Power: The Making of Solidarity at the Lenin Shipyard in Gdansk, Poland, August 1980." In *Passionate Politics: Emotions and Social Movements*, edited by Jeff Goodwin, James M. Jasper, and Francesca Polleta, 145–94. Chicago: Univ. of Chicago Press, 2001.

Benton, Gregor. "The Origins of the Political Joke." In *Humour in Society: Resistance and Control*, edited by Chris Powell and George E. C. Paton, 33–55. London: Macmillan, 1988.

Berger, Peter L. *Redeeming Laughter: The Comic Dimension of Human Experience*. New York: Walter de Gruyter, 1998.

231

Bieber, Florian. "The Serbian Opposition and Civil Society: Roots of the Delayed Transition in Serbia." *International Journal of Politics, Culture and Society* 17, no. 1 (2003): 73–90.

Blagojević, Ivan. "Moratorijum (19.1.97–27.1.97)" [Moratorium]. In *O studentima i drugim demonima: etnografija studentskog protesta 1996/97* [The students and other demons: ethnography of the student protest 1996/97], edited by Jadranja Milanović and Vuk Šećerović, 86–98. Belgrade: TODRA, 1997.

Blagojević, Marina. "The Walks in a Gender Perspective." In *Protest in Belgrade: Winter of Discontent*, edited by Mladen Lazić, 113–30. Budapest: Central European Univ. Press, 1999.

Bleiker, Roland. *Popular Dissent, Human Agency and Global Politics.* Cambridge: Cambridge Univ. Press, 2000.

Bogad, Laurence M. *Electoral Guerrilla Theatre: Radical Ridicule and Social Movements.* New York: Routledge, 2005.

———. "Tactical Carnival: Social Movements, Demonstration, and Dialogical Performance." In *A Boal Companion: Dialogues on Theatre and Cultural Politics*, edited by Jan Cohen-Cruz and Mady Schutzman, 46–58. London: Routledge, 2006.

Bond, Doug. "Nonviolent Action and the Diffusion of Power." In *Justice without Violence*, edited by Paul Wehr, Heidi Burgess, and Guy Burgess, 59–80. London: Lynne Rienner, 1994.

Bondurant, Joan V. *Conquest of Violence: The Gandhian Philosophy of Conflict.* Berkeley: Univ. of California Press, 1967.

———. "Satyagraha versus Duragraha: The Limits of Symbolic Violence." In *Gandhi, His Relevance for Our Times: A Volume of Contemporary Studies in Gandhian Themes Presented to Sri R. R. Diwakar on His Seventieth Birthday by the Workers of the Gandhi Smarak Nidhi*, edited by G. Ramachandran and T. K. Mahadevan. Bombay: Bharatiya Vidya Bhavan, 1964. Accessed September 12, 2009. http://www.mkgandhi.org/g_relevance/ chap05.htm.

Bošnjak, Spasa. "Fight the Power: The Role of the Serbian Independent Electronic Media in the Democratization of Serbia." Master's thesis, Simon Fraser Univ., 2005.

Bourdieu, Pierre. *Outline of a Theory of Practice.* Cambridge: Cambridge Univ. Press, 1977.

Bringing Down a Dictator. Directed by Steve York and Peter Ackerman. Washington, DC: York Zimmerman, 2001, DVD.

Bürger, Peter. *Theory of the Avant-Garde.* Minneapolis: Univ. of Minnesota Press, 1984.

Burke, Peter. *Popular Culture in Early Modern Europe*. New York: Harper and Row, 1978.

Burrowes, Robert. *The Strategy of Nonviolent Defense: A Gandhian Approach*. Albany: State Univ. of New York Press, 1996.

Caesar, Terry. "Impervious to Criticism: Contemporary Parody and Trash." *SubStance* 20, no. 64 (1991): 69–79.

Callahan, William A. "Laughter, Critical Theory and Korea." In *Habermas and the Korean Debate*, edited by Sang-Jin Han, 446–71. Seoul: Seoul National Univ. Press, 1998.

CANVAS (Center for Applied Non-Violent Action and Strategies). *CANVAS Core Curriculum: A Guide to Effective Nonviolent Struggle*. Belgrade: CANVAS, 2007.

———. *Nonviolent Struggle: 50 Crucial Points*. Belgrade: CANVAS, 2007.

———. "Ten Years Smarter? Chronology of Events—A Brief History of Otpor." Belgrade: CANVAS, 2008.

———. "Ten Years Smarter? Otpor—Concepts and Meanings." Belgrade: CANVAS, 2008.

Case, Clarence M. *Non-Violent Coercion: A Study in Methods of Social Pressure*. New York: Century, 1923.

Chenoweth, Erica, and Maria J. Stephan. *Why Civil Resistance Works: The Strategic Logic of Nonviolent Conflict*. New York: Columbia Univ. Press, 2011.

Clark, Howard. "The Limits of Prudence: Civil Resistance in Kosovo, 1990–98." In *Civil Resistance and Power Politics: The Experiences of Non-Violent Action from Gandhi to the Present*, edited by Adam Roberts and Timothy Garton Ash, 277–95. Oxford: Oxford Univ. Press, 2009.

Clarke, Peter. "More Total than Totalitarianism: The Strategy of Neue Slowenische Kunst." Bachelor's thesis, National College of Art and Design, 1996.

Climacus, Johannes. "Concluding Unscientific Postscript." In *Philosophical Fragments*, translated by David Swenson. Princeton, NJ: Princeton Univ. Press, 1941.

Cohen, Lenard J. *Serpent in the Bosom: The Rise and Fall of Slobodan Milošević*. Boulder, CO: Westview, 2002.

Collin, Matthew. *The Time of the Rebels: Youth Resistance Movements and 21st Century Revolutions*. London: Serpent's Tail, 2007.

———. *This Is Serbia Calling*. London: Serpent's Tail, 2001.

Čolović, Ivan. "Reading a Handful of Serbian Palms." In *Šetnja u mestu: građanski protest u Srbiji* [Walking on the spot: civil protest in Serbia], edited by Darka Radosavljević, 62–74. Belgrade: B92, 1997.

———. *The Politics of Identity in Serbia*. New York: New York Univ. Press, 2002.

Connery, Brian, and Kirk Combe, eds. *Theorizing Satire*. New York: St. Martin's, 1995.

Crnković, Gordana P. *Post-Yugoslav Literature and Film: Fires, Foundations, Flourishes*. London: Bloomsbury Academic, 2012.

de Certeau, Michel. *The Practice of Everyday Life*. Berkeley: Univ. of California Press, 1984.

Dear, John. *The God of Peace: Toward a Theology of Nonviolence*. Maryknoll, NY: Orbis, 1994.

Dobson, William J. *The Dictator's Learning Curve: Inside the Global Battle for Democracy*. New York: Doubleday, 2012.

Docker, John. *Postmodernism and Popular Culture: A Cultural History*. Cambridge: Cambridge Univ. Press, 1994.

Douglas, Mary. "Jokes." In *Implicit Meanings: Essays in Anthropology*, edited by Mary Douglas, 90–114. London and Boston: Routledge, 1984.

Dragićević-Šešić, Milena. "The Art in Protest." In *The Last Decade: Serbian Citizens in the Struggle for Democracy and an Open Society, 1991–2001*, edited by Velimir Ćurgus Kazimir, 39–51. Belgrade: Media Center, 2001.

———. "The Iconography and Slogans of Civil Society and Civil Protest 96/97." In *Civil Society in the Countries in Transition*, edited by Nadia Skenderović, 527–40. Subotica, Serbia: Agency of Local Democracy Center, Subotica and Open Univ. Subotica, 1999.

———. "The Street as Political Space: Walking as Protest, Graffiti, and the Student Carnivalization of Belgrade." *New Theatre Quarterly* 17 (2001): 74–86.

Dragović-Soso, Jasna. *Saviours of the Nation: Serbia's Intellectual Opposition and the Revival of Nationalism*. London: Hurst, 2002.

Dreyfus, Hubert L., Stuart E. Dreyfus, and Tom Athanasiou. *Mind over Machine: The Power of Human Intuition and Expertise in the Era of the Computer*. Oxford: Basil Blackwell, 1986.

Dudouet, Véronique. "Nonviolent Resistance in Power Asymmetries." In Berghof Foundation, *The Berghof Handbook: Transforming Ethnopolitical Conflict*, edited by Alex Austin, Martina Fischer, and Norbert Ropers, 237–64. Wiesbaden, Germany: VS Verlag, 2004.

Džamić, Lazar. "Of Midgets and Giants." In *Šetnja u mestu: građanski protest u Srbiji* [Walking on the spot: civil protest in Serbia], edited by Darka Radosavljević, 75–85. Belgrade: B92, 1997.

Dzelatović, Maja. "Pokrenimo Sadašnjost" [Challenges of the present days]. Presented at The Third Forum of Yugoslav Non-Governmental Organizations,

Center for Democracy Foundation and Center for the Development of Non-Profit Sector, Belgrade, May 2001. Accessed November 10, 2010. http://www.greekhelsinki.gr/english/reports/yngos-31-10-1999.html.

Eyerman, Ron, and Andrew Jamison. *Social Movements: A Cognitive Approach.* Cambridge: Polity, 1991.

Fiske, John. *Understanding Popular Culture.* London: Routledge, 1989.

Flam, Helena. "Anger in Repressive Regime: A Footnote to Domination and the Arts of Resistance by James Scott." *European Journal of Social Theory* 7, no. 2 (2004): 171–88.

Foucault, Michel. *Discipline and Punishment: The Birth of the Prison.* Translated by Alan Sheridan. New York: Vintage/Random House, 1979.

———. *Madness and Civilization.* New York: Vintage/Random House, 1973.

———. *Power/Knowledge—Selected Interviews and Other Writings 1972–1977.* Edited by Colin Gordon. New York: Pantheon, 1980.

———. *The Birth of the Clinic: An Archeology of Medical Perception.* Translated by A. M. Sheridan. New York: Vintage/Random House, 1975.

———. "What Is Enlightenment." In *The Foucault Reader,* edited by Paul Rabinow, 32–50. New York: Pantheon, 1984.

Franović, Ivana. "Serbia Eight Years After." In *People Power: Unarmed Resistance and Global Solidarity,* edited by Howard Clark, 35–38. London: Pluto, 2009.

Freud, Sigmund. *Jokes and Their Relation to the Unconscious.* Translated by Angela Richard and James Strachey. New York: Norton, 1963.

Gandhi, Mohandas K. *Constructive Programme: Its Meaning and Place.* Ahmedabad, India: Navajivan Trust, 1945.

Gaventa, John. *Power and Powerlessness: Quiescence and Rebellion in an Appalachian Valley.* Oxford: Clarendon, 1979.

Gluckman, Max. *Rituals of Rebellion in South-East Africa.* Manchester, UK: Univ. of Manchester Press, 1954.

Goldberg, RoseLee. *Performance Art: From Futurism to the Present.* New York: Thames and Hudson World of Art, 2001.

Golubović, Vidosava. "The Zenit Periodical (1921–1926)." In *Zenit 1921–1926,* edited by Vidosava Golubović and Irina Subotić. Belgrade: National Library of Serbia, 2008, 83–84.

Gordy, Eric D. *The Culture of Power in Serbia: Nationalism and the Destruction of Alternatives.* University Park: Pennsylvania State Univ. Press, 1999.

Gramsci, Antonio. *Selections from the Prison Notebooks.* Translated by Quintin Hoare and Geoffrey Nowell Smith. London: Lawrence, 1971.

Gregg, Richard B. *The Power of Non-Violence*. London: George Routledge and Sons, 1935.

Griffin, Dustin. *Satire: A Critical Introduction*. Lexington: Univ. Press of Kentucky, 1994.

Handelman, Don. "The Ritual-Clown: Attributes and Affinities." *Anthropos* 76 (1981): 321–70.

Hart, Marjolein't. "Humour and Social Protest: An Introduction." In *Humour and Social Protest*, edited by Marjolein't Hart and Dennis Bos, 1–20. Cambridge: Press Syndicate of the Univ. of Cambridge, 2007.

Hiller, Harry H. "Humor and Hostility: A Neglected Aspect of Social Movement Analysis." *Qualitative Sociology* 6, no. 3 (1983): 255–65.

Horton, Andrew. "Laughter Dark and Joyous in Recent Films from the Former Yugoslavia." *Film Quarterly* 56, no. 1 (2002): 23–28.

Hutcheon, Linda. *A Theory of Parody: The Teachings of Twentieth-Century Art Forms*. Champaign: Univ. of Illinois Press, 2000.

Ilić, Dragan. "Hronika Protesta 'Zajedno'" [Chronicle of the Zajedno protest]. In *Šetnja u mestu: građanski protest u Srbiji* [Walking on the spot: civil protest in Serbia], edited by Darka Radosavljević, 114–25. Belgrade: B92, 1997.

Ilić, Vladimir. "The Popular Movement Otpor—Between Europe and Re-Traditionalization." Helsinki files, no. 5, n.d. Policy Documentation Center, Center for Policy Studies, Central European University, Budapest. Accessed October 20, 2010. http://www.pdc.ceu.hu/archive/00005016/01/Files05.doc.

Independent International Commission on Kosovo. *The Kosovo Report: Conflict, International Response, Lessons Learned*. Oxford: Oxford Univ. Press, 2000.

Iordanova, Dina. "Conceptualizing the Balkans in Film." *Slavic Review* 55, no. 4 (1996): 882–90.

Irving, Allan, and Tom Young. "Paradigm for Pluralism: Mikhail Bakhtin and Social Work Practice." *Social Work* 47, no. 1 (2002): 19–29.

Janjatović, Petar. "Their Time Is Past." In *The Last Decade: Serbian Citizens in the Struggle for Democracy and an Open Society, 1991–2001*, edited by Velimir Ćurgus Kazimir, 52–56. Belgrade: Media Center, 2001.

Janjira Sombatpoonsiri, "Playful Subversion: Red Sunday's Nonviolent Activism in Thailand's Post-2010 Crackdown." *Peace and Policy* (forthcoming).

Jansen, Stef. "The Streets of Beograd: Urban Space and Protest Identities in Serbia." *Political Geography* 20 (2001): 35–55.

———. "Victims, Underdogs and Rebels: Discursive Practices of Resistances in Serbian Protest." *Critique of Anthropology* 20 (2000): 393–419.

Jasper, James M. "The Emotions of Protest." In *The Social Movements Reader: Cases and Concepts*, edited by Jell Goodwin and James M. Jasper, 84–107. Oxford: Wiley-Blackwell, 2009.

Joas, Hans. *The Creativity of Action*. Translated by Jeremy Gaines and Paul Keast. Chicago: Univ. of Chicago Press, 1996.

Johansen, Jörgen. "Humor as a Political Force, or How to Open the Eyes of Ordinary People in Social Democratic Country." *Philosophy and Social Action* 17, nos. 3–4 (1991): 7–23.

Jovanović, Milja. "Rage against the Regime: The Otpor Movement in Serbia." In *People Building Peace II: Successful Stories of Civil Society*, edited by Paul van Togeren, Malin Brenk, Marte Hallena, and Juliette Verhoeven, 545–51. Boulder, CO: Lynne Rienner, 2005.

Jovanović, Nebojša. "*Futur antérieur* of Yugoslav Cinema, or, Why Emir Kusturica's legacy is worth fighting for." In *Retracing Images: Visual Culture after Yugoslavia*, edited by Daniel Šuber and Slobodan Karamanić, 149–70. Boston: Brill Academic, 2012.

Jovićević, Aleksandra. "Everybody Laughed: Civil and Student Protest in Serbia 1996/7, between Theatre, Paratheature and Carnival." In *Šetnja u mestu: građanski protest u Srbiji* [Walking on the spot: civil protest in Serbia], edited by Darka Radosavljević, 45–61. Belgrade: B92, 1997.

Judah, Tim. *The Serbs: History, Myth and the Destruction of Yugoslavia*. New Haven, CT: Yale Univ. Press, 2009.

Kazimir, Velimir Ćurgus. "From Islands to the Mainland." In *The Last Decade: Serbian Citizens in the Struggle for Democracy and an Open Society, 1991–2001*, edited by Group of Authors, 5–38. Belgrade: Media Center, 2001.

———. "The Photograph as Protection." In *Šetnja u mestu: građanski protest u Srbiji* [Walking on the spot: civil protest in Serbia], edited by Darka Radosavljević, 11–28. Belgrade: B92, 1997.

Kenney, Padraic. *A Carnival of Revolution*. Princeton, NJ: Princeton Univ. Press, 2002.

Kibler, Robert E. "Responses to Inhumanity in the Balkans and a Preliminary Discussion Concerning the Problem of Evil." *East European Quarterly* 38, no. 4 (2005): 463–72.

Kiremidijan, G. D. "The Aesthetics of Parody." *Journal of Aesthetics and Art Criticism* 28, no. 2 (1969): 231–42.

Kishtainy, Khalid. "Humor and Resistance in the Arab World and Greater Middle East." In *Civilian Jihad: Nonviolent Struggle, Democratization and Governace in the Middle East*, edited by Maria J. Stephan, 53–64. London and New York: Palgrave Macmillan, 2009.

Knežević, Dubravka. "Marked with Red Ink." In *Radical Street Performance: An International Anthology*, edited by Jan Cohen-Cruz, 52–64. London: Routledge, 1998.

Knight, Charles A. "Satire, Speech, and Genre." *Comparative Literature* 44, no. 1 (1992): 22–41.

Koestler, Arthur. *The Act of Creation*. London: Pan, 1964.

Kolesarić, Vladimir, Mirjana Krizmanić, and Antun Rohaček. "Humor in Yugoslavia." In *National Styles of Humor*, edited by Avner Ziv, 189–210. New York: Greenwood, 1988.

Koller, Marvin R. *Humour and Society: Explorations in the Sociology of Humour*. Houston: Cap and Gown, 1988.

Kovačev, Dušan. "Zrenjanin: trajno zaustavljanje perspektive" [Zrenjanin: permanent termination of a perspective]. *Nova Srpska Politička Misao*, December 9, 2008. Accessed June 14, 2011. http://www.nspm.rs/politicki-zivot/zrenjanin-trajno-zaustavlj anje-perspektive.html?alphabet=l.

Kronja, Ivana. "Turbo Folk and Dance Music in 1990s Serbia: Media, Ideology, and the Production of Spectacle." *Anthropology of East Europe Review* 22, no. 1 (2004): 103–14.

Kunzle, David. "World Upside Down: The Iconography of a European Broadsheet Type." In *The Reversible World: Symbolic Inversion in Art and Society*, edited by Barbara A. Babcock, 39–90. Ithaca, NY: Cornell Univ. Press, 1978.

Kuzio, Taras. "Civil Society, Youth and Societal Mobilization in Democratic Revolutions." *Communist and Post-Communist Studies* 39 (2006): 365–86.

Kuzmanović, Bora. *Studentski protest '92: socijalno-psihološka studija jednog društvenog događaja* [The student protest' 92: a social-psychological study of a social event]. Belgrade: Institut za psihologiju Filozofskog fakulteta, knižara Plato, 1993.

La Boétie, Etienne de. *The Politics of Obedience: The Discourse of Voluntary Servitude*. Translated by Harry Kurz. New York: Free Life Editions, 1975.

Landy, Marcia. *Monty Python's Flying Circus: TV Milestones Series*. Detroit, MI: Wayne State Univ. Press, 2005.

Le Goff, Jacques. "Laughter in the Middle Ages." In *A Cultural History of Humour: From Antiquity to the Present Day*, edited by Jan Bremmer and Herman Roodenburg, 40–53. Cambridge: Polity, 1997.

Levi, Pavle. *Disintegration in Frames: Aesthetics and Ideology in the Yugoslav and Post-Yugoslav Cinema*. Redwood City, CA: Stanford Univ. Press, 2007.

Lilly, Carol S. "Film Reviews." *American Historical Review* 104, no. 4 (1999): 1428–29.

Lucas, Anne M. "Strategic Nonviolence and Humor: Their Synergy and Its Limitations." Bachelor's thesis, Kent State Univ. Honors College, 2010.

MacKinnon, Mark. *The New Cold War: Revolutions, Rigged Elections and Pipeline Politics in the Former Soviet Union.* New York: Carroll and Graf, 2007.

Mallick, Krisha, and Doris Hunter. *An Anthology of Nonviolence.* London: Greenwood, 2002.

Martin, Brian. *Justice Ignited: The Dynamics of Backfire.* Lanham, MD: Rowman and Littlefield, 2007.

Marzolph, Ulrich. "Reconsidering the Iranian Sources of a Romanian Political Joke." *Western Folklore* 47, no. 3 (1988): 212–16.

Mijatović, Brana. "(Com)Passionately Political: Music of Đorđe Balašević." *Anthropology of East Europe Review* 22, no. 1 (2004): 93–102.

———. "'Throwing Stones at the System': Rock Music in Serbia during the 1990s." *Music and Politics* 2, no. 2 (2008). Accessed May 12, 2010. http://www.music.ucsb.edu/projects/musicandpolitics /archive/2008 . . . /mijatovic.pdf.

Milivojević, Zdenka. "The Media in Serbia from 1985 to 1994." In *Serbia between the Past and the Future,* edited by Dragomir Pantić and Dušan Janjić, 367–400. Belgrade: Institute of Social Sciences and Forum for Ethnic Relations, 1997.

Milošević, Dijana. "Theatre as a Way of Creating Sense: Performance and Peacebuilding in the Region of the Former Yugoslavia." In *Acting Together: Performance and Creative Transformation of Conflict,* edited by Cythia E. Cohen, Roberto G. Varea, and Polly O. Walker, 23–44. Oakland, CA: New Village, 2011.

Milošević, Milan. "The Media Wars: 1987–1997." In *Burn This House: The Making and Unmaking of Yugoslavia,* edited by Jasminka Udovički and James Ridgeway, 109–30. Durham, NC: Duke Univ. Press, 2000.

Mišina, Dalibor. *Shake, Rattle and Roll: Yugoslav Rock Music and the Poetics of Social Critique.* Surrey, UK: Ashgate, 2013.

Monroe, Alexei, and Slavoj Žižek. *Interrogation Machine: Laibach and NSK (Short Circuits).* Cambridge, MA: MIT Press, 2005.

Morreall, John. *Taking Laughter Seriously.* Albany: State Univ. of New York Press, 1983.

Mulkay, Michael. *On Humour: Its Nature and Its Place in Modern Society.* Cambridge: Polity, 1988.

Munk, Erika. "Before the Fall, Yugoslav Theaters of Opposition." *Theater* 31 (2001): 4–25.

Naess, Arne. *Gandhi and Group Conflict: An Exploration of Satyagraha Theoretical Background*. Oslo: Universitetsforlaget, 1974.

Nenadić, Danijela, and Nenad Belčević. "Serbia—Nonviolent Struggle for Democracy: The Role of Otpor." In *People Power: Unarmed Resistance and Global Solidarity*, edited by Howard Clark, 26–34. London: Pluto, 2009.

Nikolayenko, Olena. "The Learning Curve: Student Protests in Serbia, 1991–2000." Paper presented at the Eleventh Annual Graduate Workshop, Kokkalis Program on Southeastern and East-Central Europe, Harvard Univ., Cambridge, MA, February 12–13, 2009.

Otpor. "Popular Movement Otpor (Resistance): Chronology of Actions 1999–2000." In *The Last Decade: Serbian Citizens in the Struggle for Democracy and an Open Society, 1991–2001*, edited by Velimir Ćurgus Kazimir, 374–80. Belgrade: Media Center, 2001.

Paulson, Joshua. "Removing the Dictator in Serbia—1996–2000." In *Waging Nonviolent Struggle: 20th Century Practice and 21st Century Potential*, edited by Christopher A. Miller, Hardy Merriman, and Gene Sharp, 315–39. Boston: Porter Sargent, 2005.

Paunović, Žarko. "Ten Years of NGOs in the FR of Yugoslavia." In *The Last Decade: Serbian Citizens in the Struggle for Democracy and an Open Society, 1991–2001*, edited by Velimir Ćurgus Kazimir, 57–63. Belgrade: Media Center, 2001.

Pelton, Leroy H. *The Psychology of Nonviolence*. New York: Pergamon, 1974.

Petrović, Branka, Žarko Paunović, Aco Divac, Tea Gorjanc, and Vesna Nenadić. *Directory of Nongovernmental Non-Profit Organizations in the Federal Republic of Yugoslavia*. Belgrade: Centar za razvoj neprofitnog sektora, 1998.

Popov, Nebojša. "The University in an Ideological Shell." In *The Road to War in Serbia: Trauma and Catharsis*, edited by Nebojša Popov, 303–26. Budapest: Central European Univ. Press, 1996.

Popović, Srđa. "Serbia Arena for Nonviolent Conflict: An Analytical Overview of an Application of Gene Sharp's Theory of Nonviolent Action in Milošević's Serbia." Paper presented at the conference "Whither the Bulldozer? Revolution, Transition, and Democracy in Serbia," United States Institute of Peace, Belgrade, January 30–31, 2001.

Pravdić, Ivan. "Student Performances: Guidelines for Possible Analyses or Theatre of the Masses—Walking from Failureville to Never-Never Land." In *Šetnja u mestu: građanski protest u Srbiji* [Walking on the spot: civil protest in Serbia], edited by Darka Radosavljević, 37–42. Belgrade: B92, 1997.

Prosić-Dvornić, Mirjana. "Enough! Student Protest '92: The Youth of Belgrade in Quest of 'Another Serbia'." *Anthropology of East Europe Review*, nos. 1–2 (1993). Accessed September 21, 2010. http://condor.depaul.edu/rrotenbe/aeer/aeer 11_1/prosic-dvornic .html.

———. "The Topsy Turvy Days Were There Again: Student and Civil Protest in Belgrade and Serbia, 1996/1997." *Anthropology of East Europe Review* 16, no. 1 (1998). Accessed September 21, 2010. http://www.scholarworks.iu.edu/jour nals/index.php/aeer/article/view Article/691.

Radonić, Maša. "Chronology of the Student Protest 96/97." In *Šetnja u mestu: građanski protest u Srbiji* [Walking on the spot: civil protest in Serbia], edited by Darka Radosavljević, 126–33. Belgrade: B92, 1997.

Radosavljević, Darka, ed. *Šetnja u mestu: građanski protest u Srbiji* [Walking on the spot: civil protest in Serbia]. Belgrade: B92, 1997.

Radosavljević, Vladan. *Pištaljke i jaja* [Whistles and eggs]. Belgrade: Medija Centar, 1997.

Ramet, Sabrina P. *Balkan Babel: The Disintegration of Yugoslavia from the Death of Tito to the Fall of Milošević*. Boulder, CO: Westview, 2002.

Rose, Alexander. "When Politics Is a Laughing Matter." *Policy Review* (December 2001/January 2002): 59–71.

Routledge, Paul. "Backstreets, Barricades, and Blackouts: Urban Terrains of Resistance in Nepal." *Environment and Planning: Society and Space* 12 (1994): 550–78.

———. "Entanglements of Power: Geographies of Domination / Resistance." In *Entanglements of Power: Geographies of Domination / Resistance*, edited by Paul Routledge, Joanne P. Sharp, Chris Philo, and Ronan Paddison, 1–42. London: Routledge, 2000.

Sales, Roger. *English Literature in History, 1780–1830: Pastoral and Politics*. London: Palgrave Macmillan, 1983.

Schock, Kurt. "Nonviolent Action and Its Misconceptions: Insights for Social Scientists." *Political Sciences and Politics* 36, no. 4 (2003): 705–11.

Scott, James C. *Domination and the Arts of Resistance*. New Haven, CT: Yale Univ. Press, 1990.

Sekelj, Laslo. "Parties and Elections: The Federal Republic of Yugoslavia—Change without Transformation." *Europe-Asia Studies* 52, no. 1 (2000): 57–75.

Sharp, Gene. *Social Power and Political Freedom*. Boston: Porter Sargent, 1980.

———. *The Politics of Nonviolent Action*. Boston: Porter Sargent, 1973.

———. *There Are Realistic Alternatives*. Boston: Albert Einstein Institution, 2003.

————. *Waging Nonviolent Struggle: 20th Century Practice and 21st Century Potential.* Boston: Porter Sargent, 2005.

Shepard, Ben. *Queer Political Performance and Protest: Play, Pleasure and Social Movements.* New York: Routledge, 2010.

————. "The Use of Joyfulness as a Community Organizing Strategy." *Peace and Change* 30, no. 4 (2005): 435–68.

Sherrod, Lonnie R. "Youth Activism in Serbia." In *Youth Activism: An International Encyclopedia,* edited by Lonnie R. Sherrod, Constance A. Flanagan, Ron Kassimir, and Amy K. Syvertsen, 562–68. Westport, CT: Greenwood, 2005.

Sørensen, Majken Jul. "Humor as a Serious Strategy of Nonviolent Resistance to Oppression." *Peace and Change* 33, no. 2 (2008): 167–90.

Sørensen, Maiken Jul, and Stellan Vinthagen. "Nonviolent Resistance and Culture." *Peace and Change* 37 (3): 444–70.

Speier, Hans. "Wit and Politics: An Essay on Laughter and Power." *American Journal of Sociology* 103, no. 5 (1998): 1352–401.

Spencer, Metta, Chris Miller, and Gene Sharp. "Gene Sharp and Serbia, Introduction: Nonviolence versus a Dictatorship." *Peace Magazine,* October–December 2001, 4–14.

Sretenović, Dejan. "Noise." In *Šetnja u mestu: građanski protest u Srbiji* [Walking on the spot: civil protest in Serbia], edited by Darka Radosavljević, 86–94. Belgrade: B92, 1997.

Steinberg, Marc W. "When Politics Goes Pop: On the Intersections of Popular and Political Culture and the Case of Serbian Student Protests." *Social Movement Studies* 3, no. 1 (2004): 3–29.

Stephenson, Richard. "Conflict and Control Function of Humour." *American Journal of Sociology* 56, no. 6 (1951): 569–74.

Stevanović, Lada. "Ridiculed Death and the Dead: Black Humor: Epitaphs and Epigrams of the Ancient Greece." *Glasnik Etnografskog Instituta SANU* 55, no. 1 (2007): 193–204.

"Sticker Shock," short film based on excerpts from "The New World of Power," an episode in *A Force More Powerful: A Century of Nonviolent Conflict* (multi-part documentary). Directed by Peter Ackerman and Jack DuVall. Columbus, OH: Santa Monica Pictures LLC and A Force More Powerful Films, 1999–2000. Accessed May 25, 2011. http://www.aforcemorepowerful.org/films/bdd/story/otpor/sticker-shock.php.

Subotić, Irina. "Avant-Garde Tendencies in Yugoslavia." *Art Journal* 49, no. 1 (1990): 21–27.

Subotić, Irina, and Ann Vasić. "'Zenit' and Zenitism." *Journal of Decorative and Propaganda Arts* 17 (1990): 14–25.

Summy, Ralph. "Gandhi's Nonviolent Power Perspective." Paper presented at the International Peace Research Association Conference, Univ. of Sydney, Sydney, Australia, July 6–10, 2010.

Šušak, Bojana. "An Alternative to War." In *The Road to War in Serbia: Trauma and Catharsis*, edited by Nebojša Popov, 479–508. Budapest: Central European Univ. Press, 2000.

Thomas, Robert. *Serbia under Milošević / Politics in the 1990s*. London: Hurst, 1999.

Turner, Victor. *The Anthropology of Performance*. New York: PAJ Publications, 1988.

Udovički, Jasminka. "Neither War nor Peace." In *Burn This House: The Making and Unmaking of Yugoslavia*, edited by Jasminka Udovički and James Ridgeway, 281–313. Durham, NC: Duke Univ. Press, 2000.

Van de Port, Mattijs. *Gypsies, Wars and Other Instances of the Wild*. Amsterdam: Amsterdam Univ. Press, 1998.

Vejvoda, Ivan. "Civil Society versus Slobodan Milošević: Serbia 1991–2000." In *Civil Resistance and Power Politics: The Experience of Non-Violent Action from Gandhi to the Present*, edited by Adam Roberts and Timothy Garton Ash, 295–316. Oxford: Oxford Univ. Press, 2009.

Vinthagen, Stellan. "Power as Subordination and Resistance as Disobedience: Nonviolent Movements and the Management of Power." *Asian Journal of Social Science* 34, no. 1 (2006): 1–21.

Vladisavljević, Nebojša. *Serbia's Anti-Bureaucratic Revolution: Milošević, the Fall of Communism and Nationalist Mobilization*. New York: Palgrave Macmillan, 2008.

Vučetić, Radina. *Koka-Kola socijalizam. Amerikanizacija jugoslovenske popularne kulture šezdesetih godina* [Coca-Cola socialism: the Americanization of Yugoslav popular culture in the 1960s]. Belgrade: Službeni glasnik, 2012.

Vučetić, Srđan. "Identity Is a Joking Matter: Intergroup Humor in Bosnia." *Space of Identity* 4, no. 1 (2004). Accessed April 2, 2010. http://www.pi.library.yorku.ca/ojs/index.php/soi/article/view/ 8011/7168.

Vujkov, Milana. "Black Humour in Serbian Films of the Early Eighties and Its Cultural Consequences: The Cinema of Slobodan Šijan and Dušan Kovačević." Master's thesis, Univ. of London, 2005.

Vujović, Sreten. "Protest as an Urban Phenomenon." In *Protest in Belgrade: Winter of Discontent*, edited by Mladen Lazić, 193–210. Budapest: Central European Univ. Press, 1999.

Vukanović, Maša. "Faktografija studentskog protesta 1996/97" [Facts about the student protest 1996/97]. In *O studentima i drugim demonima: etnografija studentskog protesta 1996/97* [The students and other demons: ethnography of the student protest 1996/97], edited by Jadranja Milanović and Vuk Šećerović, 10–18. Belgrade: TODRA, 1997.

Weber, Thomas. *Conflict Resolution and Gandhian Ethics*. New Delhi: Gandhi Peace Foundation, 1991.

Zijderveld, Anton C. *Reality in a Looking-Glass: Rationality through an Analysis of Traditional Folly*. London: Routledge, 1982.

Newspapers, Magazines, Online News, and Reports

"Akcija studentskog pokreta 'Otpor' u Novom Sadu" [Actions of the student movement 'Otpor' in Novi Sad]. *Danas*, November 5, 1999.

"Aktivisti Otpora određen istražni pritvor" [Otpor activists detained]. *B92*, June 22, 2000. Accessed April 8, 2011. http://www.b92.net/info/vesti/index .php?yyyy=2000&mm=06&dd=22&nav_category=1&nav_id=8157&version =print.

"Aktivisti studentske organizacije Otpor najavljuju: oblačenje Zmaj Jove u 'Otpo-rovu' majicu" [Activists from the students organization Otpor announce: dressing of Zmaj Jova in Otpor t-shirt]. *Danas*, December 23, 1999.

Balkan Peace Team. "The Protests in Belgrade and throughout Yugoslavia," December 7, 1996. Peace Brigades International Archive, London. Accessed November 10, 2010. http://www.peacebrigades.org/archive/bpt/bpt96-14 .html.

Bilefsky, Dan. "Dark One-Liners Shine a Light on the Mood of Serbs." *New York Times*, December 2, 2007. Accessed May 8, 2011. http://www.nytimes .com/2007/12/02/world/europe/02serbia.html.

Bjelovuk, Milica. "Jedan dinar u zamenu za slobodu" [One dinar in exchange for freedom]. *Glas javnosti*, January 14, 2001. Accessed October 20, 2010. http:// arhiva.glas-javnosti.co.yu/arhiva/2001.

———. "Otpor i opozicija, kokoška il jaje" [Otpor and the opposition, chicken or the egg]. *Glas javnosti*, January 22, 2001. Accessed October 20, 2010. http:// arhiva.glas-javnosti.co.yu/arhiva/2001.

———. "Otpor sa novim likom" [New image of Otpor]. *Glas javnosti*, January 10, 2001. Accessed October 20, 2010. http://arhiva.glas-javnosti.co.yu/ arhiva/2001.

————. "Pesnica stvorena iz ljubavi" [The fist created out of love]. *Glas javnosti*, January 12, 2001. Accessed October 20, 2010. http://arhiva.glas-javnosti .co.yu/arhiva/ 2001.

————. "Rađanje Otpora u Srbiji" [The birth of Otpor in Serbia]. *Glas javnosti*, 11 January 2001. Accessed October 20, 2010. http://arhiva.glas-javnosti.co.yu /arhiva/2001.

"'Blic' Daily is Helping 'Beta' Agency." *Blic*, April 21, 2000. Accessed October 20, 2010. http://www.blic.rs/stara_arhiva/naslovna/129785/Blic-daily-is-helping -Beta-agency.

Cohen, Roger. "Who Really Brought Down Milosevic." *New York Times Magazine*, November 26, 2000. Accessed October 20, 2010. http://www.nytimes .com/2000/11/26/magazine/whoreallybroughtdownmilosevic.html?scp=3 &sq=OTPOR&st=cse&pagewanted=4&pagewanted=prin.

"Dear Readers." *Blic*, May 17, 2000. Accessed October 20, 2010. http://www.blic.rs /stara_arhiva/naslovna /130375/Dear-readers.

"'Defense' of Pozarevac on Victory Day." *Free Serbia News*, May 9, 2000. Accessed September 20, 2010. http://www.xs4all.nl/~freeserb/specials/report/09052 000/e-index.html.

Di Giovanni, Janine. "Blueprint for a Revolution." *Financial Times Magazine*, March 18, 2011. Accessed April 15, 2011. http://www.ft.com/cms/s/2/0ad005b450431 1e09ad100144feab49a.html#axzz1HEy0vQHi.

Erlanger, Steven. "Rally in Belgrade Protests Early Closing of Serbian Universities." *New York Times*, May 27, 2000. Accessed October 20, 2010. http://www .nytimes.com/2000/05/27/world/rally-in-belgrade-protests-early-closing-of -serbian-universit ies.html?pagewanted=1.

————. "Serbian Government Seizes TV Station in a Drive to Crush the Opposition to Milosevic." *New York Times*, May 18, 2000. Accessed October 20, 2010. http://www.nytimes.com/2000/05/18/world/serbian-government -seizes-tv-station-drive-crush-opposition-milosevic.html?Pagewanted=all &src=pm.

"First Big Anti-War Protests in Serbia. *Radio Free Europe*, May 19, 1999. Accessed May 24, 2011. http://www.rferl.org/content/article/1141909. html.

Gibson, Carl, and Steve Horn. "Exposed: Globally Renowned Activist Collaborated with Intelligence Firm Stratfor." *Occupy*, February 12, 2013. Accessed May 14, 2015. http://www.occupy.com/article/exposed-globally-renowned -activist-collaborated-intelligence-firm-stratfor.

"Grdelica: NATO Bombing Victims Remembered." *B92*, April 12, 2008. Accessed May 24, 2011. http://www.b92.net/eng/news/societyarticle.php?yyyy=2008 &mm =04&dd =12& nav_id=49352.

Grujičić, Nebojša. "Koncert Đorđa Balaševića" [Đorđe Balašević's concert]. *VREME*, December 7, 2000. Accessed October 20, 2010. http://www.vreme .com/arhiva_html/ 518/20.html.

———. "R'n'R i protesti: kamenje na sistem" [Rock 'n' roll and protests: rocking the system]. *VREME*, December 27, 1999. Accessed September 20, 2010. http:// www.vreme.com/arhiva_html/464/14 .html.

Grytting, Wayne. "Gandhi Meets Monty Python: The Comedic Turn in Nonviolent Tactics." *Waging Nonviolence*, October 28, 2011. Accessed November 3, 2011. http://wagingnonviolence.org/2011/10/gandhi-meets-monty-python-the -comedic-turninnonviolenttactics/?utm_source=feedburner&utm_medium =feed&utm_campaign=Feed%3A+WagingNonviolence+%28Waging+Non violence%29.

Hockenos, Paul. "Serbia's New New Wave." *In These Times*, March 5, 2001. Accessed October 20, 2010. http://www.inthesetimes. com/issue/25/07/hockenos2507 .html.

"Hronologija lokalnih izbora u Srbiji" [Chronology of the local elections in Serbia]. *B92*, November 30, 2004. Accessed May 16, 2010. http://www.b92.net /specijal/lokalni 2004/enciklopedija.php?nav_id=151196.

Human Rights Watch. "Deepening Authoritarianism in Serbia and the Purges of the Universities." *Human Rights Watch* 11, no. 2 (January 1999). Accessed December 12, 2010. http://www.hrw.org /legacy/reports/1999/serbia/.

———. "The Crisis in Kosovo." Report. *Human Rights Watch*, February 2000. Accessed April 2,2010. http://www.hrw.org/legacy/reports/2000/nato/Natbm 200-01.htm.

Humanitarian Law Center. "Izveštaj: strah vlasti od Otpora u Srbiji" [Investigation: state terror against Otpor in Serbia]. Belgrade: Humanitarian Law Center, 2000. Accessed May 22, 2011. http://www.hlcrdc.org/Izvestaji/577 .sr.html.

———. "Police Crackdown on Otpor, Report No. 31." Belgrade: Humanitarian Law Center, 2001.

"Ivan Novković—simbol Otpora" [Ivan Novković—the symbol of resistance]. *B92*, October 2, 2010. Accessed May 24, 2011. http://www.b92.net/info /vesti/index.php?yyyy=2010&mm=10&dd=02&nav_category=12&nav_id =462459.

Jakovljević, Snezana. "Srdjan Milivojevic (Otpor): I Want to Be a Free Man." *Republika*, September 25, 2000. Accessed October 20, 2010. http://www.exyupress .com/republika/republika6.html.

Kaljević, Branka. "'96 Students' Protest: We Know What We Want." *AIM*, December 3, 1996. Accessed April 24, 2011. http://www.aimpress.ch/dyn/trae /archive/data/199612/61205-004-trae-beo.htm.

———. "Parents and Children: Family Resistance." *VREME*, June 3, 2000. Accessed September 20, 2010. http://www.ex-yupress.com/vreme/vreme77.html.

———. "Police Torture in Belgrade: Brutal Beating Up of Citizens." *AIM*, December 31, 1996. Accessed April 24, 2011. http://www.aimpress.ch/dyn/trae /archive/data/199612/61231-002-trae-beo.htm.

Klub, Crna, Gora Medija, and Pat FitzPatrick. "Paper Shortage Forces Closure of Dailies." *Central European Review*, July 1, 2000. Accessed May 22, 2011. http:// www.cereview.org/00/27/ serbianews27.html.

Knell, Yolande. "Egypt Protest: 'Carnival Atmosphere' among Demonstrators." *BBC*, January 31, 2011. Accessed February 28, 2011. http://www.bbc.co.uk /news/world-africa-12328506?print=true.

"Kod Zmaj Jovinog spomenika akcija pokreta 'Otpor': misli, pruži Otpor" [Near the monument of Zmaj Jova was the action of the Otpor movement: think, resist]. *Danas*, December 17, 1999.

Komlenović, Uroš, Zorica Miladinović, and Zoran Radovanović. "What Audiences in Belgrade, Nis, Kragujevac, Pancevo, Cacak . . . See and Hear: Air over Serbia." *VREME*, July 31, 2000. Accessed September 20, 2010. http://www .ex-yupress.com/vreme/vreme77.html.

Kosanović, Zoran, and Uroš Komlenović. "The Rebelled Nis: A Week without Mile." *VREME*, December, 14 1996. Accessed September 12, 2010. http:// www.scc.rutgers.edu/serbian_digest/.

Lekić, Bojana. "Rebellion of Provincial Towns." *AIM*, January 16, 1997. Accessed April 24, 2011. http://www.aimpress.ch/dyn/trae/archive/data/199701/70112 -003-trae-beo.htm.

"Maki zbog teškog zdravstvenog stanja nije mogao da daizjavu" [Because of severe illness, Maki could not make a statement]. *B92*, August 19, 2000. Accessed May 16, 2010. http://www.b92.net/info/vesti/index.php?yyyy=1999 &mm=08&dd=19 &nav_category=1&nav_id=1398.

Maliqi, Sqelzen. "Elections, Demonstrations and Kosovo: Belgrade as a Foreign Capital." *VREME*, December 7, 1996. Accessed September 20, 2010. http:// www.scc.rutgers.edu /serbian_digest/.

Marković, Petra. "L'humour, pas la guerre" [Humor, not war]. *Liberation*, July 4, 2000. Accessed August 20, 2010. http://www.liberation.fr/monde/010134129 2-l-humour-pas-la-guer re.

Marović, Ivan. "Opposition as Tool." *VREME*, May 26, 2000. Accessed September 20, 2010. http://www.exyupress.com/vreme/vreme72. html.

Marović, Ivan, and Dejan Ranđić. "Resistance (Otpor!) Info: After the Action Dinar for His Resignation Two Activists of Otpor Have Been Taken into Custody." Justwatch Archive, University of Buffalo, Buffalo, New York, September 17, 1999. Accessed October 20, 2010. http://groups.yahoo.com/group/balkans /message/353?l=1.

Matić, Boris. *Dribbling Pictures*. Accessed July 9, 2011. http://www.dribbling pictures.com/flash_eng/drbbpct.html.

"Meeting in Pozarevac." *Blic*, May 5, 2000. Accessed October 20, 2010. http://www .blic.rs/stara_arhiva/naslovna /130095/Meeting-in-Pozarevac.

"Members of Pro-NATO Organization 'Otpor' Are Mentally Disturbed Persons, Infamous for Their Criminal Acts." *Politika*, August 25, 2000. Accessed May 13, 2011. http://www.ex-yupress.com/politika/politika36.html.

"Message in a Bottle by 'Otpor' to President Milosevic." *Blic*, April 21, 2000. http://www.blic.rs/stara_arhiva/naslovna/129782/Message-in-a-bottle-by -Otpor-to-President-Milosevic.

Milosević, Milan. "Koštunica na prkosima" [Koštunica in defiance]. *VREME*, August 26, 2000. Accessed September 20, 2010. http://www.vreme.com / arhiva_html/503/index.html.

———. "Shell Them with Eggs!" *VREME*, December 1, 1996. Accessed September 20, 2010. http://www.scc.rutgers.edu/serbian_digest/.

———. "The Civic Movement: Civic Resistance, Month One." *VREME*, December 21, 1996. Accessed September 20, 2010. http://www.scc.rutgers.edu /serbian_digest/.

Monroe, Alexei. "Balkan Hardcore: Pop Culture and Paramilitarism." *Central European Review*, June 19, 2000. Accessed June 15, 2011. http://www.cereview .org/00/24/monroe24.html.

Mowat, Jonathan. "Coup d'Etat in Disguise: Washington's New World Order 'Democratization' Template." *Global Research on Globalisation*, February 9, 2005. Accessed May 10, 2012. http://globalresearch.ca/articles/MOW502A.html.

Nardone, Ali. "Humor as a Tool of Protest in Belarus." *New Tactics*, December 15, 2010. http://www.newtactics.org/en/blog/ali-nardone/humor-tool-protest -belarus.

"New Rally on May 27." *Blic*, May 20, 2000. Accessed October 20, 2010. http://www.blic.rs/stara_arhiva/naslovna/13 0464/New-rally-on-May-27.

Nikolić, Zoran B. "Students Divided: Belgrade—Struggle against Genes." *AIM*, September 8, 1997. Accessed February 12, 2011. http://www.aimpress.ch/dyn/trae/archive/data/199709/70912-029-trae-beo.htm.

Ninčić, Roksanda. "Down by Law." *VREME*, December 14, 1996. Accessed September 20, 2010. http://www.scc.rutgers. edu/serbian_digest/.

"Niški Otpor će zatražiti prijem kod Đukanovića" [Otpor from Niš will request the reception from Đukanović]. *B92*, July 28, 2000. Accessed May 23, 2011. http://www.b92.net/info/vesti/index.php?yyyy=2000&mm=07&dd=28&nav_category=1&nav_id=9588.

Omestad, Thomas. "Ten-Day Wonder: Czechoslovakia's Instant Mass Movement." *New Republic*, December 25, 1989. Accessed December 2, 2011. http://www.tnr.com/article/world/ten-day-wonder?page=0,1.

"Onemogućen protest u Leskovcu" [Protests hindered in Leskovac]. *B92*, June 22, 2000. Accessed April 8, 2011. http://www.b92.net/info/vesti/index.php?yyyy=2000&mm=06&dd=24&nav_category=1&nav_id=8213.

"Opposition Petition Drive Calls for Milosevic's Resignation: General Strike." *CNN*, July 7, 1999. Accessed May 24, 2011. http://articles.cnn.com/1999-0707/world/9907_07_yugo.opposition.01_1_party-leader-zoran-djindjic-police-banuzice/2?_s=PM: WORLD.

"Otpor organizuje proslavu Srpske nove godine" [Otpor organizes the celebration of Serbian New Year]. *Danas*, December 27, 1999.

"Otpor: Rođendanom na rođendan" [Birthday on a birthday]. *B92*, August 19, 1999. Accessed April 8, 2011. http://www.b92.net/info/vesti/index.php?yyyy=1999&mm=08&dd=19& nav_category=1&nav_id=1396.

"Otpor simbolično zatvorio župsku berbu 2000" [Otpor closed the vineyard in Župa symbolically in 2000]. *B92*, September 18, 2000. Accessed April 8, 2011. http://www.b92.net/info/vesti/index.php?yyyy=2000&mm=09&dd=18&nav_category=1& nav_id=11963.

"Otpor: To nije smak sveta, samo režim pada" [It's not the end of the world, only the regime falls]. *B92*, August 18, 1999. Accessed April 8, 2011. http://www.b92.net/info/vesti/index.php?yyyy=1999&mm=08&dd=16&nav_category=1&nav_id=1143.

Pančić, Teofil. "Election in FRY: Socialists Going On." *AIM*, November 6, 1996). Accessed March 20, 2011. http://www.aimpress.ch/dyn/trae/archive/data/199611/61106-005-trae-beo.html.

————. "Reports from Cities in Serbia." *VREME*, November 24, 1996. Accessed on May 16`, 2010. http://www.scc.rutgers.edu/serbian_digest/.

"Parties and Citizens Mark October 5." *B92*, October 5, 2007. Accessed April 8, 2011. http://www.b92.net//eng/news/politicsarticle.php?yyyy=2007&mm=10 & dd=05&nav_category=90&nav_id=44315.

Philby, Charlotte. "Exit Festival, Novi Sad, Serbia." *The Independent*, July 16, 2008. Accessed May 22, 2011. http://www.independent.co.uk/arts-entertainment /music/reviews/ exit-festival-novi-sad-serbia-868551.html.

Plavšić, Dragan "Manufactured Revolutions?" *International Socialism*, June 27, 2005. Accessed April 20, 2011. http://www.isj.org.uk/?id=122.

"Ponovo proradila TV Kraljevo" [TV Kraljevo re-opened]. *B92*, March 25, 2000). Accessed May 16, 2010. http://www.b92.net/info/vesti/index.php?yyyy=2000 &mm=03&dd=25 &nav_category=1&nav_id=5610.

Pritchard, Eleanor. "Anti-Opposition Activities." *Central European Review*, September 4, 2000. Accessed May 22, 2011. http://www.ce-review.org/00/32 /serbianews32.html.

Putnik, Milena. "Novi Sad without the Socialists: Slightly Dramatic, with Remote Control." *AIM*, December 21, 1996. Accessed April 24, 2011. http://www.aim press.ch/dyn/trae/archive/data/199612/61221-005-trae-beo.htm.

"Rally of Serbian Opposition for Freeing Studio B." *Free Serbia News*, May 17, 2000. Accessed September 20, 2010. http://www.xs4all.nl/~freeserb/specials /broadcasts/17052000 /e-index.html.

"Revolution of Scrambled Eggs and Great Plunder of the Nation." *AIM*, November 28, 1996. Accessed March 30, 2011. http://www.aimpress.ch/dyn/trae /archive/data/199611/61128-006-trae-beo.htm.

Rosenberg, Tina. "Revolution U: What Egypt Learned from the Students Who Overthew Milosevic." *Foreign Policy*, February 16, 2011. Accessed August 20, 2011. http://www.foreignpolicy.com/articles/2011/02/16/revolution_u?sms _ss=gmail&at_xt=4d61f7e3d198e602%2C0.

Salomonsson, Annika. "Art Action Group Speaks to the World: Humble Artists Create Touching Work on the Trials of Humanity." *Culturebase*, International Artist Database, May 28, 2003. Accessed June 15`, 2011. http://www.culture base.net/artist.php?677.

Shadow [pseud.]. "CANVAS, Otpor, Pora: Serbia's Brand Is Non-Violent Revolution." *Cafébabel*, March 31, 2011. Accessed August 20, 2011. http://www.cafebabel .co.uk/article/37103/egypt-revolution-serbia-otpor-pora-canvas-youth.html.

Stefanović, Nenad Lj. "What Is Otpor? Fist in the Eye of Regime." *VREME*, May 13 2000. Accessed September 20, 2010. http://www.ex-yupress.com/vreme /vreme39.html#otpor.

"Stevanović ponovo izabran sa gradonačelnika Kragujevaca" [Stevanović elected as the mayor of Kragujevac]. *B92*, June 30, 2000. Accessed April 8, 2011. http://www.b92.net/info/vesti/index.php?yyyy=2000&mm=06&dd=30&nav _category=1&nav_id=8462.

Stojanović, Dušan. "Serbs Offer Nonviolent Revolution Advice." November 11, 2004. *Charter 97*, November 11, 2004. Accessed February 28, 2011. http://charter 97.org/eng/news/2004/11/01/serb.

"Studenski pokret 'Otpor': Dinar za smenu" [The student movement Otpor: dinar for a change]. *Danas*, October 11, 1999).

Suša, Vana. "A Serbian Protest Leader Has Made a Dramatic Reappearance." *Central European Review*, March 31, 2000. Accessed May 23, 2011. http://www .ce-review.org/00/13/serbianews13.html.

Sussman, Anna Louie. "Laugh, O Revolution: Humor in the Egyptian Uprising." *Atlantic*, February 26, 2011. Accessed February 28, 2011. http://www.the atlantic.com/international/archive/2011/02/laugh-o-revolution-humor-in-the -egyptian-uprising/71530/.

———."Studio B Has Been Fined Twice." *Central European Review*, May 12–June 11, 2000. Accessed May 23, 2011. http://www.cereview.org/00/20/serbianews20 .html.

———. "The Democratic Party (DP) Held Its Sixth Party Convention." *Central European Review*, March 4, 2000. Accessed May 23, 2011. http://www.cere view.org/00/9/serbianews9.html.

———. "Thousands of Serb Workers and Supporters Gathered in Central Belgrade on International Workers Day." *Central European Review*, May 6, 2000. Accessed May 23, 2011. http://www.cereview.org/00/18/serbianews 18.html.

Tancons, Claire. "Occupy Wall Street: Carnival against Capital? Carnivalesque as Protest Sensibility." *E-Flux Journal* 30 (December 2011). Accessed May 10, 2012. http://www.e-flux.com/journal/occupy-wall-street-carnival-against-capital -carnivalesque-as-protest-sensibility/.

Todorović, Dragan. "Ko je Bogoljub Arsenijević Maki" [This is Bogoljub Arsenijević Maki]. *VREME*, June 24, 1999. Accessed September 20, 2010. http://www .vreme.com/arhiva_html/446/12.html.

"Twelve Die as NATO Hits Passenger Train." *Southnews*, April 12, 1999. Accessed May 24, 2011. http://south movement.alphalink.com.au/southnews/990412 -trainhit.html.

"U Kragujevcu se formira štab za odbranu lokalne TV" [The headquarters for the defense of the local TV is founded in Kragujevac]. *B92*, March 21, 2000. Accessed May 16, 2010. http://www.b92.net/info/vesti/index.php?yyyy=2000 &mm=03&dd=21&nav_cat egory=1&nav_id=5503.

"United towards the Victory over Regime." *Blic*, May 27, 2000. Accessed October 20, 2010. http://www.blic.rs/stara_arhiva/naslovna/130711/United-towards -the-victory-over-regime.

"We Shall Not Allow Civil War." *Blic*, May 16, 2000. Accessed October 20, 2010. http://www.blic.rs/stara_arhiva/naslovna/130318/We-shall-not-allow-civil -war.

"Who's Who: Milošević Family." *BBC*, March 14, 2006. Accessed May 13, 2011. http://news.bbc.co.uk/2/hi/europe/747130.stm.

York, Steve. "How Did We Succeed: Superior Propaganda for Advertising Freedom" (excerpted from an interview with Steve York). *Centre for Applied Non-Violent Action and Strategies* (CANVAS), November 30, 2000. http://www .canvasopedia.org/legacy/content/serbian_case/otpor_propaganda.htm#01.

"Yugoslavia: NATO Reports Anti-War Demonstrations in Serbia." *Radio Free Europe*, May 9, 1999. Accessed May 24, 2011. http://www.rferl.org/content /article/1091345.html.

Zunes, Stephen. "The Leftist Attack on Nonviolent Action for Democratic Change." *Centre for Applied Non-Violent Action and Strategies* (CANVAS), 2008. Accessed April 15, 2010. http://www.canvasopedia.org/legacy/files/various /Leftist_Attack_on_NVA.doc.

Personal Records of Protest Events

Glišović, Dalibor. "Otpor! Actions—Aleksandrovac (District of Župa)" (personal records).

Lacmanović, Petar. "Personal Records of Street Actions by Otpor Zrenjanin."

Pavlović, Alexandar. "Spisak akcija Novosadskog Otpor-a" [personal records of Otpor's action in Novi Sad].

Protest Magazines and Pamphlets

Boom! (student protest magazine). Accessed October 2010. http://www.yurope .com/mirrors/protest96/pmf/index.html.

Lekić, Slaviša. *Svi u napad iz BGD protesta* [All for attack from Belgrade protests]. Vol. 1. Belgrade: BiS, 1997.

Students of Belgrade University and of University of Arts. *Beograd je Svet: Studentski Protest '96* [Belgrade is the world: student protest '96]. Belgrade: Ušće-Print [Fast Print], 1996.

VREME Demokratije. *Vreme Foto Dokument 1–3*. Belgrade: VREME, 1997.

Index

Niš, xi, 46–47, 49, 106–8, 116–17, 134,
142–45, 154, 161, 176–78, 181, 247, 249,
223n71

nongovernmental organizations (NGOs),
xiv, xv, 13, 118, 130–32, 134–35, 138,
141–42, 144–46, 150–51, 153–54, 157–61,
168–69, 176–77, 179, 209n47, 218n1,
220n20

nonviolence, xii, xiii, 2, 54, 124, 170–71;
commitment to, 47, 49–51, 73, 88; pragmatic, 2, 4, 72; principled, 2, 72

nonviolent discipline, 51, 72–75, 93,
124. *See also* carnivals: decrease
antagonism

nonviolent revolution. *See* carnivals: as
alternative realities; carnivals: and
parallel polity

Noordung (Scipion Nasice Sisters Theater), 18

North Atlantic Treaty Organization
(NATO), xv, 25, 79, 82–85, 100, 125, 134,
149, 155–56, 182, 209n45

nostalgia, 28, 115

Novi Sad, xi, 46, 49–50, 85, 92, 100, 102,
111, 116, 118–20, 122, 134–36, 139–41,
149–51, 161, 176

Novi Sad University, 92

obedience, 3, 4, 6, 27, 36, 70

OHO, 18

opposition coalition, 79–81; and election, 12, 44–50; and Otpor, 12, 93, 96,
139–43, 147, 168, 176, 182, 205n1, 205n5,
223n71; and protest, 50–52, 62, 69

oppression, 23, 26, 41–42, 124, 127, 185n8,
191n24, 192n41; and carnivals, 2–3,
73 10, 13, 128–29, 163–67; and parody,
18, 23

Orange Alternative, 1

Orthodox, 39

Orthodox Celts, 119

Orthodox New Year, 54, 112, 182

Otpor, xii, xiii, 2, 8, 11–12; characteristics,
85–94; emerged, 47, 79–85; and local
area, 155–61; and recruitment 91–93,
111, 116, 119, 123, 146, 166; strategized
humorous protest, 94–98, 99–129;
subverted terrorist accusation, 92, 99,
108–9, 183, 210

outrage. *See* anger

parallel institutions. *See* carnivals: and
parallel polity

parody, 7–9, 163; and 1990s protest, 24, 37,
40, 41, 42, 70; distorts propaganda, 13,
18, 19; strategized by Otpor, 99, 111–17,
122–23, 128–29

Partisan Rebellion Day, 40. *See also* Yugoslav United Left

Patak, 146

Pavićević, Borka, 179

Pavlov, Vladimir, 84, 92

Pavlović, Aleksandar, xiii, 85, 117, 136,
178

peace movement, 38–40, 44, 59–60

peasants, 10, 21

People's Resistance Movement, 182

Perošević, Boško, 136, 183

Pešić, Dušan, 108, 154–55, 178

Pešić, Vesna, 80

pessimism, 73, 162, 168

Petrovaradin, 100

Petrović, Vukašin, 84

Piletić, Dragana, 141, 179

Podunavlje district, 152

police. *See* security forces

political jiu-jitsu, 124–25

Politika, 52, 60, 248

Janjira Sombatpoonsiri completed her doctoral degree at Melbourne's La Trobe University. Currently, she is a lecturer of international relations and peace studies at Thailand's Thammasat University and co-secretary general of the Asia Pacific Peace Research Association (APPRA). Her most recent publications are: "'If You Use Nonviolence, I will Respond with Nonviolence': A Nonviolent Conflict in the Case of the 2007 Pattani Protest, Southern Thailand," in *Conflict Transformation: New Voices, New Directions*, eds. Rhea DuMont, Tom Hastings, and Emiko Noma (Jefferson, NC: McFarland, 2013); and "Playful Subversion: Red Sunday's Nonviolent Activism in Thailand's Post-2010 Crackdown," *Peace and Policy* 20 (2015, forthcoming).